CROFTING LAW

CROFTING LAW

DONALD J MacCUISH MA, LLB

former Secretary and Solicitor to
the Crofters Commission

and

DEREK FLYN LLB

Solicitor in Private Practice

Butterworths/Law Society of Scotland
Edinburgh
1990

Butterworths

United Kingdom	Butterworth & Co (Publishers) Ltd, 88 Kingsway, LONDON WC2B 6AB and 4 Hill Street, EDINBURGH EH2 3JZ
Australia	Butterworths Pty Ltd, SYDNEY, MELBOURNE, BRISBANE, ADELAIDE, PERTH, CANBERRA and HOBART
Canada	Butterworths Canada Ltd, TORONTO and VANCOUVER
Ireland	Butterworth (Ireland) Ltd, DUBLIN
Malaysia	Malayan Law Journal Sdn Bhd, KUALA LUMPUR
New Zealand	Butterworths of New Zealand Ltd, WELLINGTON and AUCKLAND
Puerto Rico	Equity de Puerto Rico, Inc, HATO REY
Singapore	Butterworth & Co (Asia) Pte Ltd, SINGAPORE
USA	Butterworth Legal Publishers, ST PAUL, Minnesota, SEATTLE, Washington, BOSTON, Massachusetts, AUSTIN, Texas and D & S Publishers, CLEARWATER, Florida

Law Society of Scotland
26 Drumsheugh Gardens, EDINBURGH EH3 7YR

A CIP Catalogue record for this book is available from the British Library.

ISBN 0 406 17912 3

Typeset by Phoenix Photosetting, Chatham
Printed and bound by Bookcraft (Bath) Ltd, Midsomer Norton, Avon

PREFACE

The code of legislation making special provision for crofters as tenants of small agricultural holdings in the seven crofting counties of Scotland first took shape in simple form in the Crofters Holdings (Scotland) Act 1886. It became less simple in 1912 when the Small Landholders (Scotland) Act 1911 (incorporating previous Acts) extended the statutory tenure to tenants of small holdings throughout the whole of Scotland. Further legislation followed and by 1933 James Scott in the preface to his *Law of Smallholdings in Scotland* was able to say that 'the Landholders Acts rival even the Income Tax Acts in number, legislation by reference and general complexity'.

For the seven crofting counties there was some clarification when, following the Report of the Taylor Commission of Enquiry into Crofting Conditions, the Crofters (Scotland) Act 1955 restored to them their own special code, being partly a consolidation and re-enactment of existing statutory provisions from 1886 on and partly fresh provisions reflecting some of that Commission's recommendations. Further development was brought about by the Crofting Reform (Scotland) Act 1976 which recognises that crofting tenure has many of the characteristics of ownership. That Act introduced an optional right to the crofter to acquire an ownership title to his crofting subjects and to share in the development value of croft land that is resumed by the landlord or acquired by compulsory purchase.

The foregoing brief outline explains the layout in the first three parts of this book on crofting law. Part I is primarily devoted to a historical introduction which is essential to a proper understanding of current law. The 1955 Act does not exclude from current law all the legislation that preceded the Act and much of the judicial interpretation of enactments from 1886 onwards is still relevant.

Part II deals with crofting tenure as it now exists after some one hundred years of development, a species of leasehold tenure with tenancy conditions and the rights and obligations of the tenant statutorily defined. Part III deals mainly with the changes brought about by the 1976 Act, including the procedures for the decrofting of land.

Although cottars have also had statutory status since 1886, the legislation has made little provision for them and there is no reliable information as to how many still exist. There is urgent need for those who do to be made aware of their precarious standing in law and of how this can be remedied, as explained in Part IV.

The project, which is completed by the publication of this book, has been helped by many people and to all of them we express our gratitude. As authors, our quest for information has been made easier by the ready willingness of fellow practitioners and officials to help but we, of course, must bear the responsibility for the directions in which the subject matter has taken us and for the conclusions reached. As in the statutes, we have given the terms 'landlord', 'crofter' and 'cottar' the masculine gender. We are happy to acknowledge that this is frequently not the case.

We are deeply indebted to the several secretaries who have toiled to convert our separate writings to legibility and especially to Mrs June Coleman who has patiently collected and controlled the product of our joint exertions and given it a presentable appearance. These several ladies along with the other members of staff and of course the partners of Messrs Macleod & MacCallum, Solicitors, Inverness, have shown great interest in the project and supported it unhesitatingly throughout. Mention must also be made of the debt due to our long-suffering wives to whom we dedicate this work as a token of our affection. Finally, we have to thank Butterworths and the Law Society of Scotland for this opportunity to bring our subject matter into print.

There has been a long-felt desire to make this unusual area of law more accessible to parties and their advisers. In 1933 James Scott was hoping that his volume would assist in the framing of a Consolidation Act and he was writing a mere forty-seven years after the crofters' code was first introduced. Our ambition, more than a century after that belated introduction, is simply to clarify the code for the benefit of the modern reader and our effort is likely to have to speak for itself, at least in the immediate future.

Donald J MacCuish
Derek Flyn

Inverness
May 1990

CONTENTS

BIBLIOGRAPHY

(a) Textbooks

CN Johnston *The Small Landholders (Scotland) Acts, 1886–1911* (2nd edn, 1914)
James Scott *Law of Smallholdings* (1933)
The Laws of Scotland: Stair Memorial Encyclopaedia vol 1, 'Crofting and smallholdings', paras 797–860, and vol 6, 'The Scottish Land Court', paras 952–980

(b) Reports of the Crofters Commission

 (i) Annual reports of first Commission 1886–1912
 (ii) Annual reports of present Commission 1955–

(c) Annual reports of the Scottish Land Court 1913–

ABBREVIATIONS

Statutes

1886 Act	Crofters Holdings (Scotland) Act 1886
1911 Act	Small Landholders (Scotland) Act 1911
1931 Act	Small Landholders and Agricultural Holdings (Scotland) Act 1931
1955 Act	Crofters (Scotland) Act 1955
1961 Act	Crofters (Scotland) Act 1961
1964 Act	Succession (Scotland) Act 1964
1968 Act	Law Reform (Miscellaneous Provisions) (Scotland) Act 1968
1976 Act	Crofting Reform (Scotland) Act 1976

Law Reports

SC	Session Cases 1907–
SLCR	Scottish Land Court Reports in Scottish Law Review (1913–63) (preceded by year and volume number), and Scottish Land Court Reports 1982– (preceded by year)
SLCR App	Appendix to the annual reports of the Scottish Land Court 1963–
SLT	Scots Law Times
SLT (Land Ct)	Scottish Land Court Reports in Scots Law Times 1964–

TABLE OF STATUTES

References are to paragraph numbers; numbers in square brackets refer to material in the appendices.

Table of statutes

TABLE OF CASES

N

P

R

Part I INTRODUCTION

CONTENTS

CHAPTER 1

HISTORICAL INTRODUCTION

1.01 The Napier Commission

A convenient starting-point for the study of crofting law is the Report of
the Royal Commission known as the Napier Commission[1] which was
appointed in 1883 and reported to Parliament in 1884. Their remit was, 'to
enquire into the condition of the crofters and cottars in the Highlands and
Islands of Scotland and all matters affecting the same or relating thereto'.
They travelled rapidly and extensively throughout the crofting areas and
held a large number of meetings in public. The oral and written evidence
they collected is recorded in five large volumes. They concluded that even
if the evidence of specific events was not accurate in detail, nevertheless
the general impression conveyed was a true one. They accepted that the
economic transformation brought about throughout the Highlands and
Islands in the preceding hundred years (the era of the notorious
'Clearances') had not been anywhere accomplished without 'some
constraint, resistance and distress'. The Commission's uncovering of the
conditions prevailing in the crofting areas proved conclusively the
compelling need for Parliament to intervene in crofting affairs and the
breakthrough to special legislation for which crofters had been struggling
so strenuously was accomplished.

The Napier Commission identified the basic causes for complaint as (a)
size of holdings, (b) lack of security of tenure, (c) lack of compensation for
tenant improvements, (d) high rents, and (e) loss of land to sporting
purposes. But when it came to devising remedies, the Commission's
proposals found little place in the Act that followed. They had concluded
that 'to grant at this moment to the whole mass of poor tenants in the
Highlands and Islands fixity of tenure in their holdings would be to
perpetuate social evils of a dangerous character'. However, political
expediency and the urgent need to halt continuing unrest led the
Government to seek a solution akin to that already applied to the
somewhat similar situation in Ireland, and the Crofters Holdings
(Scotland) Act 1886 that followed extended its benefits to all crofting
tenancies, large and small.

The history of crofting legislation thus begun can conveniently be
divided into four periods, each introduced by a major Act of Parliament,
being the Acts of 1886, 1911, 1955 and 1976[2]. The first two periods are
treated at some length because the matters recorded still have relevance to
the position today. A brief outline of the progress of events in the third
and fourth periods is sufficient as the detailed exposition is dealt with in
the chapters on current law that follow.

1 1884 Report and Minutes of Evidence C3980, London: HMSO.
2 Crofters Holdings (Scotland) Act 1886 (c 29); Small Landholders (Scotland) Act 1911 (c 49); Crofters (Scotland) Act 1955 (c 21); Crofting Reform (Scotland) Act 1976 (c 21).

(1)   FIRST PERIOD: 1886–1912

1.02   Crofters Holdings (Scotland) Act 1886

The 1886 Act introduced a form of tenure that was unique, founded on the three principles of (a) security of tenure subject to compliance with specific statutory conditions[1], (b) payment by the crofter of a fair rent[2], and (c) payment to the crofter on termination of tenancy of compensation for permanent improvements provided by himself or his family predecessors[3]. There was reserved to the landlord a right to apply for authority to resume croft land (ie recover it from crofting tenancy) for a reasonable purpose, subject to payment of compensation to the crofter[4].

The Act also conferred on the crofter a right to bequeath his croft to any one member of his family, being his wife or any person who, failing nearer heirs, would succeed him in case of intestacy[5]. In the absence of a valid bequest or on intestacy, the croft passed to the heirs of the crofter according to the rules of intestate succession in heritage, except that if the heirs were heirs portioners the eldest succeeded without division[6].

The statutory conditions (for the breach of any of which the crofter could be removed from his croft following action in the sheriff court)[7] inter alia required the payment of rent and prohibited the subdivision or subletting of the holding without the landlord's written consent. The crofter was also forbidden to assign his tenancy but, in practice, assignation with the consent of the landlord was accepted as valid[8]. The landlord had the right to enter upon the holding, subject to payment of compensation for damage occasioned, for a variety of purposes such as mining and quarrying, making roads, fences and drains, and hunting, shooting and fishing.

The Act was applied to every crofter in the same manner as if his tenancy were a lease[9]. 'Crofter' was defined as meaning any person who at 25 June 1886 was tenant of a holding from year to year, who resided on his holding the annual rent of which did not exceed £30 in money, and which was situated in a crofting parish, and the successors of such person in the holding, being his heirs or legatees[10]. 'Holding' meant any piece of land held by a crofter, consisting of arable or pasture land, or of land partly arable and partly pasture, and which had been occupied and used as arable or pasture land (whether such pasture land was held by the crofter alone or in common with others) immediately preceding the passing of the Act. It included the site of his dwelling-house and any offices or other conveniences connected therewith, but not including garden ground only appurtenant to a house. Excluded from the Act were certain categories of holdings or buildings, such as holdings or buildings let to the landlord's employees during their employment or as a pension to old servants, or let to ministers of religion or schoolmasters during their tenure of office, or to any innkeeper or tradesman placed in the district by the landlord[11]. 'Crofting parishes' were such parishes within the counties of Argyll, Inverness, Ross and Cromarty, Sutherland, Caithness, Orkney and Shetland as the Commission constituted under the

Act should determine to be crofting parishes. Only twelve parishes in the seven counties failed to qualify[12].

The qualifying condition that the tenant should be resident on the holding was construed to be a continuing condition that applied throughout the tenancy. There was no qualifying condition as to who had provided the buildings and other permanent improvements on the holding. In addition to those tenants who were admitted as crofters at 25 June 1886 and their heirs or legatees, a number of crofters were admitted by agreement between landlord and tenant in the period preceding the 1911 Act. There was nothing in the 1886 Act to prevent a croft from falling out of the Act if it became vacant. The landlord was free to relet it on any tenure he chose or it could remain unlet.

1 Crofters Holdings (Scotland) Act 1886, ss 1, 3.
2 Ibid, s 6.
3 Ibid, ss 8, 10, 34 and Sch.
4 Ibid, s 2.
5 Ibid, s 16.
6 Ibid, s 19.
7 Ibid, s 3.
8 *Mason v Anderton* (1940) 28 SLCR 38.
9 Crofters Holdings (Scotland) Act 1886, s 19.
10 Ibid, s 34.
11 Ibid, s 33.
12 Being 8 parishes in Argyll (Cambeltown, Dunoon and Kilmun, Gigha and Cara, Inverchaolain, Killean and Kilkenzie, Kilmartin, Kilmodan, Southend); 2 parishes in Inverness (Cawdor, Croy); 2 parishes in Ross and Cromarty (Cromarty, Rosemarkie). See CN Johnston *Small Landholders (Scotland) Acts, 1886–1911* (1914) p 195.

1.03 The first Crofters Commission

To administer the 1886 Act, a Crofters Commission was appointed consisting of three Commissioners of whom one (the Chairman) was required to be an advocate of the Scottish bar of not less than ten years' standing and one had to be a person who could speak the Gaelic language[1]. The Commission's decision in regard to the matters committed to their determination was final but decisions on points of law could be set aside by a court of law[2]. In Sheriff Clerks' offices throughout the crofting counties a book called the 'Crofters' Holdings Book' had to be kept in which Commission orders and relative proceedings in every application coming before them required to be recorded by the Sheriff Clerk of the county concerned[3]. The Commission were required to make an annual report of their proceedings to the Secretary for Scotland for presentation to Parliament[4].

The 1886 Act was followed by two short Acts, the Crofters Holdings (Scotland) Act 1887 and the Crofters Commission (Delegation of Powers) Act 1888. The first dealt with the stay of legal proceedings for payment of rent and the second with the delegation of Commission duties to individual Commissioners.

These Acts fell far short of what crofters had been demanding, especially by reason of failure to provide for restoration to crofting of lands lost in the Clearances. Some provision was made for enlargement of existing crofts but none for creating new crofts. Most disappointed were the cottars, the landless or near landless occupiers of dwelling-houses, who either paid no rent or occupied on a year to year tenancy at an annual rent not exceeding £6[5]. They were denied the statutory rights accorded to crofters, apart from a limited right to compensation for permanent improvements when their occupancy came to an end[6]. There was no security of tenure, no right to apply for a fair rent and no right of succession to the cottar holding. In response to complaints the Royal Commission on the Highlands and Islands was appointed in 1892 with the task of ascertaining what further scope there might be for land settlement. Their report was eventually followed by the Congested Districts (Scotland) Act 1897 which set up a Board to administer a Government fund for the improvement of congested districts in crofting parishes. The Board was empowered to aid and develop agriculture and fishing and rural industries in various ways and in particular to acquire and equip land for subdivision among, or for enlargement of the holdings of, crofters and cottars in congested districts. The Congested Districts Board collaborated closely with the Crofters Commission and a measure of land settlement was promoted, frequently on land cleared of crofters in former times.

Although common grazings were an important feature of crofting townships, the 1886 Act made no provision for their regulation and management. The Crofters Common Grazings Regulation Act 1891 repaired the omission. It provided for the appointment of grazings committees who could make regulations, subject to Crofters Commission approval, regulating the fair exercise of crofters' joint rights in grazings. If the crofters failed to appoint a committee, the Commission themselves, on the request of any two crofters interested or of the landlord, could do so and also make regulations. A further effort to deal with this difficult subject produced the Crofters Common Grazings Regulations Act 1908 which authorised the Commission to take the initiative in appointing committees and making regulations. It also prescribed monetary penalties for breach of the regulations and provided for the appointment by the Commission of a person to advise and assist grazings committees (a Grazings Officer).

For the first few years this first Crofters Commission were largely concerned with their function of fixing fair rents (which were subject to revision every seven years) and dealing with arrears of rent which they had authority to reduce or cancel. Both rents and arrears were substantially reduced. Gradually the Commission evolved as a quasi-judicial body dealing with a multiplicity of issues such as claims to crofter status, boundary disputes, compensation claims on termination of tenancy, competing claims to tenancy, alleged contravention of statutory conditions, common grazing disputes and all manner of questions affecting crofting rights. By the time the first Crofters Commission came to be dissolved in 1912 a fair body of case law had accumulated, including a number of Court of Session decisions[7]. The proceedings of the Commission are recorded in twenty-five Annual Reports to Parliament, ending on 31 March 1912. At that date both the Commission and the Congested Districts Board ceased to exist. Subject to the provisions of the Small Landholders (Scotland) Act 1911, the Commission's powers and duties were transferred to a Scottish Land Court and the Board's powers and duties to a Board of Agriculture for Scotland[8].

1 Crofters Holdings (Scotland) Act 1886, s 17.
2 Ibid, s 25; *Johnston* pp 98, 99.
3 Crofters Holdings (Scotland) Act 1886, s 27.

4 Ibid, s 18.
5 Ibid, s 34.
6 Ibid, s 9.
7 *Johnston* pp 182 et seq; J Scott *Law of Smallholdings in Scotland* (1933) pp 380 et seq.
8 Small Landholders (Scotland) Act 1911, s 28.

(2)   SECOND PERIOD: 1912–1955

1.04   Small Landholders (Scotland) Act 1911

The second period was introduced by the 1911 Act, entitled an Act 'to encourage the formation of small agricultural holdings in Scotland and to amend the law relating to the tenure of such holdings (including crofters' holdings); to establish a Board of Agriculture for Scotland, and for other purposes connected therewith'. It came into operation on 1 April 1912. Some of the previous enactments relative to crofting were repealed to the extent specified in the Second Schedule to the 1911 Act. That Act was directed to be read and construed along with the 'Crofters Acts'[1], defined as meaning the Acts of 1886, 1887, 1891 and 1908. The five Acts are cited together as the 'Small Landholders (Scotland) Acts, 1886 to 1911'.

The Scottish Land Court set up under the 1911 Act was to consist of not more than five persons, including a Chairman having the same rank as a judge of the Court of Session and one person who could speak the Gaelic language[2]. The Court is final on matters of fact and law but it can state a special case for the opinion of either Division of the Court of Session on any question of law and is bound to do so at the request of any party to a case[3]. The Court of Session's determination of the question is final.

The 1911 Act extended throughout the whole of Scotland, with some amendment, the special tenure previously confined to the seven crofting counties. The term 'landholder' in place of 'crofter' was introduced to describe the protected tenant[4]. In addition to holdings which as crofts were already qualified under the 1886 Act, the 1911 Act brought into the full statutory tenure existing agricultural holdings of a certain size and also provided for admission into the tenure of new holdings to be constituted.

1 Small Landholders (Scotland) Act 1911, ss 31, 36.
2 Ibid, s 3.
3 Ibid, s 25(2).
4 Ibid, s 1.

1.05   Existing holdings

The full tenure was applied to every holding in Scotland which at 1 April 1912 was held by a tenant who resided on or within two miles from the holding and who by himself or his family cultivated the holding with or without hired labour[1], provided
(a) the current annual rent of the holding did not exceed £50 whatever the area, or alternatively that the area of the holding (exclusive of common grazing rights) did not exceed 50 acres whatever the rent[2], and

(b) the tenant or his predecessors in the same family had provided or paid for the whole or the greater part of the buildings or other permanent improvements oń the holding without receiving from the landlord or any predecessor in title payment or fair consideration therefor[3].

Where the tenant at 1 April 1912 was a tenant from year to year he became a landholder from that date; where he was a tenant under a lease for longer than one year he became a landholder from the termination of his lease. In each case the successors of the tenant, being his heirs or legatees, qualified as landholders. The qualification of residence on or within two miles of the holding had to be satisfied as at 1 April 1912 but the Court of Session held that it was not a continuing condition of the statutory tenancy[4]. A tenant was barred from qualifying as a landholder in respect of certain categories of land, such as land that was garden ground only appurtenant to a house, land within a burgh, market garden land, glebe land, woodland and home farm land, or any land that was not a holding within the meaning of the Agricultural Holdings (Scotland) Act 1908[5].

1 Small Landholders (Scotland) Act 1911, s 2(1).
2 Ibid, s 26(3)(a). For the Island of Lewis the limits set were £30 rent or 30 acres (s 27).
3 Ibid, s 2(1)(2).
4 *Rogerson v Viscount Chilton* (1917) 5 SLCR 16; on appeal sub nom *Rogerson v Viscount Chilston* 1917 SC 453, 1917 1 SLT 217, 54 SLR 366.
5 Small Landholders (Scotland) Act 1911, s 26.

1.06 New holdings

The full tenure was also applied to every new holding in Scotland which was constituted by the registration of an applicant on his application to the Land Court and the recording in the Landholders Holdings Book (formerly the Crofters Holding Book) of the application and the Court's order granting registration[1]. Any landlord and tenant could enter into an agreement whereby the tenant could apply to the Court for an order granting registration[2]. The tenure extended to the tenant's successors, being his heirs or legatees. To qualify for registration the holding had to be within the limits of £50 rent or 50 acres (exclusive of grazings) and certain categories of land were barred, as in the case of existing holdings. A person was not admissible to registration in respect of land belonging to more than one landlord or in respect of more than one holding[3]. There was no qualifying condition as to residence or as to who had provided the permanent improvements.

1 Small Landholders (Scotland) Act 1911, ss 2(1)(iv), 15.
2 Ibid, s 7(1).
3 Ibid, s 26(2).

1.07 Land settlement[1]

The creation of new holdings received a massive boost under the provisions of the 1911 Act providing for the constitution of new holdings. The new Board of Agriculture[2] was vested with extensive land settlement functions, including functions previously exercised by the Congested Districts Board.

Restrictive procedures combined with the effects of the 1914–18 war slowed down progress until the Land Settlement (Scotland) Act 1919 provided new powers and improved procedures. Thereafter the Board were able to make rapid progress, using the following two methods:

(a) Requisitioning land from private landowners for the establishment of new holdings

After preparing a land settlement scheme including terms of compensation to the landowner and others affected, the Board, with the consent of the Secretary for Scotland, would make an order confirming the scheme and record it in the Landholders Holdings Book. This had the same effect as an order of the Land Court and the selected tenants would be registered as landholders, leaving the landowner as landlord of his new tenants. The Board would adapt existing buildings on the land and provide new buildings as necessary. Assistance to take over the buildings was given to the tenants by way of loan repayable by instalments of principal and interest spread over periods of 50 or 80 years.

(b) Exercising the Board's powers to acquire land by agreement or compulsory purchase

After carrying out necessary works and providing equipment on the land acquired, the Board settled on the holdings qualified tenants who received assistance to take over buildings and were registered as landholders by the Court. This became the preferred method of land settlement and the Board (now the Secretary of State) became the largest landlord of landholder holdings in Scotland.

There was much land settlement activity in the 1920s, gradually tapering off in the 1930s and into the early 1940s, by which time a substantial amount of the land lost to crofting by the Clearances was in the occupation of landholders.

1 *Scott* pp 186 et seq.
2 Small Landholders (Scotland) Act 1911, s 4. As from 1 January 1929 the Board was superseded by the Department of Agriculture for Scotland (Reorganisation of Offices (Scotland) Act 1928); as from 4 September 1939 the functions of the Department were transferred to the Secretary of State for Scotland (Reorganisation of Offices (Scotland) Act 1939).

1.08 Joint tenancies

Where a holding (including a former croft) was held on joint tenancy when it became subject to the landholder provisions of the 1911 Act, the joint tenants qualified as joint landholders and the joint tenancy could be continued through statutory successors[1]. But when a new landholder's holding was constituted, not more than one person could be registered as tenant of the holding. Where at any time after 1 April 1912 a holding was held by a single landholder or a holding ceased to be held on joint tenancy, it was not competent for more than one person to be the landholder of such holding[2]. These provisions were mandatory and could not be set aside by agreement between landlord and tenant. Two houses were allowed on a joint tenancy holding[3].

1 Small Landholders (Scotland) Act 1911, s 26(8); *Scott* pp 60, 61.
2 *Niven v Cameron* (1939) 27 SLCR 23.
3 *MacKinnon v Duke of Hamilton's Trs* 1918 SC 274, 1918 1 SLT 288, 55 SLR 359, (1918) 6 SLCR 119.

1.09   Assignation of tenancy

The statutory condition of tenancy prohibiting assignation was slightly relaxed by the 1911 Act which allowed a landholder who was unable to work his holding through illness, old age or infirmity, with the consent of the Land Court, to assign his tenancy to a member of his family[1].

1 Small Landholders (Scotland) Act 1911, s 21.

1.10   Vacant holdings

The 1911 Act introduced a control designed to prevent the relet of vacant landholder holdings outwith the statutory tenure[1]. The landlord was required to give notice of vacancies to the Board of Agriculture and, if he relet on other than the statutory tenure without the consent of the Board (later the Department of Agriculture and later still the Secretary of State), the Board could declare the relet null and void. The introduction of this control, which developed into the current stricter procedures governing notification of vacant crofts and reletting, has an important place in the history of crofting tenure.

1 Small Landholders (Scotland) Act 1911, s 17, later fortified by the Land Settlement (Scotland) Act 1919, s 12 and the Small Landholders and Agricultural Holdings (Scotland) Act 1931, s 6; see *Scott* pp 124 et seq.

1.11   Statutory small tenants

The 1911 Act created a new class of tenants termed 'statutory small tenants'. These were tenants from year to year or leaseholders who would have qualified as landholders except for the fact that the whole or the greater part of the buildings or other permanent improvements on the holding had not been provided or paid for by the tenant or a predecessor in the same family without receiving payment or fair consideration therefor[1]. Where at 1 April 1912 the tenancy was held from year to year it became a statutory small tenancy from that date. Where it was held under a lease for a term longer than one year it became a statutory small tenancy on termination of the lease. The statutory small tenancy could be continued through heirs, legatees and assignees (if assignation was permitted by the lease). These provisions also applied in the case of a holding which at 1 April 1912 was held by joint tenants[2].

Notwithstanding the terms of section 32(1) of the 1911 Act, it has been held in a series of cases that a statutory small tenant could assign his tenancy with his landlord's consent even where the lease prohibited assignation. The same result could follow without the landlord's express consent if by his acting he treated a new tenant as successor to the previous one[3].

The statutory small tenant qualified only for limited rights of which the principal ones were a right to claim renewal of tenancy for a period (usually seven years) and to have an equitable rent (as distinct from a fair rent) fixed, failing agreement, by the Land Court[4]. In other respects the tenancy was an ordinary tenancy to which the Agricultural Holdings (Scotland) Acts applied as if it were a lease. Renewal of tenancy could be refused if the landlord could satisfy the Land Court that he had reasonable grounds of objection to the tenant. If the tenancy ever came to be terminated the holding was no longer subject to the provisions of the Landholders Acts, but there was a prohibition against amalgamating it with any other holding, as defined under the Agricultural Holdings Acts, except with the sanction of the Board of Agriculture[5].

In certain circumstances a statutory small tenancy could be converted into a landholder tenancy. The tenant could apply to the Land Court to be declared a landholder in any case where the landlord failed to implement his legal obligations to provide buildings or to maintain buildings and permanent improvements[6]. This provision was later reinforced by the Small Landholders and Agricultural Holdings (Scotland) Act 1931 (section 14) which enabled a statutory small tenant to become a landholder if his landlord, on being called upon to do so, failed to give an undertaking that the tenant would have the same rights to compensation for permanent improvements as if he were a landholder.

1 Small Landholders (Scotland) Act 1911, ss 2(1), 32.
2 *Carmichael v Maccoll* 1913 SC 916, 1913 1 SLT 480, 50 SLR 693, (1913) 1 SLCR 105.
3 *Matheson (Representatives of the late Hugh) v Master of Lovat* 1984 SLCR 82.
4 Small Landholders (Scotland) Act 1911, s 32; *Roscoe's Trustees v Macrae* 1982 SLCR 129.
5 Small Landholders (Scotland) Act 1911, s 32(3).
6 Ibid, s 32(11).

1.12   Non-agricultural uses and apportionment

The 1911 Act introduced an additional statutory condition of tenure to the effect that a landholder shall, by himself or his family, with or without hired labour, cultivate his holding[1]. Combined with this condition was a provision conferring on the landholder a new right to make use of his holding for non-agricultural occupations. These were described as 'subsidiary or auxiliary' and must be such as were not inconsistent with the agricultural uses of the holding. It was not until 50 years later that the Crofters (Scotland) Act 1961 (section 5) conferred on the crofter the right to make permanent improvements required for non-agricultural pursuits and to claim compensation therefor at the end of the tenancy.

The 1911 Act also introduced the right to apply to the Land Court for apportionment of common grazings into separate parts for the exclusive use of the several townships or shareholders interested[2]. In more recent times apportionment has come to assume great importance as a means of initiating schemes of pasture improvement.

1 Small Landholders (Scotland) Act 1911, s 10(1).
2 Ibid, s 24(5) for which a new sub-s (5) was substituted by the Land Settlement (Scotland) Act 1919, s 14.

1.13 Small Landholders and Agricultural Holdings (Scotland) Act 1931

Part I of the 1931 Act made sundry amendments to preceding Acts. It provided that action for removal for failure to pay rent or for the breach of any other statutory condition should be taken before the Land Court instead of the sheriff court as hitherto[1]. It included an important provision for the protection of a landholder entering into a contract or agreement which purported to contract out of the Landholders Acts. It declared that any such contract or agreement, to the extent that it deprived him of any right conferred on him by any provision of the Acts, was void unless it was approved by the Land Court[2].

1 Small Landholders and Agricultural Holdings (Scotland) Act 1931, s 3; *Scott* supra, p 77.
2 Small Landholders and Agricultural Holdings (Scotland) Act 1931, s 25.

1.14 The Taylor Commission

The quest for fresh legislation was again set in train by the Government with the appointment in 1951 of a Commission of Enquiry (the Taylor Commission) whose remit was, 'To review crofting conditions in the Highlands and Islands with special reference to the secure establishment of a small-holding population making full use of agricultural resources and deriving the maximum economic benefit therefrom'. When the Taylor Commission came to make their report in January 1954 they had reached the conclusion that there was need for a new Crofters Commission charged with the duty of stimulating the development of the crofting communities in all possible ways[1]. The time had come, they maintained, when crofting matters required the undivided attention of a responsible executive authority able to keep in intimate touch with the crofting areas. The Taylor Commission pointed out that the Land Court had in course of time come to exercise a very wide jurisdiction over all kinds of agricultural holdings and recommended that, while the Court should retain its proper judicial function in respect of crofting questions, those of its duties which were essentially administrative in character should be transferred to a new Commission. The Act that followed, (the Crofters (Scotland) Act 1955) giving effect to some only of the Taylor Commission's far reaching recommendations, introduced the third period of crofting legislation.

1 Report of the Commission of Enquiry into Crofting Conditions, Cmnd 9091.

(3) THIRD PERIOD: 1955–1976

1.15 Crofters (Scotland) Act 1955

A new Crofters Commission (the present Commission) was constituted by the 1955 Act. Section 1 and the First Schedule to the Act deals with the constitution and general functions of the Commission, being the reorganising, developing and regulating of crofting and keeping under review matters relating to crofting. Particular duties and powers are dealt with in section 2, giving the Commission a wide range of specific functions involving Commission investigation into crofting affairs and advising the Secretary of State thereon and the exercise of controls designed to ensure that croft land continues to be occupied as far as possible to the benefit of crofting communities.

What is dealt with in the third and fourth periods of legislation is current crofting law, with continuing need to refer back to previous enactments in which the current law is rooted. In this introduction the statutory provisions for these periods are sketched out in broad outline only, leaving the detailed exposition and relevant statutory references to be dealt with in the chapters that follow.

The 1955 Act restored to the crofting counties their own special code regulating the statutory tenure while leaving intact the existing statutory provisions for the rest of Scotland. Enactments specified in Part I of the Sixth Schedule to the Act ceased to have effect in the crofting counties and some provisions of the 1911 Act which continue to apply with modifications are set out in Part II of the Schedule. Much of the legislation which ceased to have effect in the crofting counties reappears in the Act and the judicial interpretation of previous legislation is still relevant when construing the provisions of the Crofters Acts. It is also necessary from time to time, when the crofting status of a holding is in question, to trace the history of the holding, sometimes as far back as the 1886 Act, and to do so having regard to the statutory law as it stood at the time.

1.16   Crofting tenure as revised

The various provisions in regard to crofting tenure contained in the series of Acts from 1886 onwards are brought together in sections 3–14 of the 1955 Act, subject to amendments and new provisions reflecting the recommendations of the Taylor Commission so far as adopted. The protected holding is now designated 'croft' and the protected tenant is designated 'crofter' in place of 'landholder' or 'statutory small tenant'. All existing landholders became crofters and all existing statutory small tenants, who had hitherto enjoyed restricted rights, were admitted into the full tenure as crofters. In each case the tenancy of the tenant, so far as consistent with the provisions of the Act, was deemed to be a continuance of his tenancy as a landholder or statutory small tenant. New crofts could be created as hitherto by registration by the Land Court on the joint application of landlord and tenant, or on the application of the Secretary of State where the new croft was constituted under land settlement powers. The limited right to assign his tenancy to a member of his family conferred on the crofter by the 1911 Act was extended to allow assignation to any person with the consent of the Commission. The crofter's right of bequest was extended to allow bequest outwith the family subject to Commission approval. To avoid prolonged delay in settling the succession to a croft arising on intestacy, the Commission were given power, failing timeous entry of an heir, to intervene by searching for a successor and declaring the croft vacant if the search failed.

Far reaching changes in the rules for determining the right of succession to the property of anyone who died intestate in Scotland were enacted by the

Succession (Scotland) Act 1964. It was not until 1968 that the new rules were applied to the succession to crofts by the Law Reform (Miscellaneous Provisions) (Scotland) Act 1968. The new rules apply in relation to the estate of a crofter dying after 25 November 1968.

1.17 Administration of crofts

Sections 15–23 of the 1955 Act deal with the administration of crofts. The Commission were required to compile a register of crofts and to keep it revised. Section 16 makes provision for vacant crofts. The landlord of a vacant croft is prohibited from letting it without the consent of the Commission, or of the Secretary of State if the Commission withhold consent. The Commission themselves can negotiate a relet if the landlord fails to produce acceptable proposals for reletting. Power to grant a direction that a vacant croft should cease to be a croft rested with the Secretary of State until the function was transferred by the Crofting Reform (Scotland) Act 1976 to the Commission, with right of appeal to the Land Court. There was provision for dealing with absentee crofters with dispossession as the ultimate sanction. An aged crofter unable to work his croft, who was willing to renounce his tenancy, could with the consent of the Commission acquire the ownership of his croft house and garden ground. Provisions enabling dispossessed absentee crofters and aged crofters to acquire ownership of the croft house were subsequently repealed as unnecessary when the 1976 Act conferred on all crofters the absolute right to acquire such ownership.

1.18 Common grazings

Sections 24–27 of the 1955 Act deal with common grazings. The Commission took the place of the Land Court as administrative authority dealing with common grazing matters and handling applications for apportionment of grazings for the exclusive use of individual townships or of individual shareholders. Existing statutory provisions as contained in the 1891 and 1911 Acts were re-enacted with major modifications and additions aimed at promoting proper use and development of common grazings. Every grazings committee was required to make new regulations with respect to the management and use of the grazings and providing for recovery from shareholders of expenses incurred in maintaining the grazings and providing equipment therefor. The committee had to submit satisfactory regulations to the Commission for confirmation and where a committee failed to do so the Commission themselves could make the regulations. The regulations have effect notwithstanding anything contrary thereto or inconsistent therewith contained in any lease or other agreement, whether entered into before or after the regulations come into force.

1.19 Cottars

The 1955 Act devotes only one section (section 28) to cottars, for whom the Taylor Commission made no recommendations. The definition of cottar remains substantially as in the 1886 Act.

1.20   Crofters (Scotland) Act 1961

The 1961 Act supplemented and sought to improve the 1955 Act in various particulars. In place of registration by the Land Court, the creation of new crofts was now brought under the control of the Secretary of State where it remained until it was abolished altogether by the 1976 Act. On the joint application of landlord and tenant of a holding the Secretary of State could, if he thought fit, make a direction that the holding should be a croft. The permitted size of a new croft was now stated as an area not exceeding 75 acres (exclusive of common grazings) or an annual rent not exceeding £50. Crofters and owners of non-crofting land could enter into an agreement for the enlargement of existing crofts and common grazings.

The Act introduced a new method for the assessment of compensation payable by the landlord to a crofter for permanent improvements on termination of tenancy. This was based on the amount which a landlord might reasonably be expected to receive for the improvements from the incoming tenant of the croft on relet, replacing the previous basis which assumed that there would be an incoming tenant irrespective of the probable demand or lack of demand for the tenancy. Subletting, which hitherto had been prohibited except with the consent of the landlord, could now take place with the consent of the Commission. The Act expressly provided for the first time that a crofter is entitled to erect buildings or other structures and to execute works on his croft required in connection with use of the croft for subsidiary or auxiliary occupations. These rank as permanent improvements qualifying for compensation on termination of tenancy. The powers of grazings committees to attend to the maintenance and improvement of common grazings and fixed equipment thereon were substantially increased.

The 1955 Act had provided for the stating of a case by the Commission for the opinion of the sheriff on any question of law arising in the course of their determination of matters under the Act. This provision was repealed by the 1961 Act which provided that the Land Court have power to determine any question of fact or law arising under the Crofters Acts. This was made subject to the proviso that the Land Court shall not have power to determine any question (other than a question of law) decided by the Secretary of State or the Commission in the discharge of any of their functions under these Acts.

The Taylor Commission had laid great stress on the importance of reorganisation schemes which would provide for reallocation of township lands among those who were able and willing to work them. The procedures and qualifying conditions for such schemes laid down in the 1955 Act proved too cumbersome and restrictive. The 1961 Act revised the requirements and procedures but the results of attempts at reorganisation have proved disappointing.

1.21   Crofting reform

In exercise of their function to keep crofting matters under review and to advise the Secretary of State thereon, the Commission carried out an extensive study of the extent to which crofting tenure in its traditional form might be inhibiting development of the crofting economy in modern conditions. They recommended conversion of crofting tenure to ownership, subject to safeguards, as a means of overcoming the obstacles to development that existed. A reform Bill eventually reached the statute book as the Crofting Reform (Scotland) Act 1976 and this marked the beginning of the fourth and latest period of crofting legislation.

(4) FOURTH PERIOD: 1976–1990

1.22 Crofting Reform (Scotland) Act 1976

In the 1976 Act the crofter's claim to a status higher than that of a protected tenant is recognised and the principle of conversion of crofting tenure to ownership is established. The Act allows the crofter to continue his crofting tenure undisturbed if he so wishes but he is free to apply for an ownership title as and when it suits his interests to do so, with recourse to the Land Court in the event of failure to agree terms with his landlord. He may claim title to the whole or any portion of his inbye land (land in individual occupancy) subject to limited rights of objection by the landlord and safeguards for sporting interests. He has an absolute right to acquire ownership of the croft house site and suitable garden ground. A similar right to acquire ownership of cottar subjects is extended to a cottar. Before deciding whether to exercise his right of acquisition, the crofter or cottar should consider carefully how his eligibility for the financial aids available to crofter tenants and cottars may be affected. The change in the crofter's status is also reflected in his right to share in the development value of land, whether inbye land or common grazings, resumed by the landlord or taken over under compulsory purchase powers.

There is no provision for acquisition by a crofter of common grazing land save only any apportionment thereof adjacent or contiguous to his croft that may have been granted to him for his own exclusive use. Such an apportionment can be treated as forming part of the inbye land of the croft. When the crofter becomes owner of his inbye land he remains a crofter tenant of any share he may have in common grazings.

The 1976 Act continues in an extended form the safeguards designed to ensure that land will not be taken out of the control of the Crofters Acts so long as it is in the general interest of crofting communities to retain it under control. To secure release of croft land from the Acts the owner of the land (whether the landlord of a vacant croft or a crofter who acquires ownership of croft land) requires to apply to the Commission for a decrofting direction, with right of appeal to the Land Court against the Commission's proposed decision.

The 1976 Act extends the crofter's right of assignation by allowing assignation of a part only of the croft, being the part consisting of a right in pasture or grazing land. It also enables a crofter to dispense with the consent of the Commission when assigning his croft (or the grazing right) to a member of his family provided he has obtained the consent of the landlord. The procedure whereby new crofts could be created by direction of the Secretary of State, as prescribed in the 1961 Act, was repealed and not replaced. The maximum size to which a croft can be enlarged by private agreement between a crofter and the owner of non-crofting land has been revised to thirty hectares of inbye land and an annual rent of £100, or such area and rent not substantially larger than these limits as the Commission may approve on application being made to them by the owner of the land and the crofter.

The number of crofts entered in the Register of Crofts at 31 December 1988 is recorded in the Commission's Annual Report for 1988 as 17,648 including 2,615 owner-occupied crofts. The Commission point out that a crofter is often the tenant of two or more crofts worked together as a unit. The total numbers of purchases of crofting subjects notified to the Commission in terms of the 1976 Act since 10 June 1976 were: 1,305 house sites, 282 part crofts and 2,062 whole crofts. These figures may not be wholly accurate because of failure to notify[1].

1 Crofters Commission Report 1988, para 51.

CHAPTER 2

ADMINISTRATIVE AND LEGAL FUNCTIONS

The principal bodies involved with crofting are (A) the Crofters Commission, (B) the Scottish Land Court and (C) the Secretary of State and the Department of Agriculture and Fisheries for Scotland.

(A) THE CROFTERS COMMISSION

2.01 Membership and function

The Crofters Commission are a body corporate with a common seal constituted under the Crofters (Scotland) Act 1955, with the general functions of reorganising, developing and regulating crofting in the seven crofting counties and promoting the interests of crofters there[1]. The Act provides that the Commission shall consist of not more than nine members appointed by the Secretary of State, who also appoints one member as chairman. They must include members with knowledge of crofting conditions and at least one member who can speak the Gaelic language. They are required to carry out their functions in accordance with such directions of a general character as may be given by the Secretary of State to whom they make an annual report of their proceedings which he lays before each House of Parliament[2].

In exercise of their general functions, the Commission have a duty[3]:

(1) to keep under general review all matters relating to crofts and crofting conditions and to make such recommendations thereon as they think fit;

(2) to collaborate so far as their powers and duties permit with any body or person in carrying out any measures for the economic development and social improvement of the crofting counties;

(3) to advise the Secretary of State on any crofting matters which he may refer to them or on which they think fit to advise him; and

(4) to exercise the specific powers conferred on them by the Crofters (Scotland) Acts 1955 and 1961, and the Crofting Reform (Scotland) Act 1976.

The Land Court have power to determine any question of fact or law arising under these Acts, except[4]

(a) any question reserved by the Acts to another court (eg a question as to the validity of a crofter's will), and

(b) any question (other than a question of law) decided by the Secretary of State or the Commission in the discharge of their functions under the Acts.

Any person having an interest may apply to the Court to determine any question of fact or law within these limits and the Commission may themselves refer such questions to the Court. The Court are required to intimate to the Commission their determination on questions coming before them whether under the Crofters Acts or under the Landholders Acts (in their application to the crofting counties). The Commission must send to the principal clerk of the Court for recording in the Crofters Holdings Book every order or other proceeding of theirs which they think proper to record[5].

There is a right of appeal to the Land Court against the Commission's decision or proposed decision in certain decrofting proceedings and in such appeals the Court may hear or consider such evidence as they think fit[6]. The Court have ruled that the Commission are entitled to appear before them and take part in the appeal proceedings[7]. A landlord may also apply to the Land Court for a variation of terms and conditions of re-let of a vacant croft where the Commission have negotiated a re-let on the landlord's failure to do so[8].

An important function of the Commission is the administration as agents of the Secretary of State of schemes of financial assistance for the purpose of aiding and developing agricultural production on crofts. The major scheme currently in operation is the Crofting Counties Agricultural Grants (Scotland) Scheme 1988. The various forms of assistance and the rates and conditions are fully explained in leaflets available from the Commission.

1 Crofters (Scotland) Act 1955, s 1 (as amended).
2 Ibid, s 2(4) (as amended).
3 Ibid, s 2(1) (as amended).
4 Crofters (Scotland) Act 1961, s 4 (as amended), *Mackenzie v Crofters Commission* 1966 SLT (Land Ct) 13, 1965 SLCR App 56; *Vestey v Holmes* 1967 SLT (Land Ct) 7.
5 Crofters (Scotland) Act 1955, s 2(3) (as amended).
6 Ibid, s 16A(8) (as added); see para 2.04.
7 *Moray Estates Development Co v Crofters Commission* 1988 SLT (Land Ct) 14, 1987 SLCR 14; see also *MacColl v Crofters Commission* 1986 SLT (Land Ct) 4, 1985 SLCR 142.
8 Crofters (Scotland) Act 1955, s 16(5); see para 6.03.

2.02   Constitution, proceedings and management

The constitution of the Commission is contained in the First Schedule to the 1955 Act[1]. The Commission *quorum* is three or such larger number as they may from time to time determine. If at any meeting of the Commission the votes are equally divided on any question, the person acting as chairman of the meeting has a second or casting vote. The Commission can refer to one or more of their number for report and recommendation such matters as they may determine and, with the approval of the Secretary of State, may delegate any of their statutory functions to one or more of their number. They may order that the evidence be taken on oath in any application or other proceeding coming before them. In certain proceedings (eg applications for consent to assign crofts, objections by landlords to receive legatees and proposals to dispossess absentee crofters) the Commission are required by the 1955 Act before taking action to afford those with an interest an opportunity to make representations in writing and also to be heard by a person appointed by the Commission for the purpose[2]. In certain other proceedings a similar requirement is prescribed in the Commission's Rules of Procedure.

The application of the seal of the Commission to any document must be attested by at least one member and by the person for the time being acting as secretary to the Commission[3]. Every document purporting to be an instrument issued by the Commission and to be so sealed and attested or to be duly signed on behalf of the Commission shall be received in evidence and shall be deemed to be such an instrument without further proof unless the contrary is shown.

The Commission at present comprise a chairman and six part-time members, each with responsibility for a defined geographical area. They have their head office in Inverness at which communications and notices will be received. Apart from headquarters staff, they have the services of the professional field staff of the Department of Agriculture and Fisheries for Scotland at area offices in Lerwick, Kirkwall, Thurso, Lairg, Inverness, Oban, Portree, Benbecula and Stornoway. They also have the assistance of a panel of assessors who form a two-way channel of communication between crofting communities and the Commission[4]. The assessors, numbering over a hundred, are appointed by the Commission, mostly on the nomination of grazing committees and including liaison officers nominated by the Scottish Crofters Union and the National Farmers' Union for Scotland.

Subject to the provisions of the First Schedule to the 1955 Act the Commission have power to regulate their own procedure. The current Rules (which can be found in Appendix C of this book) are dated 4 September 1980. They were made by the Commission in consultation with the Scottish Committee of the Council on Tribunals, under whose supervision the Commission come by virtue of the Tribunals and Inquiries Act 1971.

1 Crofters (Scotland) Act 1955, s 1(5).
2 Ibid, s 33(4).
3 Ibid, First Sch, paras 13, 14.
4 Ibid, s 2(2).

(B) SCOTTISH LAND COURT

2.03 Introduction

The Scottish Land Court was constituted on 1 April 1912 as statutory successor to the first Crofters Commission[1]. It is a body corporate with a common seal which is to be judicially noticed and any order or other instrument purporting to be so sealed shall be received as evidence without further proof. The members (who are not to exceed seven in number) have appointed from them a chairman of the same rank and tenure of office as if he had been appointed a judge of the Court of Session[2]. One of the members of the Court must be able to speak the Gaelic language[3].

Three members of the Court are a quorum but it may delegate such of its powers as it considers expedient to any one member or any two members of the Court (often referred to as a 'Divisional Court'). It may also appoint land valuers, assessors or other skilled persons to sit with the Court as required[4].

An order made by a Divisional Court can be reviewed upon appeal by three or more members of the Court (including where such court of review consists of three members, not more than one member who was a party to such order as is appealed against). This 'Full Court' shall include the chairman as a member[5].

The Secretary of State appoints a fit person to act as principal clerk to the Court and this is in practice a qualified solicitor[6]. In addition the Court may itself appoint further clerks of court, solicitors, surveyors, assessors or valuers in addition to clerical staff and messengers for the due performance of its duties[7]. In practice the administration of the Scottish Land Court forms part of the general Scottish Courts Administration.

The Land Court has jurisdiction to hear and determine all matters, whether of law or fact, which arise under the Crofters Acts in addition to any other jurisdiction conferred on it by statute[8]. The decision of the Land Court in any case is final, subject to the power that it may, if it thinks fit, or on the request of any party, state a special case on any question of law arising in any proceedings before it for the opinion of the Inner House of the Court of Session which is authorised finally to determine that question[9].

1 Small Landholders (Scotland) Act 1911, s 3(1) as amended by the Agriculture (Scotland) Act 1948, s 70.
2 Small Landholders (Scotland) Act 1911, s 3(2).
3 Ibid, s 3(3).
4 Ibid, s 25(5).
5 Ibid, s 25(5).
6 Ibid, s 3(6).
7 Ibid, s 3(8).
8 Crofters (Scotland) Act 1961, s 4(1).
9 Small Landholders (Scotland) Act 1911, s 25(2); Crofters (Scotland) Act 1961, s 4(3).

2.04 Procedure

The facts in any case may be ascertained by the Court by hearing parties and examining witnesses or by means of affidavits or such other mode of enquiry as it deems appropriate. The Court may require the production of all books, papers, plans and documents relating to the case and it may summon and examine on oath such witness as it thinks fit to call or allow to appear before it[1]. All orders and determinations of the Land Court shall be in writing[2]. The Court may also determine the amount of expenses in any proceedings before it and the proportion to be borne by the different parties[3]. When sitting in open court, the Land Court may report in writing to the Lord Ordinary any person who has been guilty of contempt of court and the Lord Ordinary may punish such person as if the contempt has been committed in his own Court. However, when the chairman of the Land Court is sitting in open Court, he shall have the same power as the Lord Ordinary to punish such contempt of court[4]. Any order or determination of the Land Court may be enforced as if it were a decree of the sheriff having jurisdiction in the area where the order or determination is to be enforced[5].

The Land Court is empowered to make its own rules for conducting business before it and the current rules are to be found in Appendix B of this book[6]. In addition the Land Court may, subject to the approval of the Secretary of State, prescribe such forms of application and other forms of procedure as they think proper and, with the approval of the Treasury, fix a scale of fees to be charged, organise the taxation of such fees and determine the persons by whom and the manner in which such fees are to be paid[7].

The Scottish Land Court at present comprises a chairman and three members. The principal clerk is assisted by two assistants who are also qualified solicitors. The Court is situated in Edinburgh and shares its premises and chairman with the Lands Tribunal for Scotland.

Hearings of Divisonal Courts take place in the locality of the croft land involved as do normally appeals. However, arguments of a legal nature may be heard at a suitable location, either the Land Court building or at Inverness or Oban or some other appropriate centre. It should be remembered that the value of a decision by the Court will depend to some extent on the make up of the Court making the decision. A Divisional Court decision will hold less weight than that of a Full Court and this should be borne in mind when utilising reported cases.

1 Small Landholders (Scotland) Act 1911, s 25(3).
2 Ibid, s 25(1).
3 Ibid, s 25(4).
4 Ibid, s 25(3).
5 Crofting Reform (Scotland) Act 1976, s 17(1).
6 Small Landholders (Scotland) Act 1911, s 3(12).
7 Crofters Holdings (Scotland) Act 1886, s 19.

(C) SECRETARY OF STATE AND DEPARTMENT OF AGRICULTURE AND FISHERIES FOR SCOTLAND

2.05 Introduction

The 1911 Act established a Board of Agriculture for Scotland. To it were transferred the powers and duties of the Congested Districts Board set up under the Congested Districts (Scotland) Act 1897 for the improvement of congested districts in the crofting counties[1]. The 1911 Act vested in the Board of Agriculture important new powers and duties (extended by subsequent legislation) for promoting the interests of agriculture generally and in particular for the creation of small agricultural holdings throughout Scotland both on private estates and on land acquired by the Board by agreement or compulsorily[2]. Under the Reorganisation of Offices (Scotland) Act 1928 the Board's functions were transfered to the Department of Agriculture for Scotland[3]. The Reorganisation of Offices (Scotland) Act 1939 in turn transferred to the Secretary of State for Scotland the functions of the Department (now the Department of Agriculture and Fisheries for Scotland). The Department thus lost its separate legal identity as a statutory body but continues as an organisation for the administration of the Secretary of State's statutory functions.

1 Small Landholders (Scotland) Act 1911, ss 4, 28.
2 Historical Introduction, para 1.07.
3 J Scott *Law of Small Holdings in Scotland* (1933) p 182 et seq.

2.06 Secretary of State's statutory functions

In so far as they relate to the crofting counties, these include the following:
  (1) The Secretary of State appoints the Chairman and members of the Crofters Commission and the Commission are required to carry out

their functions in accordance with such directions of a general character as he may give them[1]. He defrays the expenses of the Commission[2] and provides the services of such officers and servants as they may require[3].

(2) The Commission make an annual report to the Secretary of State, a copy of which he lays before each House of Parliament with such comments as he thinks fit[4].

(3) The Secretary of State may make schemes for providing financial assistance to crofters and others in the crofting counties[5].

(4) The Commission have a duty to advise the Secretary of State on any crofting matter which he may refer to them or on which they may think fit to advise him[6].

(5) There is a right of appeal by the landlord to the Secretary of State if the Commission withhold consent to the letting of a croft[7].

(6) The amount of compensation for permanent improvements payable to a crofter on termination of tenancy may be less when assessed on the new basis introduced by the 1961 Act than it would have been had the amount been assessed on the old basis under the 1955 Act. Where this is so and the tenancy of the croft began before the 1961 Act commenced, the crofter can recover the difference between two amounts from the Secretary of State[8].

(7) Where an absentee tenant has been dispossessed and the croft has remained unlet for six months, the landlord may require the Commission to decroft the croft and the Secretary of State to purchase the croft buildings[9].

(8) Where the Commission have relet a vacant croft as an enlargement of another croft and any of the buildings on the vacant croft cease to be required for the enlarged croft, the landlord may require the Secretary of State to purchase the buildings[10].

(9) Townships reorganisation schemes prepared by the Commission require to be submitted to the Secretary of State for further investigation and assessment prior to confirmation[11].

(10) The Secretary of State may be required by the owner to purchase land and buildings affected by a township reorganisation scheme[12].

The Land Court has no power to determine any question (other than a question of law) decided by the Secretary of State in the discharge of his functions under the Crofting Acts[13].

---

1 Crofters (Scotland) Act 1955, s 1.
2 Ibid, s 35; Crofters (Scotland) Act 1961, s 16; Crofting Reform (Scotland) Act 1976, s 20.
3 Crofters (Scotland) Act 1955, Sch 1, para 12.
4 Ibid, s 2(4) (as amended).
5 See paras 3.13–3.14.
6 Crofters (Scotland) Act 1955, s 2(1).
7 Ibid, s 16(3); see para 6.03.
8 Crofters (Scotland) Act 1961, s 6 (as amended); see para 5.15.
9 Crofters (Scotland) Act 1955, s 16(7), (8) (as amended); see para 6.15.
10 Ibid, s 16(6), (8) (as amended); see para 6.03.
11 Crofters (Scotland) Act 1961, ss 8, 9 and Second Sch.
12 Ibid, s 9.
13 Crofters (Scotland) Act 1961, s 4 (as amended).

Part II CROFTING TENURE

CONTENTS

CHAPTER 3

CROFTS AND CROFTERS

3.01 Earlier Acts

The crofter's tenure of his croft is basically that of a tenant from year to year[1] whose conditions of tenancy and rights and obligations have been laid down in a series of Acts of Parliament, commencing with the Crofters Holdings (Scotland) Act 1886 and of which the latest is the Crofting Reform (Scotland) Act 1976. Chapter one 'Historical Introduction' is referred to for an exposition of the main Acts and this is essential reading if one is to get a proper grasp of crofting tenure as it exists today. The earlier Crofters Acts were administered by the first Crofters Commission. At that time the statutory tenure was confined to small agricultural holdings (designated 'crofts') within the seven crofting counties, being the former counties of Argyll, Caithness, Inverness, Orkney, Ross and Cromarty, Sutherland and Zetland. As from 1 April 1912 the 1911 Act extended the tenure to existing smallholdings throughout the whole of Scotland and made provision for the creation of new holdings. The Crofters Commission were replaced by the Scottish Land Court. The fully protected tenant was designated 'landholder' in place of 'crofter'. A new class of tenants, with restricted rights, termed 'statutory small tenants', was created. The 1911 Act and the earlier Acts were cited together as the 'Small Landholders (Scotland) Acts 1886 to 1911'.

1 *MacDonald v Dalgleish* (1894) 21 R 900, 2 SLT 67, 31 SLR 751; *Sutherland v Sutherland* 1986 SLT (Land Ct) 22, 1984 SLCR 94.

3.02 The Crofters (Scotland) Act 1955 and later Acts

In 1955 fresh legislation was introduced to make special provision again for the seven crofting counties. The Crofters (Scotland) Act 1955 constituted the present Crofters Commission as the administrative body charged with the duty of reorganising, developing and regulating crofting. The Land Court continued as the judicial body. The Act consolidated the existing statutory provisions and applied them with some amendments and additions to the tenure in the crofting counties. The expressions 'crofter' and 'croft' were revived to describe the protected tenant and holding and statutory small tenants were admitted into the full tenure. Thus crofters have again their own special code as contained in the 1955 Act together with the Crofters (Scotland) Act 1961 and the Crofting Reform (Scotland) Act 1976. Provisions of earlier enactments ceasing to have effect in the crofting counties and provisions of the Small Landholders (Scotland) Act 1911 having effect subject to modifications are scheduled in the 1955 Act[1]. It is still sometimes necessary to refer to the statutory provisions in their original context and judicial decisions construing these provisions are still relevant. The Acts apply to land belonging to the Crown and to government departments subject to such modifications as may be prescribed by regulations made by the Secretary of State[2].

In the 1955 Act the expression 'crofter' is defined as the tenant of a croft[3]. The expression 'landlord' means any person for the time being entitled to receive the rents and profits or to take possession of a croft[4]. Where there were heritable creditors in possession of an estate, they and not the owners were held to be the 'landlords' entitled to let a vacant holding on the estate[5]. It has long been established that, in order to qualify as a crofter, a tenant must be a principal tenant holding direct from the proprietor of the land and not merely a subtenant[6]. This is so even where the subtenancy has been granted by a leaseholder holding under a long lease[7].

1 Crofters (Scotland) Act 1955, s 38 and Sixth Sch.
2 Ibid, s 38(1).
3 Ibid, s 3(2).
4 Ibid, s 37(1).
5 *Adie's Trs v Harrison* (1939) 27 SLCR 65.
6 *Livingstone v Beattie* (1891) 18 R 735, 28 SLR 518; *Dalgleish v Livingston* (1895) 22 R 646, 2 SLT 564, 32 SLR 347; see Scott *Smallholdings* (1933) p 134.
7 *MacDonald v Bennet* (1949) 37 SLCR 24.

3.03   Definition of croft

The definition of the expression 'croft' falls under three heads[1]:

(a) Former landholder holdings

> Every holding (whether occupied by a landholder or not) in the crofting counties which was, immediately before 1 October 1955 (when the 1955 Act came into operation), a holding to which any of the provisions of the Landholders Acts relating to landholders applied.

The great mass of crofts in existence today qualified as such because they were previously landholders' holdings. The phrase 'whether occupied by a landholder or not', occurring in the statutory definition, takes account of the fact that when a landholder's holding fell vacant it still remained subject to the Landholders Acts in the sense that, if the landlord relet it on other than landholder tenure without the consent of the Secretary of State (originally the Board, afterwards the Department, of Agriculture) the Secretary of State was entitled to declare the relet null and void[2]. The Land Court (Divisional Court) held that a landholder's holding which had been owner-occupied for 31 years continued to be subject to the Landholders Acts and hence became a croft at 1 October 1955[3]. So far as consistent with the provisions of the 1955 Act, the tenancy of a former landholder who became a crofter is deemed to be a continuance of his tenancy as a landholder[4].

(b) Former statutory small tenancy holdings

> Every holding in the crofting counties which was immediately before 1 October 1955 a holding to which the provisions of the Landholders Acts relating to statutory small tenants applied[5].

When a statutory small tenancy fell vacant the provisions of the Landholders Acts ceased to apply. Hence holdings at any time held on a statutory small tenancy that were at the said date vacant or held on any other tenure (other than landholder tenure) did not become crofts[6]. Subject to the provisions of the 1955 Act, the tenancy of a former statutory small tenant who became a crofter is deemed to be a continuance of his tenancy as a statutory small tenant[7].

(c) New crofts

(1) Every holding in the crofting counties which, between 1 October 1955 and 27 August 1961 (when the 1961 Act came into operation), was constituted a croft by the registration under section 4 of the 1955 Act of the tenant as a crofter by the Land Court on the joint application of landlord and tenant or on the application of the Secretary of State in exercise of land settlement functions[8].

The qualifying size of a new croft constituted under this provision was the same as for holdings admitted to the statutory tenure for the first time under the 1911 Act, namely, a holding of which the annual rent did not exceed £50 irrespective of area, or of which the area (exclusive of common grazing) did not exceed 50 acres irrespective of rent. Not more than one person could be registered as a crofter in respect of any holding.

(2) Every holding in the crofting counties as to which, after 27 August 1961, the Secretary of State directed under section 2(1) of the 1961 Act that the holding should be a croft[9].

Application for the direction could be made jointly by the landlord and tenant of any holding of which the area did not exceed 75 acres (exclusive of common grazing) or of which the annual rent did not exceed £50. The Secretary of State could make the direction if he saw fit. This provision for constituting new crofts was repealed by the 1976 Act[10] and was not replaced.

1 Crofters (Scotland) Act 1955, s 3(1) (as amended).
2 Small Landholders (Scotland) Act 1911, s 17 (as amended by the Land Settlement (Scotland) Act 1919, s 12 and the Small Landholders and Agricultural Holdings (Scotland) Act 1931, s 6), s 6; see *Scott* pp 124 et seq. *Doxford Estates Co Ltd v Macdonald* (1943) 31 SLCR 16; *MacNee v Stroyan's Trs* 1970 SLCR App 29; *Whyte v Garden's Trs* (1926) 14 SLCR 73; see also the more recent case of *Palmer's Trustees v Crofters Commission* 1989 SLCR 98 1990 SLT (Land Ct) where it was argued (under reference to the cases of *Countess of Seafield's Trs v Sutherland* (1935) 23 SLCR 53 and *Secretary of State for Scotland v Shareholders of Lealt and Culnacnock Common Grazings* 1982 SLT (Land Ct) 20, that, following a break in a lease to a landholder and the relet of the holding outwith the Landholders Acts, these Acts ceased to apply. The Court however did not need to consider this argument in disposing of the case before them.
3 *Laird, Applicant* 1973 SLT (Land Ct) 4, but see *Palmer's Trs v Crofters Commission* supra.
4 Crofters (Scotland) Act 1955, s 39(1).
5 See para 1.11.
6 *Roscoe's Trs v Macrae* 1982 SLCR 129.
7 Crofters (Scotland) Act 1955, s 39(1).
8 Crofters (Scotland) Act 1955, 3(1)(c) (as amended).
9 Ibid, s 3(1)(d) (as amended).
10 Crofting Reform (Scotland) Act 1976, Sch 3.

3.04 Meaning of 'holding'[1]

It will be observed from the foregoing statutory definition of 'croft' that, except for new crofts created after 1 October 1955, the question whether a holding is a croft turns on whether immediately before that date it was a landholder's holding or a statutory small tenant's holding. When defining the holdings which were to qualify for the statutory tenure[2], the 1911 Act repealed the earlier definition of holding contained in the 1886 Act[3] and adopted by reference the definition provided by section 35 of the Agricultural Holdings (Scotland) Act 1908 (repeated in section 49(1) of the Agricultural Holdings (Scotland) Act 1923). This described a holding as 'any piece of land held by a tenant which is either wholly agricultural or wholly pastoral, or in part agricultural and as to the residue pastoral . . .'. Applying this definition in an important test case[4] relating to the fixing of fair rents for landholder holdings, the full Court of Session by a narrow majority decided that any dwelling-house or other buildings which were not required for agricultural or pastoral purposes on the holding did not form part of the statutory tenancy. To resolve the difficulty the Court further decided that they were faced with a *casus improvisus* and that such buildings must be excised from the holding. This excluded the buildings from the statutory protection and left the remainder to stand as the statutory tenancy. But the Land Court, in a case dealing with the acquisition of croft land under the 1976 Act, have since displaced that decision[5]. They have ruled that supervening legislation has removed the difficulties faced by the Court of Session and that their decision is no longer authority in the crofting counties for the proposition that non-agricultural buildings on a croft should be excised therefrom, whether for the purpose of fixing a fair rent or for the purpose of acquisition of croft land. The legislation referred to is the Agricultural Holdings (Scotland) Act 1949 where a holding is simply defined as 'the aggregate of the agricultural land comprised in a lease'[6], with a wide definition given to the word 'agriculture'[7]. The Court referred to the statutory condition which confers on a crofter the right to make use of his croft for subsidiary or auxiliary occupations[8], combined with the further right to erect buildings or other structures required for such uses[9], as placing the matter beyond doubt.

1 See *Scott* pp 42 et seq.
2 Small Landholders (Scotland) Act 1911, s 26(3)(f).
3 Crofters Holdings (Scotland) Act 1886, s 34.
4 *McNeill v Duke of Hamilton's Trs* 1918 SC 221, 1918 1 SLT 265, 55 SLR 329, 6 SLCR 71.
5 *Cameron v Duke of Argyll's Trs* 1981 SLT (Land Ct) 2.
6 Agricultural Holdings (Scotland) Act 1949, s 1(1).
7 Ibid, s 93(1).
8 Crofters (Scotland) Act 1955, Second Sch, para 3 (as amended).
9 Crofters (Scotland) Act 1961, s 5.

3.05   Grazing rights

For the great majority of crofters, grazing rights are an important part of the croft and in some cases of more importance than the inbye land. These rights have been recognised as forming part of the statutory tenancy from 1886 onwards. For the purposes of the Crofters Acts any right in pasture or grazing land held or to be held by the tenant of a croft, whether alone or in common with others, is deemed to form part of the croft.[1] This right has been described as being not a tenancy of land but an ancillary right outside the croft which constitutes a pertinent of the croft and belongs to the tenant of the croft as such. It is an incorporeal right in contrast to a real right such as is created by a lease[2]. Where a crofter and his predecessors had exercised an undefined right of grazing throughout living memory over land that was not proved to be a common grazing, it was held that the grazing right formed part of his croft[3].

Grazing rights may be held by a crofter on an arrangement entirely separate from his tenancy of the croft and not forming a pertinent of it. The subjects may be worked together but they remain on separate tenures and do not become one crofting subject[4].

The subordinate right of peat cutting which can also form a pertinent of the croft is dealt with under 'Security of Tenure'[5] and 'Common Grazings'[6].

Where by virtue of the acquisition provisions of the 1976 Act a crofter has acquired his entire croft other than a right in pasture or grazing land effeiring to the croft, the crofter continues to hold this right in tenancy until such time as it is held otherwise and the right by itself is deemed to be a croft[7]. It is competent for a crofter to assign a right in common grazings separately from his croft[8].

1 Crofters (Scotland) Act 1955, s 3(5).
2 *Ross v Graesser* 1962 SC 66, 1962 SLT 130, (1962) 50 SLCR 9.
3 *MacDonald v Guthrie* 1971 SLCR App 23; but see *Kemp v Johnston's Trs* 1988 SLCR 115.
4 *Ross v Graesser*, supra.
5 See para 4.16.
6 See para 8.08.
7 See para 9.18.
8 See para 6.04.

3.06   Crofting enlargements

The 1961 Act makes provision for the enlargement of existing crofts and common grazings by the addition of non-crofting land[1]. The owner of such land can enter into agreement with any crofter to enlarge his croft up to an area not in excess of 30 hectares (exclusive of any common pasture or grazing held therewith) provided the rent of the enlarged croft is not in excess of £100. No procedure is required to effect the enlargement other than notification by the owner of the land to the Crofters Commission. Where the area and rent of the enlarged croft would exceed these limits, the owner of the land and the crofter may make joint application to the Commission for a direction that the land shall form part of the croft. The Commission may make the direction only if they are satisfied that such direction (a) would be of benefit to the croft, and (b) would not result in the croft being substantially in excess of these limits. If the direction is granted the statutory tenure will apply to the croft as enlarged.

Where the owner of non-crofting land agrees to grant rights in any pasture or grazing land to crofters sharing in any common grazing and the owner and crofters agree that such land will form part of the common grazing it will be enlarged accordingly and the statutory tenure will apply. The owner is required to notify the Commission of the enlargement.

Non-crofting land can also be brought into a township reorganisation scheme by the Commission for the purpose of enlarging crofts and common grazings[2]. Even where croft land has been decrofted, this does not bar the subsequent exercise of any statutory powers for the enlargement of existing crofts[3].

1 Crofters (Scotland) Act 1961, s 2 (as amended).
2. See para 6.16.
3 Crofters (Scotland) Act 1955, s 16(9) (as substituted).

3.07 Rights of access

A right of access over non-crofting land may be claimed as forming a pertinent of a croft and as such the Land Court have jurisdiction to adjudicate on the claim[1]. It is well established that where a crofter claims a right of access over another part of the same estate as a pertinent of his croft, the Court have jurisdiction to determine the question. Founding on previous authority the Court decided that they had jurisdiction to determine that a crofter had established a pertinential right of access over the land of a neighbouring proprietor, being land which formerly formed part of the same estate as that on which the croft was situated[2]. But they dismissed a crave to authorise the crofter to enter on that land to carry out work for the widening and improvement of the access as being a matter affecting heritable title over which they had no authority.

To establish the claim to access it is necessary to prove that the right is founded on an express grant by the person entitled to grant it, or that the access is one of necessity serving a landlocked croft, or that the right has been acquired by reason of use over a long number of years[3]. It must not be merely a privilege depending on the tolerance of the tenant whose land is being crossed. Once a right of access has been established by the person claiming it, the onus of proof will shift and it will be for the person challenging the right to show why the *status quo* should be disturbed[4]. Any necessary upkeep of the access requires to be shared by those having rights thereto according to user. Where the right includes use for vehicular traffic there can be a progression from former use, such as from carts to tractors[5].

Right of access must be distinguished from a right of way which is a heritable right burdening the property of a servient proprietor and vests in the public at large[6]. As such the rules of prescription apply and the Land Court have no jurisdiction. But the Court have held that while these rules do not apply to a tenancy, a right of access in favour of a croft which has been enjoyed for more than 60 years must be assumed to have some substantial foundation and requires some strong reasons to be adduced before the right can be displaced[7].

1 *Adamson v Sharp's Trs* (1917) 5 SLCR 76.
2 *Maclean v Fletcher* 1965 SLT (Land Ct) 5.
3 *Tait v Abernethy* 1984 SLCR 19, 1985 SLCR 147; *Stewart v MacRitchie* 1955 SLCR App 233; *MacKenzie v Cameron* 1953 SLCR App 133.
4 *Little v Countess of Sutherland's Trs* 1979 SLCR App 18.
5 *Tait v Abernethy* supra; *Malcolm v Lloyd* (1886) 13 R 512, 23 SLR 371.
6 *Tait v Abernethy* supra; *Jeffrey v Dixon* 1983 SLCR 69; *Little v Countess of Sutherland's Trs* supra.
7 *Munro v Forbes* (1933) 21 SLCR 31.

3.08 Crofting boundaries

Among the functions of the Land Court is the power to determine, either on the application of any person having an interest or on a reference made to them by the Crofters Commission, any question arising under the Crofters

Acts as to the boundaries of a croft or of any pasture or grazing land a right in which forms part of a croft[1].

When fixing boundaries the Court may have to examine data from various sources such as estate maps and rent records, entries in the Commission's Register of Crofts and oral evidence. Some of these are often at variance with each other[2]. Where the information from such sources proved particularly unreliable the Court preferred to base their decision on evidence of possession with some corroboration from aerial evidence[3]. A boundary line between two common grazings which had been recognised by both townships for over 40 years was accepted by the Court although the estate plan showed a different line[4]. By way of clearing the way for an application to fix croft boundaries, landholder tenants challenged the accuracy of the areas of their holdings. The areas had been recorded 26 years earlier in an agreement for enlargement of holdings to which the Court had interponed authority at the instance of the landlord and tenants. The Court held that the tenants were barred by acquiescence, *mora* and taciturnity from disputing the accuracy of the figures recorded in the agreement[5].

1 Crofters (Scotland) Act 1961, s 4(1)(c).
2 *Ross v Master of Lovat* 1979 SLCR App 127; *MacLean v MacLeod* 1978 SLCR App 41; see also *Shetland Islands Council v Jamieson* 1988 SLCR 97.
3 *Macaskill v Taylor* 1970 SLCR App 34.
4 *Borve Grazings Committee v Rushgarry Grazings Committee* (1946) 34 SLCR 47.
5 *Garenin Grazings Committee v Garenin Tenants* (1950) 38 SLCR 16.

3.09   Fencing and maintenance of fencing

One question frequently at issue concerns the liability of crofters to fence boundaries of crofts and common grazings and to maintain boundary fences. The legal principles applicable have been stated in a number of cases. A crofter cannot be compelled by a neighbour to fence his croft or to co-operate with him in the erection of a fence between their crofts[1]. In the absence of proof that an existing fence or dyke between neighbours is a mutual one or that the crofter is under specific obligation to maintain it, the Court cannot order him to do so[2]. The crofter has no right to call on his landlord to provide new fencing unless they have agreed otherwise. Where there is existing fencing between land occupied by the landlord and land occupied by the crofter, the obligation to maintain is mutual but if the fences are renewed by the crofter, they become his improvement and the entire future maintenance falls on him[3]. In law every tenant is responsible for the herding of his own stock and the Winter Herding Act 1686 enacts certain penalties where stock is allowed to stray on to neighbouring land[4].

In a special case stated by the Land Court, the Court of Session held that the grazings committee had a duty to maintain, repair and if necessary replace the existing fences and dykes separating the holdings of individual crofters from the common grazings[5]. Where a boundary fence separating two common grazings on the same estate had been erected to replace an old turf dyke as to one-half by each of the two townships concerned, the liability for maintenance was allocated by the Land Court in the same proportions[6]. This was in accord with township regulations and long established custom. The Court observed that responsibility in such matters, failing agreement or regulations otherwise, fell to be decided according to long usage and a continuous course of practice.[7]. On the other hand the Court held that tenants of holdings originally constituted under a land settlement scheme were entirely responsible for the maintenance of fences separating their common grazings from the common grazings of two adjoining townships. They failed to prove any agreement in their contracts of tenancy that the adjoining townships would share the responsibility and in the intervening twenty-seven years no call had been made on them to do so[8].

A distinction has to be drawn between the internal fences on an estate and a march fence separating two estates. The law is well settled that agricultural tenants on each side of a march fence are bound at common law to maintain such fence to the extent of one-half each. A landlord may be compelled by a neighbouring proprietor to erect a fence on the march by legal process under the old Scots Act, the March Dykes Act 1661 (cap 41), or they may both agree to erect the fence at mutual expense. Whenever the march fence is erected the obligation on tenants on each side to maintain the fence to the extent of one-half naturally follows[9]. The Land Court applied this statement of the law to landholder tenants in a case where the tenants on one side of the march fence were taken bound by their conditions of let to maintain it to the extent of one-half and the tenants on the other side were not[10]. The Court held that in the absence of stipulation to the contrary a similar liability fell upon the neighbouring tenants and any relief from this liability granted by their landlord in the past must be assumed to have been an indulgence. The Court have no jurisdiction to order a landlord to erect a march fence.

1 *Peto v Macrae* (1945) 33 SLCR 40.
2 *Manson v Goodlad* (1941) 29 SLCR 33.
3 *Macdonald v Lord Breadalbane* (1944) 32 SLCR 60, 1943 SLCR App 50.
4 *Manson v Goodlad* supra.
5 *Crofters Commission v Cameron of Garth* 1964 SC 229, 1964 SLT 276 (applying s 25(1)(a) of the Crofters (Scotland) Act 1955 (as amended), see para 8.03; *Sikorski v Noble* 1985 SLCR 139.
6 *Totescore Common Grazings Committee v Idrigill Common Grazings Committee* (1961) 49 SLCR 44.
7 Citing *Falconer v Murray* (1913) 1 SLCR 53.
8 *Tenants of Dunans v Department of Agriculture for Scotland* (1938) 26 SLCR 67.
9 *Dudgeon v Howden* Nov 23, 1813 FC 458.
10 *Balemore Landholders v Orde's Trs* (1933) 21 SLCR 11; see also *Ross v Secretary of State for Scotland* (1953) 41 SLCR 39 and *Harrold v Secretary of State for Scotland* (1953) 41 SLCR 37, 1953 SLCR App 256.

3.10 Register of crofts[1]

It is true to say that the vast majority of crofts can be easily identified and are now entered in the Register of Crofts kept by the Crofters Commission in Inverness. The Register was recently computerised. The Commission have a duty to compile and keep up-to-date a register containing particulars of individual crofts[2]. They have authority to serve notice on the owner or the occupier of any holding requiring him to provide them with information as to the extent, rent and tenure of the holding and as to such other matters relating to ownership or occupation as they may reasonably require[3]. Failure without reasonable cause to provide accurate information within three months after service of the notice renders the owner or occupier concerned liable on summary conviction to a fine not exceeding £10[4]. Another source of information is the Land Court who are required to intimate to the Commission the Court's determination on questions coming before them under the Landholders Acts (in their application to the crofting counties) and the Crofters Acts[5].

The data to be entered in the Register include the name, location, rent and extent of every croft, the name of the tenant and landlord, and such other matters as the Commission may, with the approval of the Secretary of State, decide are proper to be entered[6]. The figures quoted for extent are not always reliable as not all crofting estates have accurate records of the areas of individual crofts. Many of the areas and common grazing rights shown in the Register were extracted from the Annual Reports of the first Crofters Commission and the Appendices to the Annual Reports of the Land Court. The Court have observed that these sources are not in themselves authoritative[7].

The Commission are required from time to time to insert new entries in the Register or alter or omit existing entries as may be necessary to ensure its accuracy[8]. They must notify the parties concerned of new entries and changes in the Register, except such entries and changes as have been made on information provided by the parties themselves. Any person showing good reason is entitled to be provided with an extract from the Register certified by the secretary or acting secretary to the Commission and this provides sufficient evidence of the entry in the Register[9].

The Register is an administrative record and if a holding lacks the necessary qualifications entry will not by itself confer on the holding the status of croft[10]. This was held to be so even when the entry had been made on the authority of a return made by the landlord to the Commission which the tenant had not contradicted[11]. In a recent case the Land Court confirmed in general terms the view taken in these earlier cases of the effect of entry in the Register[12]. They observed that the only possible exception to their general statement concerned the entry of holdings in the Register made under section 15(4) of the 1955 Act. These were entries made between 1955 and 1961 by the Commission themselves in the absence of agreement by landlord and tenant and of any decision by the Land Court that the tenant was a crofter. The Court did not pursue the point which did not affect the decision of the case before them.

If a question arises (other than a question decided by the Secretary of State or the Commission in discharge of functions under the Acts) as to whether a holding is a croft or who is the tenant or as to the particulars of tenancy it can be referred for determination to the Land Court on the application of any person having an interest or on a reference made to the Court by the Commission[13]. Initially the onus is normally on a tenant to prove that his holding is a croft but the onus may shift to the landlord to invert the status quo where he has acquiesced over a lengthy period in allowing the holding to be treated as a croft[14]. Detailed investigation into the history of a holding may be necessary to determine whether it ever qualified for the statutory tenure and if so whether it remained subject to the tenure throughout its history[15].

1 The Small Landholders (Scotland) Act 1911, s 33 provided for a Register of Smallholdings throughout Scotland to be compiled by the Board of Agriculture but it never came to fruition. The Crofters Commission were required to compile and maintain a Register of Crofts by the Crofters (Scotland) Act 1955, s 15. Section 15 was partially repealed by the Crofters (Scotland) Act 1961 (s 3(4)) and s 3 of that Act re-enacted with some modifications and additions the repealed provisions. The current provisions for the Register are now to be found in the Crofters (Scotland) Act 1955, s 15(1), (5) and in the Crofters (Scotland) Act 1961, s 3, with minor amendments by the Crofting Reform (Scotland) Act 1976. The original

Register compiled under the Crofters (Scotland) Act 1955, in so far as it contains particulars required by the Crofters (Scotland) Act 1961, is deemed to have been compiled under the 1961 Act (s 3(4)).

2 Crofters (Scotland) Act 1961, s 3(1).
3 Crofters (Scotland) Act 1955, s 15(1) (as amended).
4 Ibid, s 15(5).
5 Crofters (Scotland) Act 1961, s 4(2) (as amended).
6 Crofters (Scotland) Act 1961, s 3(2) (as amended).
7 *Lockerby v Mackinnon* 1968 SLCR App 117; *Williamson v Foster* 1968 SLCR App 123.
8 Crofters (Scotland) Act 1961, s 3(2) (as amended).
9 Crofters (Scotland) Act 1961, s 3(3).
10 *Wallace v Stewart* (1961) 49 SLCR 18; *Elder v Manson* 1964 SLT (Land Ct) 15.
11 *Holbourn's Representatives v Gear* 1967 SLT (Land Ct) 5.
12 *Palmer's Trs v Crofters Commission* 1989 SLCR 98, 1990 SLT (Land Ct) 21.
13 Crofters (Scotland) Act 1961, s 4(1) (as amended); see para 2.01.
14 *Matheson (Representatives of the late Hugh) v Master of Lovat* 1984 SLCR 82.
15 *Elder v Manson* supra; *Shetland Islands Council v Jamieson* 1988 SLCR 97.

3.11 Subsidiary or auxiliary occupations

A crofter has the right to make such use of his croft for subsidiary or auxiliary occupations as, in case of dispute, the Land Court may find to be reasonable and not inconsistent with the cultivation of the croft[1]. This provision left in doubt the extent, if any, to which a crofter might be entitled to carry out permanent improvements suitable for these occupations and also whether compensation therefor would be payable at the end of the tenancy.

These doubts were resolved by the 1961 Act[2]. It provides that a crofter may erect any buildings or other structures or execute any works on his croft which

(1) are reasonably required for subsidiary or auxiliary occupations, and
(2) will not interfere substantially with the use of the croft as an agricultural subject.

Such buildings or structures (if they are fixtures on the land) and such works shall be permanent improvements deemed suitable to the croft and so qualify for compensation at the end of the tenancy (see paras 5.11–5.12). This provision is retrospective to the extent that, if a claim is otherwise valid, the right to compensation extends to improvements executed before as well as after the 1961 Act came into operation.

A typical subsidiary use of croft land is use for the accommodation of tourists. When this takes the form of providing a caravan site there is a special relaxation of licensing and planning permission requirements open to all occupiers of land in the crofting counties[3]. Such occupiers do not require a site licence or planning permission for use of land as a caravan site provided:

(a) the land extends to not less than two acres of unbuilt on land;
(b) the use of the land for a caravan site falls within the period 1 April to 30 September in any year; and
(c) during that period there are not more than three caravans on the land at any one time.

1 Crofters (Scotland) Act 1955, Second Sch, para 3.
2 Crofters (Scotland) Act 1961, s 5.
3 Caravan Sites and Control of Development Act 1960 (c 62) Sch 1; Caravan Sites (Exemption from Licensing) (Scotland) Order 1961, SI 1961/976; Town and Country Planning (General Development) (Scotland) Order 1981, SI 1981/830.

3.12   Record of croft

The Land Court are required, on the application of a landlord or crofter, to make a record of the croft[1]. The application is intimated to the other party by the Court and each party is given an opportunity of being heard. The Court records the condition of the cultivations and of the buildings and other permanent improvements on the croft and by whom the permanent improvements have been executed or paid for. Such a record can prove useful when, for example, a fair rent is being fixed or a crofter is subletting his croft and it is desired to preserve reliable evidence of the state of the croft.

1 Crofters (Scotland) Act 1955, s 6.

FINANCIAL ASSISTANCE

3.13   (a) Agricultural improvement grants

For the purpose of aiding and developing agricultural production on crofts the Secretary of State may make schemes for providing grants and loans to crofters and other eligible occupiers[1]. Such schemes may be administered through the agency of the Crofters Commission. The current scheme which is so administered is the Crofting Counties Agricultural Grants (Scotland) Scheme 1988. Those eligible for grants under the scheme include crofters, the legal sub-tenants of crofts (or parts of crofts), common grazings committees or grazings constables and the owner-occupiers of registered crofts who are of substantially the same economic status as crofters.

Assistance is available for a wide variety of agricultural operations including land improvement, drainage and fencing and the provision of farm equipment and agricultural buildings. Leaflets explaining the procedure for obtaining grants, the operations eligible and the rates and main conditions of grant are obtainable from the Commission and from area offices of the Department of Agriculture and Fisheries for Scotland.

1 Crofters (Scotland) Act 1955, s 22(1); Crofters (Scotland) Act 1961, s 14(1) (as amended); Crofting Reform (Scotland) Act 1976, s 12(5).

3.14   (b) Building grants and loans

The Secretary of State may provide assistance by way of grant or loan towards the erection, improvement or rebuilding of dwelling-houses and other buildings for crofters[1]. He may also provide assistance by way of loan to the incoming tenant of a croft to enable him to pay to the outgoing tenant or to the landlord the compensation for permanent improvements due to the outgoing tenant[2]. The current schemes of assistance are administered by the Department of Agriculture and Fisheries for Scotland.

The giving of building grants for dwelling houses is regulated by the Crofters etc Building Grants (Scotland) Regulations 1990, which prescribe the conditions of grant, including conditions as to occupation and maintenance[3].

These apply to the dwelling house for a period of twenty years where the grant is for erection or rebuilding and five years where the purpose is improvement. In the event of breach of conditions the Secretary of State may require repayment of a proportion of the grant and release from the conditions before the expiry of the period of the grant may be obtained by a like repayment.

Whenever the Secretary of State makes payment of a building grant, he is required to have recorded in the Register of Sasines a notice specifying the conditions which then apply to the building. If the conditions of the grant cease to apply by reason of recovery of a proportion of the grant for breach of conditions or repayment before the period of grant has expired, the Secretary of State requires to have recorded a notice to that effect in the Register.

During the period of the grant, any compensation payable to the crofter for permanent improvements falls to be reduced by so much of the value of the improvements as is attributable to the grant and the landlord shall not be entitled to any rent in respect of value so attributable.

1 Crofters (Scotland) Act 1955, s 22(2) (as extended by the Crofting Reform (Scotland) Act 1976, s 12(1), (2)).
2 Crofters (Scotland) Act 1955, s 22(3).
3 SI 1990/944 (in force 16 May 1990) made under the Crofters (Scotland) Act 1955, s 22(4) and the Crofters (Scotland) Act 1961, s 14(2).

3.15 Removal of crofter by Secretary of State

Where assistance is given by way of loan, the Secretary of State is required to give notice thereof to the landlord and to record the loan agreement in the Crofters Holdings Book. This has the effect of transferring to the Secretary of State all rights of the crofter and his statutory successors to compensation for permanent improvements up to the amount of any outstanding liability under the agreement[1]. Any amount eventually found to be due by the landlord to the Secretary of State may, if the Secretary of State so determines, be deemed to be a loan by him to the landlord and shall be secured by a heritable security over the land[2]. The loan agreement also entitles the Secretary of State to apply to the Land Court for removal of the crofter on the occurrence of any of the following events[3]:

(1) the crofter has abandoned his croft;
(2) the crofter has broken any of the statutory conditions other than the condition as to payment of rent; or
(3) the crofter has broken any of the conditions of repayment contained in the loan agreement.

The Land Court may order removal after considering any objections stated by the crofter or by the landlord[4]. It has been held a reasonable ground of objection by the landlord that removal for breach of conditions of repayment should not be ordered unless all the remedies available at common law for recovery of the debt have been exhausted[5].

Where the outgoing tenant of a croft is under any liability to the Secretary of State in respect of a loan, the incoming tenant may agree with the Secretary of State to assume such liability as a loan to him[6].

1 Crofters (Scotland) Act 1955, s 23. A crofter's right to compensation for permanent improvements can also be transferred to the Highlands and Islands Development Board in security of a loan to a crofter (but postponed to the security rights of the Secretary of State) – Highlands and Islands Development (Scotland) Act 1965, s 8(3)(a).

2 Crofters (Scotland) Act 1955, s 23(4) (as amended).
3 Ibid, s 13(2).
4 *Secretary of State for Scotland v Campbell* 1971 SLCR App 35.
5 *Department of Agriculture for Scotland v Macpherson* (1934) 22 SLCR 37.
6 Crofters (Scotland) Act 1955, s 23(5).

CHAPTER 4

SECURITY OF TENURE

4.01 Introduction

Security of tenure, fair rent and compensation for permanent improvements are the basic statutory rights on which crofting tenure was founded and of these the most important is security of tenure.

4.02 Removal of crofter

While a crofter is entitled, on giving one year's notice in writing to the landlord, to renounce his tenancy at any term of Whitsunday (28 May) or Martinmas (28 November)[1], he himself enjoys a large measure of security of tenure. This rests on section 3(3) of the Crofters (Scotland) Act 1955 which provides that a crofter shall not be subject to be removed from his croft except:
- (a) where one year's rent of the croft is unpaid;
- (b) in consequence of the breach of one or more of the statutory conditions, other than the condition as to payment of rent; or
- (c) in pursuance of any enactment, including any contained in the Act.

Action under heads (a) and (b) can be taken by the landlord by way of application to the Land Court for an order for removal of the crofter[2]. The form of action under head (c) is governed by the enactment concerned and is dealt with where the relevant statutory provisions are discussed. These include the provisions for:
- (i) resumption of croft land by the landlord (see para 10.02 et seq);
- (ii) dispossession of an absentee crofter (see para 6.12 et seq);
- (iii) removal at the instance of the Secretary of State under a loan agreement (see para 3.15); and
- (iv) compulsory acquisition of croft land (see para 10.14).

1 Crofters (Scotland) Act 1955, s 7(1).
2 Ibid, s 13(1).

4.03 Contracting out

The crofter's security is further safeguarded by a provision aimed against contracting out of statutory rights. Any contract or agreement made by a crofter shall be void to the extent that it deprives him of any rights under the

Crofters Acts unless the contract or agreement is approved by the Land Court[1]. This provision is in similar terms to that in section 25 of the Small Landholders and Agricultural Holdings (Scotland) Act 1931 against contracting out of rights under the Landholders Acts.

The landlord and tenant of a croft cannot contract that the holding is to cease to be a croft and the Land Court have no power to approve of such an agreement[2]. The character which the Crofters Acts impose upon the holding cannot be destroyed at the will of the landlord and tenant.

The shareholders in a common grazings entered into an agreement whereby the landlords would enclose and plant a portion of the grazings and the shareholders undertook that no grazing of livestock would take place within the area. As an agreement depriving crofters of statutory rights it required Land Court approval to make it valid. In granting approval of the agreement as being reasonably beneficial to the present shareholders, the Court stressed that it was not binding on successor shareholders (or possibly even landlords), nor could it affect the powers and duties of the grazings committee under section 25 of the 1955 Act[3].

1 Crofters (Scotland) Act 1955, s 3(4): see *Hamilton v Noble* 1989 SLCR 51.
2 *MacVarish v Becher* 1970 SLCR App 26; *Whyte v Garden's Trs* (1925) 13 SLCR 99, (1926) 14 SLCR 73.
3 *Stornoway Trust v Mackay* 1989 SLT (Land Ct) 36; see para 8.03.

STATUTORY CONDITIONS OF TENURE

4.04 General

The statutory conditions, for the breach of any of which a crofter is liable to be removed from his croft, are set out at length in the Second Schedule to the 1955 Act[1]. It is well established that a tenant may purge an irritancy of a statutory condition of let and it has been the invariable practice of the Land Court to allow a tenant in breach of such a condition an opportunity of remedying the breach (when it is capable of being remedied) before pronouncing an order of removal[2]. These statutory conditions have changed little since they were laid down in the Landholders Acts and much of the earlier case law relating to landholders is still relevant.

The statutory conditions can be grouped and summarised as follows (with the relevant paragraph of the Second Schedule quoted in each case):

1 Crofters (Scotland) Act 1955, s 3(3).
2 *Elliot v Mackay* (1936) 24 SLCR 3; *Little v McEwan* 1965 SLT (Land Ct) 3, 1964 SLCR App 42; *MacLaren v MacLaren* 1984 SLCR 43.

4.05 Payment of rent

The crofter shall pay his rent at the due term (para 1).

An application for an order to remove one of two joint tenants for non-payment of rent was held to be incompetent since both tenants are liable for payment of rent *in solidum*[1]. Where a crofter placed on deposit receipt the net arrears of rent due (under deduction of sums claimed to be due to her by the landlord), this was held not to satisfy the statutory condition[2]. An order of removal was granted against a tenant who was more than one year in arrears with rent and against whom a sheriff court decree for payment had been obtained[3]. An offer to pay off arrears by weekly instalments came too late – it should have been made during the sheriff court proceedings.

1 *South Uist Estates Ltd v MacPherson* 1975 SLCR App 22; *Martin v Maclean* (1927) 15 SLCR 23.
2 *Park v Mackintosh* 1968 SLCR App 103.
3 *Earl of Dundonald v Campbell* (1941) 29 SLCR 43.

4.06 Assignation, subletting and subdivision

The crofter shall not assign, sublet or subdivide his croft except in accordance with the provisions of the Act (paras 2, 5 and 6).

The statutory limits within which assignation[1], subletting[2] and subdivision[3] are permissible are described below under these headings.

1 See para 6.04.
2 See para 6.05 et seq.
3 See para 6.11.

4.07 Cultivation of croft

(a) The crofter shall, by himself or his family with or without hired labour, cultivate his croft (para 3).

The duty to cultivate is without prejudice to the right within certain limits to make use of the croft for subsidiary or auxiliary occupations (see para 3.11). The expression 'cultivate' is defined in the Schedule (para 12). It includes horticulture or any purpose of husbandry including the keeping or breeding of livestock, poultry or bees, and the growing of fruit, vegetables and the like. It is not restricted to the everyday meaning of tilling the soil and growing crops. The keeping or breeding of livestock is an illustration of what is permissible. Nowhere in the statutes is it provided that the stock on the holding must be the property of the tenant. The tenant can grow a crop of grass and sell it to a person outside who will·use it by putting in stock to graze[1].

(b) The crofter shall not, to the prejudice of the interest of the landlord, persistently injure the croft by the deterioration of the soil after notice in writing has been given by the landlord to the crofter not to commit, or to desist from, the particular injury specified in the notice (para 4)[2].

1 *Little v McEwan* supra; see also *MacLaren v MacLaren* 1984 SLCR 43; *Arran Properties Ltd v Currie* 1983 SLCR 92; *Williamson v Henry* 1975 SLCR App 31.
2 *Culfargie Estates Ltd v Leslie* (1957) 45 SLCR 38; *Peto v Macrae* (1945) 33 SLCR 40; *Burton Property Trust v MacRae* 1989 SLCR 34.

4.08   Croft equipment

(a) The crofter shall provide such fixed equipment on his croft as may be
necessary to enable him to cultivate the croft (para 3A).

'Fixed equipment' has the like meaning as in section 93 of the Agricultural
Holdings (Scotland) Act 1949[1]. It is a very comprehensive definition and
includes inter alia any building or structure affixed to land, all permanent
buildings, permanent fences, ditches and drains, fanks and dippers, farm
access or service roads, water and sewage systems, electrical installations and
shelter belts.

This statutory condition marks the fundamental distinction between
crofting tenure and tenure under the Agricultural Holdings (Scotland) Acts.
There are crofts where the landlord has provided the fixed equipment or
some portion of the equipment (particularly in the case of crofts created under
land settlement schemes, and in the case of former statutory small tenancies)
but there is no obligation on a crofting landlord to do so unless he chooses. A
landlord who provided a private water supply to crofts was held entitled to
discontinue it subject to abatement of rent[2].

(b) The crofter shall not, to the prejudice of the interest of the landlord,
persistently injure the croft by the dilapidation of buildings (para 4).

In the absence of any agreement to the contrary, the crofter is entirely
responsible for the maintenance of buildings whether provided by himself or
by his landlord. There is no provision in the Acts which deals directly with
the question of maintenance but the Land Court held that the obligation is
implicit in this statutory condition[3]. The principle is long established and has
been reiterated by the Court in many cases[4].

At the end of a tenancy compensation may be payable to the landlord for
the deterioration of, or damage to, any fixed equipment provided by him (see
para 5.15).

(c) The crofter shall not, without the consent in writing of the landlord, erect
or suffer to be erected on the croft any dwelling-house otherwise than in
substitution for a dwelling-house which at 1 October 1955 was already on
the croft. If there was no dwelling-house on the croft at that date, the crofter
may erect one dwelling-house (para 7).

A distinction has to be drawn between the croft house and any buildings,
including an additional dwelling-house which the crofter may be entitled to
erect in excercise of his right to erect buildings for the purpose of a subsidiary
or auxiliary occupation[5].

1 Crofters (Scotland) Act 1955, s 37(1).
2 *Secretary of State for Scotland v Mackay* 1964 SLT (Land Ct) 2.
3 *Holman v Henderson* 1965 SLT (Land Ct) 13.
4 Eg *Harrold v Secretary of State for Scotland* (1953) 41 SLCR 37, 1953 SLCR App 256.
5 Crofters (Scotland) Act 1961, s 5; *Cameron v Duke of Argyll's Trs* 1981 SLT (Land Ct) 2; see
para 3.11.

4.09   Written conditions

The crofter shall not persistently violate any written condition signed by him
for the protection of the interest of the landlord or of neighbouring crofters

which is legally applicable to the croft and which the Land Court shall find to be reasonable (para 8).

This condition falls to be construed in light of the express provision in the 1955 Act that any contract or agreement contracting out of rights under the Crofters Acts shall be void unless the contract or agreement is approved by the Land Court[1].

A similar statutory condition is contained in section 1(5) of the Crofters Holdings (Scotland) Act 1886 and a similar provision against contracting out of statutory rights in section 25 of the Small Landholders and Agricultural Holdings (Scotland) Act 1931. In granting registration of a new tenant as a landholder under the Small Landholders Acts on the joint application of landlord and tenant, the Land Court made it clear that they were not thereby making any finding that the written agreement between parties governing the terms of tenancy was 'legally applicable' to the holding or that it was 'reasonable' or 'approved' within the meaning of the statutory provisions[2]. This could be of importance both to former landholders who, as such, became crofters under the 1955 Act and to tenants who were registered as crofters under that Act[3].

A landholder entered into an agreement with the Department of Agriculture for Scotland, who were the landlords, to take over permanent improvements on the holding at a valuation to be made by the Department and to sign a bond for the amount of the valuation. He subsequently refused to sign the bond. In refusing the Department's application for an order of removal for breach of a statutory condition, the Land Court held that the valuation was to a material extent excessive as value to the holding and that it was unreasonable to ask the tenant to sign the bond[4].

The Land Court dismissed an application by the landlord for removal of a crofter who was admittedly in breach of a condition in his missives of let prohibiting him from siting a caravan or chalet on his croft[5]. The Court held that the condition was unreasonable as preventing the crofter from using the croft for the auxiliary occupation of tourism.

A condition binding a landholder to reside on the holding was held unreasonable in a case where the holding was too small to provide a reasonable livelihood, where there was no evidence of employment in the vicinity and where the tenant was employed and resident elsewhere[6]. But a residence clause was held reasonable and binding where the holding was reasonably capable of providing full-time employment and a sufficient livelihood[7].

1 Crofters (Scotland) Act 1955, s 3(4); *Hamilton v Noble* 1989 SLCR 51; see para 4.03.
2 *Buccleuch Estates Ltd and Shaw, Joint Applicants* (1943) 31 SLCR 17.
3 Crofters (Scotland) Act 1955, ss 3(1)(c), 39(1).
4 *Department of Agriculture for Scotland v Calder* (1935) 23 SLCR 48.
5 *Bray v Morrison* 1973 SLT (Land Ct) 6.
6 *Secretary of State for Scotland v MacKenzie* (1951) 39 SLCR 19.
7 *Macleod v MacLean* (1938) 26 SLCR 82.

4.10 Bankruptcy

The crofter shall not do any act whereby he becomes notour bankrupt within the meaning of the Bankruptcy (Scotland) Act 1913 and shall not execute a trust deed for creditors (para 9).

In terms of the Bankruptcy Act notour bankruptcy continues in the case of sequestration until the debtor obtains his discharge. In granting an order of removal of a landholder for breach of this condition, the Land Court observed that the condition was clearly conceived for the protection of landlords against the danger of deterioration of their property through the inability of a tenant to farm the lands properly[1]. While they agreed that they had a discretion in the matter, it would require some very compelling reason before the Court could exercise its discretion and refuse the order of removal. In an earlier case the Court described the execution of a trust deed for creditors as 'a palpable and irremediable breach' of the statutory condition[2]. In a still earlier case the Court granted a decree of removal against a landholder who was notour bankrupt at the date of presentation of the application for removal. Payment of the debt for which he had been made notour bankrupt was held not sufficient to purge the legal irritancy as his state of insolvency and consequent status of notour bankrupt had not ceased[3].

1 *Secretary of State for Scotland v Black* 1965 SLT (Land Ct) 2.
2 *Culfargie Estates Ltd v Leslie* (1957) 45 SLCR 38.
3 *Department of Agriculture for Scotland v Muir* (1932) 20 SLCR 26.

4.11 Sale of intoxicating liquors

The crofter shall not, without the consent in writing of the landlord, open any house on the croft for the sale of intoxicating liquors (para 12).

4.12 Rights reserved to the landlord

Extensive rights are reserved to the landlord under para 10 of the Second Schedule. They are expressed in the form of a statutory condition that the crofter shall permit the landlord, or any person authorised by the landlord, to enter upon the croft for the purpose of exercising any of the rights specified and the crofter shall not obstruct such exercise. Compensation is payable for 'any damage done or occasioned by the exercise of the rights and in case of dispute the compensation will be such as the Land Court may find reasonable'. The Court have pointed to the contrast with the original wording to be found in the 1886 Act which refers to 'any damage to be done or occasioned'[1]. They observed that the 1955 Act looks only to past or existing damage and they commend a form of order awarding compensation that reserves to parties the right to re-apply to the Court for any further order that may prove necessary[2].

Where the damage is to common grazings, the claim for compensation must be made by the shareholders and not by the grazings committee[2]. Shareholders can pursue a joint action and the clerk to the committee can act as their representative or agent. Each shareholder is entitled to make a separate claim and this may be appropriate where the degree of damage suffered may vary as between different shareholders.

The rights reserved include:

1 Crofters Holdings (Scotland) Act 1886, s 1(7).
2 *Crofters Sharing in Keil Common Grazings v MacColl* 1986 SLCR 142.

4.13   Mining and quarrying

Mining or searching for minerals and quarrying or taking stone, gravel, sand or other workable minerals (para 10(a)).

Where there was delay in disposing of an application to the Land Court for authority to resume an area of croft land for the purpose of leasing it to contractors to quarry sand and gravel, the landlords authorised the contractors to commence quarrying operations on the ground. The crofter objected to the landlords exercising this right while persisting in their application for resumption. The Court rejected the objection on the ground that limited exercise of the statutory conditions procedure was an intermission *ex necessitate* in the continuing resumption procedure'[1].

In a case where the landlord had failed to implement a condition imposed by the Court that he should fence a quarry opened on the common grazings and a shareholder had suffered damage to a pony as a result, the Court awarded compensation for the damage sustained[2].

1 *Libberton Proprietors Ltd v MacKay* 1973 SLT (Land Ct) 13; see also *Duke of Argyll's Trs v MacCormick* 1988 SLCR 123, 1989 SLT (Land Ct) 58 and *Crofters Sharing in Keil Common Grazings v MacColl* 1986 SLCR 142.
2 *Maclennan v Secretary of State for Scotland* (1947) 35 SLCR 40.

4.14   Water on the croft

Using for any estate purpose springs of water rising on the croft and not required for croft use (para 10(c)).

Crofters having rights in a common grazing are by implication entitled to a supply of water on the grazing for watering stock but, apart from express grant from the owner of the common grazing, they are not entitled to a supply of water from the grazing for the domestic purposes of their crofts[1].

A landlord was held entitled to claim a supply of water for the use of a feuar on his estate from a well on the holding of his landholder tenant, but only to the extent that the supply of water from the well was more than sufficient for the use of the tenant's holding. The landlord's claim was founded on section 12 of the 1911 Act which is in terms similar to this statutory condition[2].

1 *MacColl v Downie's Trs* (1962) 50 SLCR 28.
2 *MacLeod v MacLeod* (1940) 28 SLCR 3.

4.15   Timber and other trees

Cutting or taking timber, except timber and other trees planted by the crofter or any of his predecessors in the tenancy or which may be necessary for ornament or shelter (para 10(d)).

Where a question arose between the crofter and the landlord as to the ownership of a number of trees on croft land some of which were the result of natural regeneration, there was no evidence that the crofter or his predecessors had planted or nurtured any of the trees. The Land Court held that there were no grounds for departing from the substantive law that mature timber belongs to the landlord unless otherwise provided by express stipulation or contract[1].

1 *Gilmour v Master of Lovat* 1979 SLT (Land Ct) 2; see para 9.13.

4.16 Peat supplies

> Cutting or taking peats excepting such peats as may be required for use of the croft (para 10(d)).

The legal principles governing peat cutting rights were discussed by the Land Court in a Shetland case dealing with competing claims by landholders to the right to cut peats from peat mosses on a common grazing (or 'scattald' as it is termed in Shetland)[1]. It was pointed out that the right of peat cutting, though usually associated with or included in the right of pasturage, is quite separable from that right. A right of common grazing, though it may be established by prescription, is usually founded upon a grant in the feudal title of the proprietor. On the other hand a right to peat cutting appears to be a subordinate right which may be constituted without any specific grant. Its extent is determined by possession and may be limited by the requirements of the users.

This statutory condition is in similar terms to the condition originally laid down in the 1886 Act[2]. It recognises the crofter's prior right to a supply of peats for the present and prospective requirements of his croft. There is reserved to the landlord and any person authorised by him the right, subject to payment of compensation for any damage caused, to enter on the croft (which includes any common grazings pertaining thereto) for the purpose of cutting or taking any peat surplus to the crofter's requirements that may be available. These provisions apply whether the peat moss is on the crofter's individual croft occupied by him or on common grazing or elsewhere outwith the individual croft.

While the landlord in exercise of his reserved right is entitled to take surplus peat within the limits mentioned for his own domestic or estate use, his right does not extend to commercial peat extraction[3]. If such is the landlord's purpose, the appropriate procedure is by way of an application to the Land Court under section 12 of the 1955 Act for authority to resume the ground for that purpose.

1 *Smith v Bruce* (1925) 13 SLCR 8, (1927) 15 SLCR 83.
2 Crofters Holdings (Scotland) Act 1886, s 1(7).
3 *MacAskill v Basil Baird & Sons Ltd* 1987 SLT (Land Ct) 34, 1986 SLCR 133.

4.17 Opening roads, drains, etc

> Opening or making roads, fences, drains and water courses (para 10(e)).

A landlord was found entitled, subject to payment of compensation, to grant permission to a crofter to construct a road suitable for modern vehicular traffic across a neighbouring croft along the line of an existing pedestrian route[1].

In response to an application by the Secretary of State, the Land Court declared that he could legally be granted power by the landlords concerned to execute certain works for the improvement of an extensive drainage system serving a number of crofting townships[2].

1 *Nicholson v Sinclair* 1968 SLCR App 121.
2 *Secretary of State for Scotland v Greig* (1963) 51 SLCR 3.

4.18　Rights of access

(1) Access with or without vehicles to and from the seashore or any loch for the purpose of exercising any right of property or other right belonging to the landlord (para 10(f)).
(2) Access at reasonable times to view or examine the state of the croft and all buildings or improvements thereon (para 10(g)).

4.19　Sporting rights

Hunting, shooting and fishing or taking game or fish, wild birds or vermin (para 10(h)).

The rights reserved do not preclude the crofter from recovering compensation for damage by game (as assessed by the Land Court) recoverable by a tenant under section 15 of the Agricultural Holdings (Scotland) Act 1949.

The expression 'game' means deer, hares, rabbits, pheasants, partridges, grouse, blackgame, capercailzie, ptarmigan, woodcock, snipe, wild duck, widgeon and teal. Permission to kill any one of the kinds of game mentioned excludes a claim for compensation for damage caused by that kind[1].

1 *Ross v Watson* 1944 SLCR 29.

CHAPTER 5

FAIR RENT AND COMPENSATION FOR IMPROVEMENTS

5.01 Introduction

Statutory security of tenure was not of itself a sufficient protection for crofting tenants. In addition it was necessary to grant two more basic statutory rights. These are the right to have a fair rent fixed and the right to compensation for tenant's improvements at the end of a tenancy.

FAIR RENT

5.02 Statutory provisions

The statutory provisions regulating the rent payable by a crofter and how such rent may be altered are now contained in section 5 of the Crofters (Scotland) Act 1955[1]. Fair rent provisions were originally enacted in sections 4, 5 and 6 of the Crofters Holdings (Scotland) Act 1886.

The rent payable by a crofter as a statutory condition of his tenancy is the yearly rent that was payable for the year current at 1 October 1955 or that rent as revised in terms of the Crofters Acts. Where the croft came to be let after that date, the rent so payable is the rent fixed at the date of the re-letting or as subsequently revised. The rent may be altered at any time by agreement in writing between the landlord and the crofter to such amount and for such period as they may agree. Such rent shall be the rent payable by the crofter so long as the agreement subsists and thereafter shall continue so long as it is not altered by a fresh agreement or replaced by a fair rent fixed by the Land Court.

1 Modified by the Crofting Reform (Scotland) Act 1976, s 7 to provide for adjustment of rent where a crofter acquires ownership of a part of his croft.

5.03 Period of rent

Application to fix a fair rent may be made to the Land Court by the crofter or the landlord. The rent fixed by the Court shall be the rent payable from the first term of Whitsunday or Martinmas following the Court's decision. A rent so fixed shall not be altered for a period of seven years from such term except by mutual agreement between landlord and crofter. Where a croft has been re-let after 1 October 1955 the rent then agreed shall not be altered by the

Court for a period of seven years or such longer period as may have been agreed[1].

Where during the currency of a septennial period a holding had suffered extraordinary damage consequent on a cloud-burst and the landlord declined to remedy the damage, the Land Court held that the landholder tenant could competently apply for an abatement of rent[2]. When a landlord resumed a portion of a croft and the rent was reduced as part of the compensation for the resumption, an application by the landlord in the following year to fix a fair rent for the remainder of the croft was held to be competent[3]. When a crofter acquires the ownership of any part of his croft, the Court may, on the application of the crofter or his landlord, determine a fair rent for the part of the croft remaining on tenancy, notwithstanding that it is less than seven years since the existing rent became payable[4].

1 *Ferguson v McLeod* 1969 SLCR App 29.
2 *Sutherland v Lyon* (1931) 19 SLCR 42.
3 *Secretary of State for Scotland v Love* 1972 SLCR App 46.
4 Crofting Reform (Scotland) Act 1976, s 7; see para 9.18.

5.04 Relevant considerations

Before determining a fair rent for a croft the Land Court are directed to hear parties and to take into consideration all the circumstances of the case, of the croft and of the district. The Land Court observed that the meaning of the word 'district' in this context is a broad direction to take into consideration the prevailing conditions in the general geographical area in which the croft is situated with distinctive conditions of its own[1]. It is not intended to mean territory defined for special administrative or official purposes such as a local government district. In particular the Court is directed to take into consideration any permanent or unexhausted improvements on the croft and suitable thereto which have been executed or paid for by the crofter or his predecessors in the tenancy (defined as 'the persons who before him have been tenants of the croft since it was last vacant')[2]. This points to the guiding principle that has ruled the fixing of fair rents from 1886 onwards[3], namely, that a crofter shall not be rented on tenant's improvements.

The question of how improvements executed by virtue of a specific agreement in writing under which the tenant was bound to execute the improvements should be treated when fixing the rent was considered by the Court of Session in two cases. One related to the equitable rent payable by a statutory small tenant[4] and the other to the fair rent payable by a landholder where the same principle applied[5]. Both classes of tenant became crofters under the Act of 1955. In each case the Court decided that improvements executed under agreement were not excluded from consideration by the Land Court and that it was for them when fixing an equitable or fair rent to decide whether payment or fair consideration had in fact been received by the tenant. If so, rent should be paid on them – otherwise not.

1 *Moray Estates Development Co v Crofters Commission* 1988 SLT (Land Ct) 14, 1987 SLCR 141.
2 Crofters (Scotland) Act 1955, s 37(1).
3 Report of the first Crofters Commission for 1886–1887, p 101.
4 *Wilkie v Hill* 1916 SC 892, 1916 2 SLT 104, 53 SLR 728, (1917) 5 SLCR 3.
5 *MacKinnon v Duke of Hamilton's Trs* 1918 SC 274, 1918 1 SLT 288, 55 SLR 359, (1918) 6 SLCR 119.

5.05   Fair rent principles

The concept of a fair rent has been examined in a number of judgments since 1886[1]. The Land Court, in discussing the principles to be applied, stated that, after excluding tenant's improvements,

> 'the most important element in arriving at the fair rent is what the landholder, working the holding by himself or his family, and such hired labour as may be required, with reasonable skill and industry, can make out of the holding. . . . The main point, after determining on what the tenant is to be rented, is to find what is a fair division between the landlord and the tenant of the annual net profits, or what are estimated to be the ordinary annual net profits, of the particular holding, taking into account the quality and situation of the land and all existing buildings and other improvements which are to be reckoned as landlord's improvements, on the footing of the holding being worked with reasonable skill and industry during the period for which the rent is fixed.'[2]

The Court, applying these principles, considered the argument that the tenant's labour should be allowed for before fixing the surplus available as 'annual net profits'[3]. They ruled against such deduction but on the other hand the tenant was entitled to the profits of the capital employed by him in connection with his agricultural business on the holding and these must be ascertained in relation to the ordinary rate of profits of farming stock in the neighbourhood. The Court also adopted Sheriff Dickson's summing up of the position in the words, 'It would appear that the reasonable principle is to fix the rent upon the basis of the agricultural value of the land to a prudent agriculturalist unhampered by the element of competition[4].'

1 Scott *Law of Smallholdings in Scotland* (1933) pp 72–75.
2 *MacAlpin v Duke of Hamilton's Trs* (1914) 2 SLCR 74 at 82.
3 *Secretary of State for Scotland v Ramage* (1952) 40 SLCR 29.
4 14 *Encyclopaedia of the Laws of Scotland* (ed Lord Dunedin and J Wark 1933) at pp 136, 137.

5.06   Application of fair rent principles in recent cases

In two more recent applications[1] the Land Court quoted with approval the principles on which fair rents for crofts are to be determined as set forth in these earlier cases. In the first of these applications the Court was dealing with the renting of small crofts in a remote location in the Western Isles where the main agricultural value of a croft lies nowadays in stock raising, the arable land consists mainly of disused lazy beds and the common grazings have limited grazing value. The general guide for fixing rents on the basis of a fair division of annual net profits proved difficult to apply. In such a case the rents were fixed on the agricultural potential of the land made available by the landlord in its unimproved state. The Court took into account the decline in the value of money since these particular rents were last judicially determined in 1890, while observing that inflation is a factor which cuts both ways in that it also inflates the prices of various items of agricultural expenditure by crofters.

Where there were material differences between the landlord and tenant as to acreages and common grazing rights, the Court would not proceed with an application to fix a fair rent until these differences had been resolved[2]. But although the data provided by parties may be sparse, the Court are entitled from their own knowledge and experience to assess the potential profitability of the subjects and determine what is a fair division of the profits between the landlord and tenant[3]. As the element of competition for the tenancy is not taken into account, the Court observed that evidence of the competitive rents at which neighbouring farms were let under the Agricultural Holdings Acts were irrelevant. The landlord's plea that the Court should take into account agricultural grants available to landholders was also rejected.

1 *Hitchcock's Trs v McCuish* 1982 SLCR 101; *W C Johnston Ltd v Fitzsimon* 1983 SLCR 95.
2 *Freswick Estates Co Ltd v Manson* 1969 SLT (Land Ct) 8, 1968 SLCR App 101.
3 *Secretary of State for Scotland v Murray* (1962) 50 SLCR 3.

5.07   Injury to crops by game

Apart from the right to compensation for damage by game which may be recoverable by a crofter under section 15 of the Agricultural Holdings (Scotland) Act 1949, the Land Court are entitled, in fixing a fair rent, to take into account that a croft is exposed to injury to crops by game and requires watching to prevent such injury, thereby diminishing the letting value of the croft[1].

1 *McKelvie v Duke of Hamilton's Trs* 1918 SC 301, 1918 1 SLT 295, 55 SLR 374, 6 SLCR 137; *Greig v Cunninghame's Trs* (1918) 6 SLCR 18.

5.08   Improvements and deterioration

While a crofter is not to be rented on his own improvements neither is he entitled to have his rent lowered if he allows his land to deteriorate through non-cultivation or failure to provide the necessary equipment[1]. It is not a relevant consideration that a crofter is unable to work his croft because of old age, illness or infirmity[2]. Where the common grazing was worked on the club stock system, the difficulty of finding tenants who would be suitable working partners in the club was taken into account in fixing fair rents[3]. In the absence of agreement to the contrary, the crofter is entirely responsible for the repair and maintenance of the buildings and other equipment even where such have been wholly or partially provided by the landlord and this is an important factor when assessing fair rent[4]. Where the landlord discontinued a private water supply to certain crofts, the tenants were held entitled to an abatement of rent[5].

1 *Harrold v Secretary of State for Scotland* (1953) 41 SLCR 37, 1953 SLCR App 256.
2 *Vestey v MacAskill* 1972 SLCR App 55.
3 *Botley v McLeod* 1971 SLCR App 35.
4 *Holman v Henderson* 1965 SLT (Land Ct) 13.
5 *Secretary of State for Scotland v Mackay* 1964 SLT (Land Ct) 2.

5.09   Subsidiary or auxiliary occupations

The extent to which the use made of the croft for subsidiary or auxiliary occupations (see para 3.11) may be taken into account when fixing a fair rent has not hitherto been the subject of much consideration by the Land Court. It may figure more prominently in future having regard to the encouragement in recent times of the crofter's non-agricultural activities and the provisions of section 5 of the 1961 Act.

5.10 Revenue from holiday visitors

The statutory condition which forbids a crofter to sublet his croft or any part of it otherwise than with the consent in writing of the Crofters Commission is made subject to the proviso that this shall not debar a crofter from subletting any dwelling-house or other building on his croft to holiday visitors[1]. This proviso to the subletting prohibition was first introduced by the 1911 Act. In a series of cases on the estate of Arran, where the practice of letting to holiday visitors was well established, the Court of Session considered among other things how houses and buildings on a holding from which this kind of revenue may be derived should be dealt with by the Land Court in fixing a fair rent[2]. The Court could see no reason for excluding from consideration in arriving at a fair rent the fact that by letting his house to holiday visitors, as was the custom of the district, the tenant could derive a return, just as he could from cultivating a field. They therefore ruled that this was a consideration which could enter into the question of fair rent. The tenant would not be charged rent on his own improvements (where the house was a tenant improvement) but the landlord was entitled to more than an agricultural rent for the value of the site of the house. The landlord's contribution to the holiday visitor enterprise was a site in an attractive locality.

1 Crofters (Scotland) Act 1955, Second Sch, para 5 (as substituted).
2 *McNeill v Duke of Hamilton's Trs* 1918 SC 221, 1918 1 SLT 265, 55 SLR 329, 6 SLCR 71.

COMPENSATION FOR IMPROVEMENTS

5.11 Statutory provisions

The crofter's right on termination of tenancy to recover from his landlord compensation for his permanent improvements has been a basic principle of crofting tenure since introduced by the 1886 Act. The principle still remains substantially as enacted in section 7 of that Act, with minor modifications. The statutory provisions are now contained in section 14 of the 1955 Act and section 6 of the 1961 Act. Certain amendments were introduced by the 1968 Act consequent on changes in the law of succession to the tenancies of crofts.

A crofter removing or being removed from his croft is entitled to compensation from his landlord for the tenant's permanent improvements, such as buildings, reclamation of land, fences and ditches, etc. The claim arises when the crofter renounces his tenancy[1], or where his tenancy is terminated by the Crofters Commission[2], or where he is removed by order of the Land Court[3], or where, following the death of the crofter, the tenancy is terminated by his landlord or his executor[4]. The claim entitles the crofter (or the executor) to a payment for any tenant's improvement on the croft[5].

1 Crofters (Scotland) Act 1955, s 7.
2 Ibid, s 17.
3 Ibid, s 13.
4 Succession (Scotland) Act 1964, s 16(3).
5 Crofters (Scotland) Act 1955, s 14(1).

5.12 Compensation criteria

To qualify for compensation a permanent improvement has to satisfy the following criteria:
(a) The improvement must be suitable to the croft[1]. Where an outgoing crofter occupies more than one croft each one must be treated as a separate agricultural unit and the improvements thereon valued in relation to the croft on which they are situated[2]. Although the Acts refer to permanent improvements 'on the croft', the improvement need not necessarily be physically on the croft (for example, piers or landing stages and access roads)[3].
(b) The improvement must have been executed or paid for by the crofter (or the deceased crofter in the case of a claim by an executor) or any of the predecessors of the crofter or deceased crofter in the tenancy[4] (defined as 'the persons who before him have been tenants of the croft since it was last vacant')[5].

The compensation is payable even where the crofter has carried out the improvement without consultation with, or even the consent of, his landlord and where no notice was given nor written agreement exists. However, if following such an agreement, the crofter did receive fair consideration for the improvement (by way of reduction in rent or otherwise) then no compensation is payable for that improvement[6]. No payment can be claimed as compensation in respect of any buildings erected by a tenant in contravention of any interdict or other judicial order[7].

A crofter, who was formerly a statutory small tenant, is not entitled to any compensation for permanent improvements made or begun before 1 October 1955 to which he would not have been entitled if his tenancy had expired immediately before that date. A statutory small tenant's rights of compensation were governed at that stage by the Agricultural Holdings (Scotland) Act 1949. Accordingly any additional rights to compensation for permanent improvements which the former statutory small tenant (or his statutory successors) can get by becoming a crofter are restricted to permanent improvements begun after 30 September 1955.

The removal of the crofter for breach of the statutory conditions is not a reason for excluding his right to compensation. Indeed it is the time when compensation requires to be assessed and paid[8]. Normally the onus of proof is on the crofter to show that the improvements for which he is claiming compensation were executed or paid for by the crofter himself or by any of his predecessors in the tenancy. He is not, however, bound to prove his landlord made no contribution to an improvement. If the landlord alleges that he did make such a contribution, then the landlord must provide evidence.

The following are permanent improvements for which a crofter is entitled to compensation:
  (1) Dwelling-house
  (2) Farm offices
  (3) Subsoil and other drains
  (4) Walls and fences
  (5) Deep trenching
  (6) Clearing the ground
  (7) Planting trees
  (8) Making piers or landing stages
  (9). Roads practicable for vehicles from the croft to the public road or the seashore
  (10) Improvement works carried out on a sub-standard dwelling-house as required by a local authority under the Housing (Scotland) Act 1974
  (11) All other improvements which, in the judgment of the Land Court, will add to the value of the croft as an agricultural subject
  (12) Buildings or other structures erected or works executed for the purposes of subsidiary or auxiliary occupations.

Any building or other structure on the croft must be a fixture to qualify as a permanent improvement. In law, all such improvements belong to the owner of the land, subject only to the crofter's right of use as tenant and to his right to claim compensation at waygo. Where the landlord has made any contribution to an improvement, the value of such contribution falls to be deducted from the value of the improvement when fixing the compensation payable to the crofter.

1 Crofters (Scotland) Act 1955, s 14(1)(a); *Stornoway Trs v Jamieson* (1926) 14 SLCR 88; *Humbert v Maciver* (1961) 49 SLCR 29.
2 *Pearson v Sumburgh Co Ltd* 1960 SLCR App 193.
3 *Mackenzie v Roger* 1964 SLT (Land Ct) 8.
4 Crofters (Scotland) Act 1955, s 14(1)(b).
5 Ibid, s 37(1).
6 Ibid, s 14(1)(c).
7 Ibid, s 14(3).
8 *Board of Agriculture v Sinclair's Trs* (1929) 17 SLCR 34.

5.13 Compensation and the Agricultural Holdings (Scotland) Act 1949

The provisions of the Agricultural Holdings (Scotland) Act 1949[1] apply to crofters with respect to the payment to outgoing tenants of compensation for improvements. This allows additional items to be claimed for, such as unexhausted manurial values. Valuations are required to be made by the Land Court unless otherwise agreed by parties in writing[2]. No such compensation is payable for any improvement for which compensation is due under the Crofting Acts[3].

1 Crofters (Scotland) Act 1955, s 14(10).   ·
2 Ibid, s 14(10)(a).
3 Ibid, s 14(10)(b).

5.14　Land Court may fix amount of compensation

The amount of compensation payable under the Crofting Acts for permanent improvements or for deterioration is fixed, failing agreement, by the Land Court[1]. The Court is entitled to bring its own opinion to any question of valuation which arises[2]. Where a crofter has given notice of renunciation of his tenancy, or the landlord either gives to, or receives from the executor of a deceased crofter a notice terminating the tenancy, the Land Court may also assess the amount of compensation due on the joint application of the landlord and the crofter or the executor (or, where the crofter's rights to compensation have been transferred to the Secretary of State, the Secretary of State) prior to the renunciation or termination[3].

1 Crofters (Scotland) Act 1955, s 14(8).
2 *Grant v Countess of Seafield's Trs* (1934) 22 SLCR 76 at 81.
3 Crofters (Scotland) Act 1955, s 14(9).

5.15　Bases of compensation

The basis of compensation laid down in the 1955 Act[1] was displaced by a new basis introduced by the 1961 Act[2]. Where the tenancy which is coming to an end began before 27 August 1961, the claim can at the request of the outgoing crofter be valued on the old basis as well as the new and the claimant can choose the more favourable valuation. The earlier basis required improvements to be assessed at such sum as fairly represented their value to an incoming tenant, irrespective of whether there was in fact any incomer or any likelihood of one. Since 1961, the improvements are valued at the amount which the landlord might reasonably be expected to receive from an incoming tenant if the croft were offered for letting on a crofting tenancy on the open market.

The 1961 Act provided the outgoing crofter with an opportunity to gain from the potential demand for his tenancy as assessed by the Court. But where there is little or no demand for the tenancy, the valuation under the 1955 Act might prove advantageous to the crofter. Since 1961 the landlord pays only the value assessed as the amount he might expect to recover from a new tenant and, if the 1955 formula produces a higher figure, the Secretary of State can be called upon to pay the difference[3].

If the crofter has been responsible for deterioration or damage to improvements provided by the landlord then the cost of making good the deterioration or damage may be assessed by the Land Court and an order made against the outgoing crofter[4]. The landlord is entitled to set off the amount due or to become due to him by the crofter against any compensation payable by him in respect of the crofter's improvements[5]. Thus the balance of any claims at the end of a tenancy may fall to be received by the landlord. In the case of a deceased crofter his executor may pursue his claim whilst the landlord's claim is good against the executry funds. The Crown may also pursue a claim as *ultimas haeres* where no successor comes forward.

Where the crofter has entered into an agreement whereby his rights to compensation for the permanent improvements have been transferred to the Secretary of State under a building loan agreement or to the Highlands and Islands Development Board in security of a loan, the landlord is liable to make payment up to the value of the loan outstanding to the Secretary of State[6] or to the Board[7]. Where the Secretary of State is called upon to pay part of the compensation he shall be entitled to set it off against any amount due to him by the crofter[8].

1 Crofters (Scotland) Act 1955, s 14(1).
2 Crofters (Scotland) Act 1961, s 6(2).
3 Ibid, s 6(3).
4 Crofters (Scotland) Act 1955, s 14(6).
5 Ibid, s 14(7).
6 Ibid, s 7(2).
7 Highlands and Islands (Scotland) Act 1965, s 8(3).
8 Crofters (Scotland) Act 1961, s 6(3)(a).

CHAPTER 6

CHANGES IN TENANCY

6.01 Introduction

This chapter deals with changes in the tenancy of a croft brought about by relet and assignation as well as changes affecting the principal tenancy resulting from subletting and subdivision. The related subjects of dispossession of absentee crofters and the reorganisation of crofting townships are also found here.

6.02 Vacant crofts

It is essential for effective administrative control by the Crofters Commission that they should receive notice of croft vacancies as they arise. The landlord of a croft is responsible for notifying the Commission whenever[1]:

(a) he receives from the crofter a notice of renunciation of his tenancy, or
(b) he obtains from the Land Court an order for removal of the crofter from the croft[2], or
(c) he either gives to the executor of a deceased crofter, or receives from such executor, notice terminating the tenancy of the croft[3].

A crofter is entitled, on one year's notice in writing to the landlord, to renounce his tenancy at any term of Whitsunday (28 May) or Martinmas (28 November)[4]. The landlord may waive his right to a written renunciation and accept renunciation in other forms but he is entitled to insist on the tenant fulfilling the statutory requirement[5]. A crofter was barred by *mora*, taciturnity and acquiescence from challenging a notice of renunciation to which his 'signature' had been adhibited by his wife[6].

The notice to the Commission of the vacancy must be given within one month of the landlord receiving notice of renunciation or of the Land Court making the order for removal or of the landlord giving or receiving notice of termination, as the case may be. In addition there is a general provision to the effect that where for any other reason a croft has become vacant the landlord shall notify the Commission within one month of the vacancy coming to his knowledge. Any person who fails to comply with the requirement to give notice is liable on summary conviction to a fine not exceeding £10[7].

After a landholder tenant had left his holding derelict and uncultivated for six years without payment of rent, the landlord relet it to a tenant who entered into occupation and fenced it. The Land Court held that there was clear abandonment of the holding and the landlord was entitled, without further process of notification, to treat it as a vacant holding[8]. In another case the applicant laid claim to the tenancy of a landholder's holding on the ground that his brother had abandoned the tenancy. The Court dismissed the application as incompetent in the absence of concurrence by the landlord[9].

What is meant by 'vacant' in the context of these provisions is precisely defined. A croft is taken to be vacant notwithstanding that it is occupied, if it is occupied otherwise than by the tenant of the croft[10]. When, for example, a crofter acquires the ownership of his croft from the landlord and so becomes the owner-occupier, the principle of *confusio* applies and the croft is deemed to be vacant[11]. For the avoidance of any doubt, the Crofting Reform (Scotland) Act 1976 added to section 16 of the Crofters (Scotland) Act 1955 (dealing with vacant crofts) a new subsection (14) declaring that the section has effect as if a person who has become owner-occupier of a croft were required within one month of becoming owner-occupier to give the Commission notice of the fact and as if any reference in the section to a landlord included reference to an owner-occupier[12].

The foregoing provisions and the provisions that follow relating to vacant crofts and re-letting apply in relation to a part of a croft as they apply in relation to a croft[13].

1 Crofters (Scotland) Act 1955, s 16(1) as amended by the Law Reform (Miscellaneous Provisions) (Scotland) Act 1968, Sch 2, Pt I, para 17.
2 See para 4.01.
3 See para 7.08.
4 Crofters (Scotland) Act 1955, s 7(1).
5 *Sutherland Estates v Mackay* (1929) 17 SLCR 23.
6 *Sutherland v Fletcher* 1977 SLT (Land Ct) 5.
7 Crofters (Scotland) Act 1955, s 16(10).
8 *Boyd v Earl of Morton* (1934) 22 SLCR 56; see also *Mackenzie v Rogers* 1973 SLCR App 22.
9 *MacNeil v MacNeil* (1943) 31 SLCR 19.
10 Crofters (Scotland) Act 1955, s 16(11A) added by the Crofters (Scotland) Act 1961, Sch 1, Pt II, para 12(c).
11 *Cameron v Bank of Scotland* 1989 SLT (Land Ct) 38, 1988 SLCR 47.
12 Crofting Reform (Scotland) Act 1976, Sch 2, para 8(d).
13 Crofters (Scotland) Act 1955, s 16(13) (as added).

6.03 Re-letting

The landlord of a croft (including an owner-occupier) is prohibited from letting the croft, or any part of it, to any person except[1]:
(a) with the consent in writing of the Commission, or
(b) with the consent of the Secretary of State if the Commission withhold consent.

Any letting of a croft otherwise than with the appropriate consent is null and void. Where any person is in occupation of a croft under such an irregular letting, a procedure is prescribed[2] whereby the Commission:
(a) may serve a notice in writing on the person requiring him to give up his occupation within one month from the service of the notice, and
(b) if he fails to do so, may take action in the Sheriff Court for his ejection from the croft similar to the action prescribed for the ejection of an absentee crofter[3].

An owner-occupier of a croft cannot validly re-let the croft to a new tenant while reserving the right of occupation to himself. Under a family arrangement the owner-occupier of a croft purported to lease it to his eldest son **by** obtaining the Commission's consent to the re-letting, followed by entry of the son's name in the Register of Crofts. The father reserved the legal occupancy to himself and the son never entered into possession. In determining that the son had not become the tenant of the croft, the Land Court observed that the Commission's consent and alteration of the entry in the Register did not of themselves create a valid lease[4].

Where a croft is vacant the Commission may initiate action for re-letting at any time after one month from the occurrence of the vacancy[5]. They may do so by giving the landlord notice requiring him to submit to them his re-letting proposals, whether as a separate croft or as an enlargement of another croft. If within two months from giving the notice no re-letting proposals are submitted, or the Commission refuse to approve any that are submitted, the Commission may themselves, if they think fit, proceed to re-let the croft. They may re-let to such person or persons and on such terms and conditions (including conditions as to rent) as, after consultation with the landlord, they may fix. The Commission may not re-let while an application for consent to re-letting proposals is being considered by the Secretary of State or while an application to release the croft from the Crofters Acts is before the Commission (see para 10.12). Any re-let by the Commission shall have effect in all respects as if it had been granted by the landlord. But the landlord himself may, within one month from the date of the re-letting, apply to the Land Court for a variation of the terms and conditions of re-let and any variation made by the Court shall have effect as from the date of the re-letting[6].

Where the re-let effected by the Commission is as an enlargement of another croft and any of the buildings on the vacant croft are not required for the enlarged croft, the Commission are required to give notice to that effect to the landlord[7]. Thereupon the surplus buildings will cease to form part of the croft and the landlord may at any time within six months thereafter give notice to the Secretary of State requiring him to purchase the buildings. Where notice has been duly given, the Secretary of State shall then be deemed to be authorised to purchase the buildings compulsorily and to have initiated procedure for the purchase. The consideration payable by him shall be such sum as he and the landlord may agree or, failing agreement, as the Land Court may determine to be the amount which an outgoing tenant who had provided the buildings would have been entitled to receive from the landlord for the buildings as compensation for permanent improvements on termination of tenancy[8].

The Commission's Rules of Procedure provide that, on receipt of an application for their consent to the let of a croft, they will investigate local crofting conditions, the demand for crofts in the locality and the quality of the landlord's nominee for the tenancy.

1 Crofters (Scotland) Act 1955, s 16(3).
2 Ibid, s 16(3A) (as added).
3 Crofters (Scotland) Act 1955, s 17(3); see para 6.14.
4 *Sutherland v Sutherland* 1986 SLT (Land Ct) 22, 1984 SLCR 94.
5 Crofters (Scotland) Act 1955, s 16(4) (as amended).
6 Crofters (Scotland) Act 1955, s 16(5).
7 Ibid, s 16(6).
8 Ibid, s 16(8) (as amended); see para 5.11.

6.04   Assignation of croft[1]

It is a statutory condition of the crofter's tenure that he shall not, except in
accordance with the provisions of the 1955 Act, execute any deed purporting
to assign his tenancy[2]. These provisions forbid assignation by the crofter[3]:
(a) to a member of his family[4] unless he obtains the consent in writing of his
       landlord or, failing such consent, the consent in writing of the Crofters
       Commission;
(b) to a person other than a member of his family, unless he obtains the
       consent in writing of the Commission.

Assignation of a croft without Commission consent, where their consent is
required, is null and void and the Commission may declare the croft to be
vacant.

Where the assignation is effected by the landlord consenting to it, he is
required to notify the Commission of the assignation and the name of the
assignee. Where the assignation is made with consent of the Commission, it
takes effect at the term of Whitsunday (28 May) or Martinmas (28 November)
first occurring not less than two months after the date on which the
consent was intimated to the crofter. At any time before such term it is open
to the crofter (or his executor[5] or legatee in the event of his death) and the
assignee jointly to give to the Commission notice in writing that they do not
intend to proceed with the assignation[6].

The Commission are required to give the landlord notice of any application made to them for consent to the assignation of a croft and to afford both
crofter and landlord an opportunity of making representations before they
decide whether or not to grant the application. This requirement is construed
in the 1955 Act[7] and the Commission's Rules of Procedure give effect to it by
providing an opportunity to parties to make representations both in writing
and at a hearing before a person (usually a Commissioner) appointed by the
Commission. The Commission must take into account the family and other
circumstances of the crofter and of the proposed assignee and the general
interests of the township in which the croft is situated. The local demand for
crofts and the proposed assignee's lack of crofting experience and inadequate
use of land already held have been given as reasons for refusing to grant an
application[8]. There is no right of appeal against the Commission's final
decision.

The crofter's right to assign his croft in accordance with the foregoing
provisions was by the 1976 Act extended to allow him in the same manner to
assign a part of his croft, being a part consisting of any right in pasture or
grazing land held by him whether alone or in common with others[9].

The 1955 Act gave the Commission power to make their consent to an
assignation subject to such terms and conditions as they thought fit[10] but this
power was withdrawn by the 1961 Act[11].

The Land Court have held that the Commission acted properly within
their statutory and discretionary powers when, after taking account inter alia
of social considerations, they consented to a crofter assigning his croft which
was of little agricultural significance to a person who became an absentee
crofter[12]. A joint tenant may competently assign his rights of joint tenancy
without the consent of the other joint tenant[13].

---

1 The Crofters Holdings (Scotland) Act 1886 (s 1) expressly provided that a crofter should
   have no power to assign his tenancy. This was not construed in practice as an absolute

prohibition provided the landlord gave his consent. The Small Landholders (Scotland) Act 1911, s 21 relaxed the prohibition in favour of a landholder who was unable to work his croft through illness, old age or infirmity. He could apply to the Land Court for leave to assign his holding to a member of his family. Further relaxation was introduced by the Crofters (Scotland) Act 1955, s 8 which allowed a crofter to assign his croft to anyone with the consent of the Crofters Commission. Finally s 8 of the 1955 Act was amended by the Crofters (Scotland) Act 1961 and the Crofting Reform (Scotland) Act 1976 and the Law Reform (Miscellaneous Provisions) (Scotland) Act 1968, leaving the statutory provisions now governing assignation of crofts as explained in what follows.

2 Crofters (Scotland) Act 1955, Second Sch, para 2.
3 Ibid, s 8; Crofting Reform (Scotland) Act 1976, s 15.
4 'Member of his family' means the wife or husband of the crofter or his son-in-law or daughter-in-law or any person who could be entitled to succeed to the crofter's estate on intestacy (see para 7.02).
5 As to the transfer of a croft tenancy by an executor in exercise of executry functions see para 7.06.
6 Crofters (Scotland) Act 1955, s 8(6).
7 Crofters (Scotland) Act 1955, s 33(4).
8 See, eg Crofters Commission Annual Reports for 1982, 1986 and 1987.
9 Crofters (Scotland) Act 1955, s 8(7) (as added); Crofting Reform (Scotland) Act 1976, s 15.
10 Crofters (Scotland) Act 1955, s 8(4).
11 Crofters (Scotland) Act 1961, Sch 3.
12 *Vestey v Holmes* 1967 SLT (Land Ct) 7.
13 *Macdonald v Stornoway Trs* (1945) 33 SLCR 32.

6.05   Subletting: Introduction

In the 1886 Act it was made a statutory condition of the crofter's tenure that he must not sublet his croft or any part of it without the landlord's written consent[1]. This prohibition, which accords with the common law, was continued throughout the Landholders Acts into the 1955 Act[2] but the 1961 Act admitted a considerable relaxation. A crofter is now entitled, with the consent in writing of the Commission and subject to such conditions (other than a condition relating to rent) as they may impose, to sublet his croft[3]. In similar manner a crofter may sublet a part of his croft[4], such as the share in common grazings effeiring to the croft or the croft with the exception of the croft house and garden ground. Any sublet entered into without the Commission's consent is declared to be null and void. The consent of the landlord is no longer required.

A special exception is made of the crofter's right to sublet to holiday visitors 'any dwelling-house or other building forming part of his croft'. This right he can exercise without the consent of anybody. The value of the right is enhanced by the provisions which now enable a crofter to make on the croft non-agricultural permanent improvements which can qualify for compensation at the end of the tenancy[5].

1 Crofters (Holdings) (Scotland) Act 1886, s 1(4).
2 Crofters (Scotland) Act 1955, Second Sch, para 5.
3 Crofters (Scotland) Act 1961, s 11 and the Crofters (Scotland) Act 1955, Second Sch, para 5 (as substituted).
4 Crofters (Scotland) Act 1961, s 13(4).
5 Ibid, s 5 and Crofters (Scotland) Act 1955, Fifth Sch, para 11 (as added); see para 5.12.

6.06   Application for consent to sublet and conditions of sublet

When applying to the Commission for consent to a sublet of his croft (or part), a crofter must provide such information as the Commission require, including the name of the subtenant and the duration and terms of the sublease. The rent to be charged need not be disclosed. The Commission will serve notice of the application on the landlord and they are required to have regard to any observations he may make to them. The Commission's Rules of Procedure provide for enquiry into local crofting conditions and the circumstances of parties as well as a hearing if necessary before the final decision is reached.

In addition to approved conditions agreed between the crofter and proposed subtenant, such as reservation of peat rights and access to the crofter's house and any land he is retaining in his own occupation, the Commission can impose their own conditions. Typical conditions imposed relate to the standard of husbandry to be practised, the provision and maintenance of fixed equipment and compensation at waygo for improvements carried out and for unexhausted values of lime and fertilisers. The Commission favour a period of sublet of at least three years and not more than seven, unless there are exceptional circumstances. The Land Court have observed that in the absence of provision in a sublease to which the Commission have consented for continuation of the sublet beyond the term of years specified in the sublease, it cannot be assumed to continue by tacit relocation[1]. It is the Commission's practice in cases where parties are not represented by a solicitor, to provide a form of missive incorporating the conditions imposed by them and any other valid conditions which parties may wish to include. Whether or not the form of missive thus provided is used, the Commission require to see the completed missive for record purposes and to satisfy themselves as to the subtenant's eligibility for grant-aid under the Crofting Counties Agricultural Grants (Scotland) Scheme 1988 (see para 3.13).

1 *Carnach Crofts Ltd v Robertson* 1973 SLT (Land Ct) 8.

6.07　Subleases in existence prior to the 1961 Act

When the 1961 Act came into operation there were in existence a number of subleases that were either valid (granted with the written consent of the landlord) or irregular (without such consent). The Act provided that a valid sublease could continue to be valid if within six months of commencement of the Act the crofter intimated particulars to the Commission. An irregular sublease could be validated if within the like period the landlord and crofter intimated particulars to the Commission[1].

1 Crofters (Scotland) Act 1961, s 11(1) (now repealed).

6.08　Common grazings and subleases

Where under a valid sublease a right in common grazing is let to the subtenant, he comes in place of the crofter in any matter concerning such right and the relevant grazings regulations apply to the subtenant[1]. Both the crofter and his subtenant are entitled to receive notice of common grazing improvement proposals and to make representations but no liability for the relevant expenditure can be imposed on the crofter while the subtenancy subsists[2]. Subject to these provisions, the subtenant is neither a crofter nor the tenant of an agricultural holding within the meaning of the Agricultural Holdings (Scotland) Act 1949[3]. The crofter's basic security of tenure is thus preserved. The terms and conditions regulating the subtenancy have to be found in the sublease as agreed between the crofter and subtenant and laid down or approved by the Commission. In other respects the sublease is subject to the common law.

1 Crofters (Scotland) Act 1961, s 13(2) (as modified), Crofters (Scotland) Act 1955 s 25(1B) (as inserted).
2 See also para 8.07.
3 Crofters (Scotland) Act 1961, s 13(1).

6.09 Termination of subleases when main tenancy ends

A sublease comes to an end when the main tenancy of the croft comes to an end (for example, by the crofter renouncing his tenancy or acquiring the ownership of the croft which extinguishes the tenancy)[1]. Likewise the sub-tenancy is ended when the landlord, in exercise of his statutory right to resume croft land, resumes land that is sublet. But in whatever manner the crofter's own tenancy comes to an end, with consequent termination at the same date of any existing subtenancy, the subtenant can apply to the Commission for an order permitting him to remain in occupation for a further period not exceeding one year, subject to such conditions as may be specified in the order. The application may be made within one month from the sublease coming to an end or such longer period not exceeding three months as the Commission think reasonable. No proceedings for removal of the subtenant can be taken before the expiry of the relevant period or before the Commission have disposed of the subtenant's application. The coming into effect of a decrofting direction given by the Commission to a crofter in anticipation of his acquiring croft land or the site of the croft house does not affect the Commission's power to permit a subtenant to remain in occupation for a further period after the sublease has come to an end[2].

1 Crofters (Scotland) Act 1961, s 13(3) (as amended).
2 Crofters (Scotland) Act 1955, s 16(9A) (as substituted).

6.10 Compulsory subletting

In addition to the foregoing provisions for voluntary subletting, section 12 of the 1961 Act provides for the subletting, if necessary compulsorily, of crofts not adequately used. The substance of the section is that the Commission, after giving one year's warning notice to a crofter who is not making adequate use of his croft, would have power to require him to submit acceptable subletting proposals. If he failed to do so the Commission themselves could effect a sublet. This section, however, has been held in abeyance and it can only be brought into operation by order of the Secretary of State approved by resolution of each House of Parliament[1].

1 Crofters (Scotland) Act 1961, s 19(2).

6.11   Subdivision

The 1886 Act[1] made it a statutory condition of a crofter's tenure that he should not subdivide his croft without the consent in writing of his landlord and the prohibition was continued in the same form in the Landholders Acts. The 1955 Act tightened the prohibition by requiring the consent in writing of the landlord and of the Commission, without which any subdivision is declared to be null and void[2].

The Commission's Rules of Procedure require that an application for their consent to a subdivision shall be accompanied by the landlord's consent in writing. The purposes for which applications for subdivision have been granted include:[3]

(a) improved agricultural management and improved lay-out and access to crofts;
(b) transfer of portions of croft land by crofters who are unable to work them to persons who can;
(c) transfer of portions of crofts to members of the family;
(d) providing suitable house sites for neighbours;
(e) enabling joint tenants to be given their own part of the croft.

1 Crofters Holdings (Scotland) Act 1886, s 1(4).
2 Crofters (Scotland) Act 1955, s 9, Second Sch, para 6.
3 See Crofters Commission Annual Reports, 1984–1988 for examples of purpose.

6.12   Absentee crofters: powers of the Crofters Commission[1]

The Crofters Commission have power to treat a crofter as an absentee if they determine:

(a) that he is not ordinarily resident on or within sixteen kilometres of his croft measured in a straight line[2], and
(b) that it is in the general interest of the crofting community in the district in which the croft is situated that the tenancy of the crofter should be terminated and the croft let to some other person or persons.

Wording somewhat similar to the above occurs in section 16A(2) of the 1955 Act whereby the Commission, when deciding whether or not to grant a decrofting direction, are required to have regard to the general interest of the crofting community in the district and to the demand for a tenancy of the croft. The Land Court, in an appeal against a Commission proposed decision, took the view (i) that 'district' in that context meant in broad terms the general geographical area in which the croft was situated with distinctive conditions of its own, and (ii) that the Commission were entitled to take account of all demand from whatever quarter, even from persons outside the local district[3].

The Commission can take action against a crofter whose permanent residence is away from the croft by making an order terminating his tenancy and requiring him to give up his occupation of the croft at a term of Whitsunday (28 May) or Martinmas (28 November) not earlier than three months after the making of the order.

The Commission's power to take action is not mandatory but permissive[4]. Before making an order of termination the Commission are required:

(a) to take into consideration all the circumstances of the case, including the extent, if any, to which the croft is being worked and, where the croft is being worked by a member of the crofter's family, the nature of the arrangements under which it is being so worked;

(b) to give the crofter and to the landlord, not less than six months before the term at which the proposed order will take effect, notice that they propose to make an order; and

(c) to afford to the crofter and the landlord an opportunity of making representations to them against the making of the order.

The action to be taken by the Commission in complying with this last requirement is prescribed in the 1955 Act[5] and set out in the Commission's Rules of Procedure (see Appendix C, rule 30).

1 In an effort to remedy the problem presented by absentee crofters, s 17 of the 1955 Act conferred on the Crofters Commission power to deal with crofters not ordinarily resident on or within two miles of their crofts. The ultimate sanction was dispossession, but coupled with a right to the dispossessed crofter in certain circumstances to claim a conveyance in feu of the croft house and garden ground. Section 7 of the 1961 Act revised the provisions relating to the conveyance in feu and increased to ten miles the limit placed on ordinary residence from the croft. As the 1976 Act confers on every crofter the right to acquire an owner's title to his croft house and garden ground, the provisions in the Acts of 1955 and 1961 relating to the granting of a conveyance of the croft house to a dispossessed crofter became unnecessary and were repealed (1976 Act, s 22(2) and Sch 3). The revised statutory provisions relating to absentee crofters are now contained in the 1955 Act, s 17(1)–(3) and (9) (as revised by the 1976 Act, Sch 2, para 9 and Sch 3).
2 *Simpson v Yool* (1919) 7 SLCR 18.
3 *Moray Estates Development Co v Crofters Commission* 1988 SLT (Land Ct) 14, 1987 SLCR 14.
4 *Vestey v Holmes* 1967 SLT (Land Ct) 7.
5 Crofters (Scotland) Act 1955, s 33(4).

6.13 Options available to the crofter prior to termination of his tenancy

Action which the crofter may choose to take in the time available to him includes subletting the croft, or assigning the croft tenancy (subject to the landlord's or the Commission's approval as required) or renouncing the tenancy and claiming such compensation for permanent improvements as may be due to him by the landlord. It is also open to him to exercise his absolute right to acquire an owner's title to the croft house and garden ground before taking action by way of sublet, assignation or renunciation of the remainder of the croft.

6.14 Notice and ejection

The Commission must give notice of the making of an order of termination of tenancy to the crofter and to the landlord not less than three months before the term at which the order takes effect. If the crofter fails to give up occupation of the croft in compliance with the order, the Commission may apply to the Sheriff for a warrant of ejection. The Sheriff shall grant the warrant unless cause to the contrary is shown and the Commission may recover from the crofter the expenses of the application and of the execution of the warrant incurred by them.

The dispossessed crofter has the same rights to compensation for permanent improvements and is subject to the same liabilities for compensation for deterioration or damage as if he had renounced his tenancy of the croft at the term at which the order takes effect.

6.15 Landlord's rights when vacant croft remains unlet

When, as a result of action against an absentee crofter, a croft has become vacant and remains unlet for a period of six months, the landlord is entitled within a further period of three months to demand that the Commission direct that the croft shall cease to be a croft[1]. If the landlord, within one month of the Commission issuing such a direction, gives notice to the Secretary of State requiring him to purchase the croft buildings, the Secretary of State must do so. When the notice is given the Secretary of State is deemed to be authorised to purchase the buildings compulsorily and to have initiated procedure for the purchase. The consideration payable is such sum as the Secretary of State and the landlord may agree or, failing agreement, as the Land Court may determine to be the amount which an outgoing tenant who had provided the buildings would have been entitled to receive from the landlord by way of compensation for permanent improvements[2].

1 Crofters (Scotland) Act 1955, s 16(7) (as substituted).
2 Crofters (Scotland) Act 1955, s 16(8) (as amended).

6.16 Reorganisation schemes

With a view to bringing about a reallocation of land to revive crofting townships, the Taylor Commission laid great stress on the need for immediate and drastic action. They proposed that the new Crofters Commission should have power to frame and implement schemes for the reorganisation of townships in an advanced state of decay. The 1955 Act that followed attempted to give effect to these proposals, with detailed provision as to the content of schemes and the procedures to be followed[1].

The Crofters Commission found that in practice the procedures laid down were slow and cumbersome and the provisions ill adapted to effect a reallocation of croft land that would bring units of suitable size into the hands of crofters who were able and willing to work them. In an attempt to remedy this, the 1961 Act made fresh provisions for reorganisation[2] but these also failed to remove the main stumbling blocks to a successful township scheme. The powers, however, are still there and the Commission can operate them provided they are satisfied that a township ought to be reorganised to secure its preservation or better development. They may do so either of their own accord or on being requested by a crofter in the township or by the grazings committee or the landlord. The following are the main features of a reorganisation scheme as laid down in the 1961 Act and the scheme may apply in relation to a group of neighbouring townships as it applies to a township:
(1) The scheme shall provide for such reallocation of land in the township as is most conducive to proper and efficient use and to the general benefit of the township.

(2) Every crofter in the township who so wishes shall be granted the tenancy of a croft which includes his existing croft house and is of no less value than his existing croft.

(3) The scheme may provide for any or all of the following:

    (a) enlargement of crofts or common grazings by the addition of non–crofting land in the vicinity of the township;

    (b) admission into the township of new crofters and allocation to them of shares in the common grazings;

    (c) apportionment for the exclusive use of the township of a part of any common grazings in which it shares;

    (d) inclusion in any croft formed under the scheme of a part of the common grazings or of any lands held runrig.

To enable a scheme to proceed, a majority of the crofters in the township or townships concerned must be in favour of it. It is unnecessary to enter into the detail of the statutory procedures as they stand at present. They are set out in the Act in two sections and a lengthy schedule[2] and, except in the absence of serious objection, a scheme may be expected to engender protracted proceedings (involving the Secretary of State and possibly a public local enquiry and an application to the Court of Session) before a scheme of any substance can reach fruition.

1 Crofters (Scotland) Act 1955, ss 19, 20 (repealed).
2 Crofters (Scotland) Act 1961, ss 8, 9, Second Sch.

CHAPTER 7

SUCCESSION

7.01 Introduction

On the death of a crofter, the right to the tenancy of his croft is indivisible. It is heritable in succession and there is a limited right of bequest available to the crofter. His tenancy is transferred to his successor only after the appropriate statutory steps have been taken. These steps are now contained in the Crofters (Scotland) Act 1955[1] and the Succession (Scotland) Act 1964[2]. Succession to a crofting tenancy was not affected by the 1964 Act (having been specifically excluded therefrom) until the Law Reform (Miscellaneous Provisions) (Scotland) Act 1968 amended the 1964 Act so that it applied to crofters dying after 25 November 1968[3].

In the vast majority of cases, the succession to a deceased crofter's tenancy poses no problems. Where there is a will, the croft tenancy can often without any difficulty be transferred to the appropriate beneficiary. Where there is no will, the crofter may be survived by a spouse, whose prior rights might well take the whole estate including the tenancy or, where there is no spouse, another single successor might be entitled to claim the whole estate. However, where the deceased's estate is subject to several claims by intestate successors, the effect is that a crofting tenancy is now in many ways to be dealt with as just another item of that intestate estate[4].

Notwithstanding the number of cases of succession to crofts which must have been settled since 1968, there remain areas of potential dispute for which the ground rules have not yet been judicially established. The most obvious is the problem of finding the value of the deceased's crofting interest which is of course initially required for confirmation purposes. Other problems include the division of the value of the deceased's interest when more than one person is entitled to share it, and what becomes of the tenancy when there is no bequest and no-one is confirmed as executor.

The Land Court have reluctantly refused to deal with executor's problems of valuation and divison for lack of statutory jurisdiction. They have pointed out that if agreement cannot be secured amongst the beneficiaries it is open to the executor to renounce the tenancy and to claim compensation[5]. Whatever was being considered when succession in crofting was brought into line with succession in other matters, it is unlikely that it was intended that any crofter's family would have to part with a tenancy on such grounds. Further it is often the case that renunciation is the method least likely to realise the true value and executors are naturally reluctant to follow such a course of action.

1 Crofters (Scotland) Act 1955, ss 10, 11; Law Reform (Miscellaneous Provisions) (Scotland) Act 1968, s 8, Sch 2.

2 Succession (Scotland) Act 1964, s 16; Law Reform (Miscellaneous Provisions) (Scotland) Act 1968, s 8, Sch 2.
3 Law Reform (Miscellaneous Provisions) (Scotland) Act 1968, s 8.
4 See M C Meston *The Succession (Scotland) Act 1964* (3rd edn, 1982), p 17.
5 *MacLennan's Exrx v MacLennan* 1974 SLT (Land Ct) 3.

7.02 Bequest of tenancy

A crofter may by will or other testamentary writing bequeath the tenancy of his croft. However, the bequest is not effective unless and until certain conditions have been fulfilled. These conditions are now contained in the 1955 Act[1] permitting a crofter to bequeath his tenancy and controlling the acceptance of such a bequest by the crofter's legatee. Failure to obey these rules might result in the actual succession to the tenancy being far removed from the deceased crofter's testamentary intentions.

Since the introduction of statutory succession in 1886 it has been implicit that, in default of a valid bequest, the right to the tenancy of a deceased crofter is to descend to one of his heirs in intestacy. A crofter failing to bequeath his interest in the tenancy for any reason is thus held to be intestate *quoad* that interest. Care must therefore be taken when drawing a crofter's will.

Where the bequest is ineffective, the right to the tenancy of the croft falls to be dealt with as intestate estate[2]. It would appear therefore that notwithstanding a will purporting to deal with the whole estate, where there is no valid bequest of the tenancy or that bequest fails, persons who would be entitled to share in intestate estate of the deceased are entitled to share the value of the tenancy no matter how the testator intended the tenancy to be dealt with.

The power to bequeath is now subject to the following statutory limitations:

(1) The bequest of the tenancy must be to '*any one person*'. It is not within the power of a crofter to leave his tenancy to more than one person either by dividing his tenancy or in joint tenancy. Nor can he bequeath the tenancy to one person in liferent and another in fee[3].

(2) A bequest to a person who is not '*a member of the crofter's family*' is null and void unless the Commission otherwise determine[4]. The expression 'member of the crofter's family' is defined[5] as meaning the crofter's spouse or any one of the persons who would in any circumstances have been entitled to succeed to the estate on intestacy by virtue of the 1964 Act, or the crofter's son-in-law or daughter-in-law. If the bequest is to a member of the crofter's family, the approval of the Commission is not required. But if the legatee is not a member of the crofter's family as defined, the legatee must make application to the Commission for their approval. No time limit is given for that application and no guidance is given to the Commission as to how to determine an application for such approval. A legatee should be encouraged to make application for approval as soon as possible after the death of the crofter.

(3) *Notice to the landlord*[6] must be given by the legatee in all cases within the two-month period following the date of death of the crofter unless he is prevented by some unavoidable cause, in which case he must give such notice within a further four month period. Failure to give the notice to the landlord renders the bequest null and void. Notice of the bequest given to the landlord must normally be in writing[7]. The giving of notice

by the legatee imports the acceptance of the bequest by him. What is an unavoidable cause, in respect of delay by a legatee in giving notice to the landlord, is not defined but it would seem important that the crofter intending to bequeath the tenancy makes provision for intimation of that bequest to the legatee before or immediately following his death[8].

It is not necessary for confirmation to be obtained before the legatee claims the tenancy nor does the granting of confirmation affect his claim[9]. The statute is silent as to how the legatee substantiates his claim. He is merely required to give notice of the bequest following the death of the crofter. The whole tenor of the statutory requirements is that bequests outwith the crofter's family are null and void unless approved by the Commission. Bequests must come before the Commission for approval when they are to a person outwith the family or to a legatee who has been objected to by the landlord.

1 Crofters (Scotland) Act 1955, s 10 (as amended).
2 Crofters (Scotland) Act 1955, s 11(1).
3 *Anderson v Barclay-Harvey* (1917) 5 SLCR 65.
4 Crofters (Scotland) Act 1955, s 10(1).
5 Ibid, s 10(7).
6 Ibid, s 10(2).
7 Ibid, s 29(1).
8 See *MacKinnon v Martin* (1958) 46 SLCR 19.
9 Succession (Scotland) Act 1964, s 16(8).

7.03 Power of objection

The landlord is empowered to object to the bequest within one month of receiving the notice from the legatee. He must state his objection in writing to both the Commission and the legatee giving his reasons for objecting[1]. The Commission will consider the objection and allow parties the opportunity of making written representations and to request a hearing. If the objection is upheld then the Commission will declare the bequest to be null and void[2].

Unless the landlord intimates his objection to the Commission, the legatee becomes the tenant as from the date of death of the deceased crofter[3]. If an objection is rejected by the Commission then the same rule applies[4]. The statute does not suggest what grounds of objection there may be to a legatee but it is probable that this must relate to the ability of the legatee to maintain the tenancy rather than being a general right in favour of the landlord to restrict the crofter's freedom of bequest[5].

1 Crofters (Scotland) Act 1955, s 10(3).
2 Ibid, s 10(4).
3 Ibid, s 10(2).
4 Ibid, s 10(4).
5 *Howie v D Lowe & Son Ltd* (1952) 40 SLCR 14.

7.04 Failure to bequeath

In the event of a bequest being null and void for any reason, the right to the croft falls to be treated as intestate estate[1]. If there is no valid bequest, the rights of those persons entitled to succeed on intestacy are bound to arise. Therefore, in every case which has no legatee successfully installed in the tenancy the value of that tenancy falls to the intestate successor or is divided between or amongst the several intestate successors.

It is made clear that any dispute regarding the validity of a bequest or the legal effect of a bequest requires to be taken before an appropriate court for determination[2]. It is not for the Crofters Commission to decide these questions nor is it within the jurisdiction of the Land Court.

1 Crofters (Scotland) Act 1955, s 10(5).
2 Ibid, s 10(6).

7.05 Confirmation

Although a legatee can give notice to the landlord of a bequest in respect of a tenancy without awaiting confirmation, it is essential for the purposes of the 1964 Act that an executor confirms to the deceased's crofting tenancy. Without confirmation the interest does not vest in the executor[1]. It appears therefore that no-one possesses or is responsible for the deceased's interest from the date of death until the granting of confirmation or the appearance and acceptance of a legatee. Whilst the landlord is entitled to know after the death of his tenant who is responsible for the croft and what claims are to be made by the deceased's successors, the duty to act will fall on the landlord and the Crofters Commission unless an executor or legatee comes forward.

The deceased's interest as tenant of a croft is heritable estate and should be entered as such in the inventory of the deceased's estate when applying for confirmation. The entry should show that interest as a separate item sufficient to identify it. The value of that item will of course include the permanent improvements on the croft provided by the deceased. However, the principles for valuing a croft tenancy on the death of the tenant are not at all clear and there has in the past been a tendency to undervalue and to allow the administration to proceed without the bother of obtaining a valuer's report when such a process would be both costly and time-consuming.

It is necessary to clearly distinguish between the value of the deceased's interest in his croft and the right to the tenancy itself. The valuation of a croft may be hotly contested by those persons entitled to share its value but the destination of the tenancy in intestacy is in the control of the executor where one has been appointed. One or more of those persons may therefore seek appointment as executor for the power of nominating the next tenant whilst several may seek the nomination themselves. Given that the value may thereafter be used for the calculation of the shares of the several persons entitled thereto, great care should be taken so as to avoid late claims for larger payments from such beneficiaries. Stock and implements on the croft are obviously moveable as is the deceased's share in any sheep stock club[2] or other co-operative venture linked to his crofting enterprise. The valuation of such items will pose additional problems for the executor and should be entered as separate items in the inventory.

The only guidance given by the 1955 Act regarding the value of a croft tenancy at death is indirect. Where a tenancy, which is part of the estate of a deceased crofter, is terminated the executor is entitled to compensation for permanent improvements. But the 1964 Act also contemplates the transfer of the tenancy by the executor to a person not entitled to share in the estate[3]. Such a transfer would no doubt demand a consideration for which there is no statutory formula and might even be a market price albeit the 'market' is restricted. It is sometimes argued that where compensation or a price has been obtained, the sum recovered can then be dealt with in terms of the deceased's will, for instance as part of the residue for the benefit of residuary legatees, but it is to be doubted whether a crofter can in his will legitimately direct his executor to renounce the tenancy or otherwise deal with it in order to give the value thereof to a testamentary beneficiary. Confirmation ought to be obtained prior to the transfer of tenancy by the executor but where the executor has succeeded in having the tenancy transferred prior to confirmation he should try to ensure that confirmation is obtained by him within one year from the date of death[4].

1 Succession (Scotland) Act 1964, s 14; *Rotherwick's Trs v Hope* 1975 SLT 187.
2 *Kennedy v MacDonald's Exors* (1959) 47 SLCR 3.
3 Succession (Scotland) Act 1964, s 14(1)(ii).
4 *Garvie's Trs v Garvie's Tutors* 1975 SLT 94.

7.06   Intestate succession

The law of intestate succession cannot be dealt with here other than in brief detail. When the statutory tenure was created by the Crofters Holdings (Scotland) Act 1886, the only modification made to the ordinary rules of intestate succession in heritage for identifying the successor to the tenancy was that in the event of the heirs-at-law being heirs portioners, the eldest would succeed without division. The 1955 Act laid down improved procedures for securing the entry of a successor on intestacy and to that end provided for the exercise of certain controls by the Crofters Commission. Major changes introduced in 1968 to the succession to crofts were the admission to the right of succession of females on an equal basis with males and of the mother and relatives of the mother on an equal basis with the father and relatives of the father. The successor to the tenancy was no longer to be found by applying the old doctrine of primogeniture and preference of males. The rights of a surviving spouse in the succession were also greatly enhanced and adopted and illegitimate children acquired rights.

One major innovation in 1968 was that several members of the deceased's family might be equally entitled to be nominated as next tenant and each might be entitled to share in his intestate estate and therefore to a division of the value of the tenancy. Executors who are exposed to such problems must seek to resolve these difficulties, if neccessary by negotiation amongst all the interested parties. As a crofter who leaves no valid bequest of his crofting tenancy must be held to have died intestate *quoad* his right to the holding, the rights of those persons entitled to share in the intestate estate cannot be ignored.

On the death of a crofter intestate or where his bequest of the tenancy of his croft has failed to receive effect, it is the duty of the executor to nominate the next tenant by furnishing the landlord with the name and address of that proposed tenant. Where two or more persons are entitled to share in the deceased's estate, it is for the executor to decide which one of them should get that portion of the estate consisting of the right to the croft tenancy and to transfer the tenancy to him or her. For his own protection, the landlord should seek to have the confirmation exhibited to him at this time. The executor is required to furnish particulars of the transferee 'as soon as may be' and the landlord must accept the transferee as the new tenant and notify the Commission accordingly[1]. Unlike the position where he is faced with a legatee, there is no opportunity for the landlord to raise an objection where the nomination has been properly made by the executor. No consent is required from the Crofters Commission where the nominee is a member of the deceased crofter's family. If, however, the tenancy is to be transferred to anyone else then the Commission's approval is required[2].

If, within a period of three months from the 'relevant date', the executor has not furnished the landlord with particulars of the transferee, the landlord is required to notify the Commission. The 'relevant date' may be any one of four different dates, namely:

(1) where there has been a bequest of the tenancy in favour of a person not being a member of the crofter's family but the Commission have refused to determine that the bequest shall not be null and void, the date of that refusal;

(2) where the deceased crofter has not bequeathed the tenancy, the date of the crofter's death;

(3) where the deceased crofter has bequeathed the tenancy but the bequest has become null and void on the legatee's failure to give the statutory notice to the landlord, the date upon which the bequest became null and void;

(4) where a bequest has been declared null and void by the Commission, the date upon which they notified the landlord and the legatee to that effect[3].

1 Crofters (Scotland) Act 1955, s 11(1).
2 Succession (Scotland) Act 1964, s 16(2).
3 Crofters (Scotland) Act 1955, s 11(3).

7.07 Nomination of successor by the Commission

If three months have elapsed since the relevant date and the executor of the deceased crofter has not furnished the landlord with particulars of the transferee, the Commission are empowered to seek a successor from amongst those claiming rights in the deceased's estate[1]. They may advertise for claims to the tenancy from persons who may be entitled to share in the intestate estate of the deceased crofter or to claim legal rights or the prior rights of a surviving spouse out of that estate.

The Commission may nominate as successor to the tenancy any of the persons who intimate a claim, but before doing so they must consult with the executor (if any) and be satisfied:

(a) that the claimant they intend to nominate is a person entitled to succeed to the intestate estate of the deceased crofter or to claim legal rights or the prior rights of a surviving spouse out of the estate, and

(b) that adequate provision is made for the settlement of the entitlement or claim of any other person known to them to be entitled to succeed to or to claim such rights out of the estate[2].

The Commission must give notice to the landlord of the person nominated by them and the landlord is required to accept him as successor to the tenancy[3]. Nomination by the Commission operates the transfer of the croft tenancy and the transfer is in or towards satisfaction of their nominee's interest in the deceased's intestate estate[4]. Nomination extinguishes the right of any other person to the croft tenancy[5].

1 Crofters (Scotland) Act 1955, s 11(4).
2 Ibid, s 11(4A).
3 Ibid, s 11(4B).
4 Ibid, s 11(4C).
5 Ibid, s 11(6).

7.08   Termination of the tenancy

If the deceased's interest in the croft is not disposed of within twelve months of the date of death or of the decision of the Commission resulting in the failure of a bequest or such longer period as may be agreed between parties or by the sheriff, it is open to the landlord or the executor to take action to terminate the tenancy[1]. Similarly the tenancy may be brought to an end by the Commission declaring the croft vacant after a further month[2] and a claim for compensation may be made within 12 months after such declaration[3].

The executor's additional right to terminate a tenancy depends upon his being satisfied that the interest in the lease 'cannot be disposed of according to law'[4] and at any time the executor may so inform the landlord. Where a tenancy is thus terminated, the landlord is required to pay compensation to the executor in the usual way and no time limit is specified for compensation to be claimed[5]. A claim for compensation might however fail if it is delayed without reasonable cause[6].

1 Succession (Scotland) Act 1964, s 16(3)(b), (4)(a).
2 Crofters (Scotland) Act 1955, s 11(5).
3 Ibid, s 11(7).
4 Succession (Scotland) Act 1964, s 16(3)(a).
5 Crofters (Scotland) Act 1955, s 14(1)(ii).
6 *Macleod v Vestey* (1962) 50 SLCR 23.

7.09   Late claims to the tenancy and other matters

Given that any possible bequest is dealt with by the Acts which impose a strict timetable, late claims to the tenancy will always be based on entitlement to succeed to intestate estate. Whereas the right to share in the value of that estate will not be time-barred, any such claim would appear to be valid only against an executor and the right to claim the tenancy itself might be lost by the passage of time[1]. The rules prior to 1968 indicated that a claim to the right of tenancy would be lost if it was not pursued within two years of the emergence of the right, except in very special circumstances[2]. A claim timeously made by the proper successor should not be ousted by the landlord's acceptance as tenant of another whose claim was invalid[3]. However, it is likely that since 1968, the executor's powers have replaced any personal claims from individual successors. Such a successor may of course be a party who could seek appointment as executor for himself.

Whatever procedure is followed to find a successor it is clear that he must account to the executor for the value of the tenancy so that adequate provision can be made to settle other parties' claims on the deceased's estate. If an executor intends to transfer the tenancy of a deceased crofter to any person where that person is not entitled to the tenancy in or towards satisfaction of his entitlement or claim to the deceased's estate, then the approval of the Crofters Commission is required[4].

The 1955 Act empowers the Crofters Commission either to identify the next tenant of a croft or to declare it vacant. The court has observed the practice of allowing a holding to be continued in the name of the representatives or heirs of a deceased tenant as being undesirable[5]. A claim against a landlord for compensation lying with a crofter prior to his death will fall to be pursued by his executor[6].

It has been the practice since 1968 for the executor of a deceased crofter to proceed to nominate himself as the next tenant of the deceased's croft. Attention should be given to this point where it is thought that there is a possibility of the executor being challenged as acting as *auctor in rem suam*. Such a challenge will require to be made in the ordinary courts.

1 *Wilson v Stewart* (1853) 16 D 106; *MacIver v MacIver* 1909 SC 639, 1909 1 SLT 258, 46 SLR 552; *MacMillan v MacLeod* (1937) 25 SLCR 45; *MacDonald v Fraser* 1965 SLCR App 51.
2 *Campbell v Duke of Sutherland* (1913) 1 SLCR 3.
3 *Smith v Barvas Estate Ltd* (1927) 15 SLCR 36.
4 Succession (Scotland) Act 1964, s 16(2)(c)(i).
5 *Sutherland v Sharp's Trs* (1928) 16 SLCR 3; *MacLeod v Barvas Estate Ltd* (1928) 16 SLCR 44; *Macdonald v Mackintosh* (1941) 29 SLCR 12.
6 *Kerr v Duke of Hamilton's Trs* (1919) 7 SLCR 92; *MacInnes v Cathcart's Trs* (1939) 27 SLCR 43; *Davidson's Exrx v Stewart* 1964 SLT (Land Ct) 6.

CHAPTER 8

COMMON GRAZINGS

8.01 Statutory provisions

The right to share in common grazings forms an important part of the great majority of crofts (see para 3.05). Since 1891 there has been statutory provision for the appointment of common grazings committees and the making of common grazings regulations. The administrative authority with responsibility for common grazings was the first Crofters Commission until the Scottish Land Court took over these functions under the Small Landholders (Scotland) Act 1911. The Crofters (Scotland) Act 1955 substantially re-enacted the existing statutory provisions with two major changes:

(a) the functions of grazings committees were extended in the direction of improved use and development of the grazings as distinct from the regulation of rights, a process that was carried further by the Acts of 1961 and 1976; and

(b) the administrative responsibility for common grazings was transferred from the Land Court to the present Crofters Commission.

The statutory provisions governing common grazings are now contained in sections 24–27 of the 1955 Act, section 15 of the Crofters (Scotland) Act 1961 and section 16 of the Crofting Reform (Scotland) Act 1976. Reference in these sections to a crofter includes reference to any person who, not being a crofter, is entitled to share in a common grazing along with crofters[1]. Thus shareholders who are not crofters (such as ordinary agricultural tenants) are subject to the grazings regulations and to the jurisdiction of the grazings committee who administer the regulations. When a crofter acquires the ownership of his entire croft other than the grazing right effeiring to it, he continues to hold the right on crofting tenancy[2]. A shareholder may also be a person to whom a grazing right has been assigned[3] or sublet[4].

1 Crofters (Scotland) Act 1961, s 15(6) (as amended).
2 See para 9.18.
3 See para 6.04.
4 See para 6.08.

8.02 Grazings committee

Detailed provision for regulating the appointment of grazings committees (or constables) and committee proceedings are contained in section 24 of the 1955 Act[1]. The shareholders may from time to time, at a public meeting called for the purpose, appoint a grazings committee of such number as the meeting shall decide. A person is eligible for membership although he is not a crofter[2]. Notice of the meeting may be given by any two crofters interested in the grazings. The notice requires to be published for two successive weeks in a local newspaper or it can be posted for two successive weeks in such public place in the district as the Commission may approve. Any dispute as to sufficiency of notice will be determined by the Commission. In practice, the committee in office make the arrangements for the election of a new committee when their own term of office is coming to an end.

The Committee must appoint a clerk, whether a member of the Committee or not, and pay him or her such annual remuneration as they may fix. This expenditure is recoverable from the shareholders. Any vacancy occurring in the membership by reason of death or resignation shall be filled by nomination of the remaining members. A majority of members of the committee is a quorum. The term of office of the committee is three years, at the end of which period a new committee falls to be appointed.

If the crofters fail to appoint a grazings committee, the Commission may themselves make the appointment and also appoint a clerk. Alternatively the Commission may appoint a grazings constable with the like powers and duties as a grazings committee. The Commission shall fix his term of office and his annual remuneration which shall be defrayed by an assessment levied on the shareholders in such manner as the Commission deem reasonable.

If the Commission are satisfied that the grazings committee or any of its members or the clerk are not properly carrying out their statutory duties, they may remove any or all of them from office and appoint or provide for the appointment of other persons (whether crofters or not) in place of the person or persons removed. In an application by a shareholder for suspension or removal of a grazings committee, which was subsequently allowed to be withdrawn, the Land Court observed on the legal position and the duties of a committee[3].

1 As amended by the Crofters (Scotland) Act 1961, s 15(1), First Sch, para 13 and the Crofting Reform (Scotland) Act 1976, s 16(1).
2 Crofters (Scotland) Act 1961, s 15(1).
3 *MacKinnon v Duke of Argyll* (1947) 35 SLCR 35.

8.03 Functions of grazings committees

The powers and duties of grazings committees fall under the three heads of maintenance, improvement and management[1]. A committee is not precluded from carrying out the duties of maintenance and improvement on land other than the common grazings[2].

(a) Maintenance

It is the duty of the committee to maintain the common grazings and to provide, maintain and, if necessary, replace the fixed equipment required in connection therewith.

'Fixed equipment' has the like meaning as in the Agricultural Holdings (Scotland) Act 1949 (section 93(1)). It includes inter alia all permanent buildings necessary for agricultural purposes, permanent fences including hedges and stone dykes, ditches and drains, fanks, dippers, pens, access or service roads, bridges, water systems and shelter belts[3]. Unless the fixed equipment is required in connection with common grazings, the grazings committee has no jurisdiction to deal with it. Where the grazings regulations provided that the committee should attend to 'township roads', the Land Court held that it had no power to deal with a road giving access only to the township arable lands and not serving the common grazings[4].

Responsibility for common grazings fencing is discussed under 'Crofting boundaries' and 'Fencing and maintenance of fencing' (see paras 3.08 and 3.09).

(b) Improvement

It is the duty of the committee to carry out works for the improvement of the common grazings and the fixed equipment thereon.

Under the 1955 Act the committee was prohibited from carrying out such works of improvement except with the consent of a majority of the crofters ordinarily resident in the township and with the approval of the Commission[5]. The 1976 Act introduced a new procedure which enables the committee to proceed without majority consent. To initiate an improvement project or scheme the committee must now give notice to each shareholder of (i) their proposals for the improvement works, and (ii) the proposed allocation among the shareholders of the expenditure to be incurred. Any shareholder may within one month of the date of the notice make representations to the Commission in respect of the proposed works or the proposed allocation of expenditure. The Commission may approve these as they stand or they may approve them subject to modification or they may reject them altogether. Where the grazing right is sublet, both the crofter who sublet and his subtenant are entitled to receive notice of the improvement proposals and to make representations, but no liability to meet expenditure shall be imposed on the crofter so long as the subtenancy subsists.

(c) Management

It is the duty of the committee to make and administer, with a view to their due observance, regulations for the management and use of the common grazings.

The Commission may appoint a person who shall have power to summon and to attend any meeting of a grazings committee for the purpose of advising them and otherwise assisting them with their duties. The Commission staff includes a Grazings Officer whose duty it is to attend to common grazings matters.

1 Crofters (Scotland) Act 1955, s 25 (as amended and added to).
2 Crofting Reform (Scotland) Act 1976, s 16(2).
3 Crofters (Scotland) Act 1955, s 37(1).
4 *MacDonald v Greig* 1964 SLT (Land Ct) 5.
5 Crofters (Scotland) Act 1955, s 25(1) proviso (repealed).

8.04 Grazings regulations

Grazings regulations made under previous legislation were not adequate to cover all the functions of a grazings committee as extended by the 1955 Act. For that reason every committee was required as soon as possible after the Act came into operation, and in any event within six months after being required by the Commission to do so, to make and submit new grazings regulations to the Commission for confirmation. The Commission could confirm them with or without modification or refuse to confirm them. If a committee failed to submit satisfactory regulations, the Commission themselves could make the regulations. In all, 750 sets of regulations have been made and confirmed in terms of these provisions. Where prior to the 1955 Act there were existing regulations in force which have not been superseded by new regulations made or confirmed by the Commission, these existing regulations continue in force[1].

A grazings committee may from time to time submit to the Commission for confirmation amendments of the current regulations. They should do so whenever the practice in the township differs from what is laid down, or is not provided for, in the regulations. The Commission may confirm with or without modification or refuse to confirm amendments submitted by the Committee. The Commission themselves may require a committee to submit amendments to current regulations within a certain time and if they fail to do so the Commission can proceed to make the amendments.

Before confirming, making or amending regulations, the Commission are required to consult the landlord of the common grazings. They must send a copy of such regulations both to the landlord and to the grazings committee.

Grazings regulations for the time being in force have effect notwithstanding anything contrary thereto or inconsistent therewith contained in any lease or other agreement whether entered into before or after the coming into force of the regulations. This is an important change from previous legislation which required the terms of such agreements to be taken into account[2]. The change is designed to prevent restrictions in leases or conditions of let from interfering with the proper management of common grazings.

The penal sanction for contravention of or failure to comply with grazings regulations is a fine not exceeding £10 on summary conviction of an offence[3]. In the case of a continuing offence a further fine can be imposed not exceeding 50 pence for each day on which the offence is continued after the committee or the Commission have served notice on the offender warning him of the offence.

1 Crofters (Scotland) Act 1955, s 26 (as amended), s 39(5); *Martin v Geddes* 1983 SLCR.77.
2 Crofters Common Grazings Regulation Act 1891, s 2.
3 Crofters (Scotland) Act 1955, s 27(1) (as amended).

8.05 Content of grazing regulations: Introduction

In addition to the general power conferred on a grazings committee to make regulations for the management and use of the common grazings, there are certain specific matters for which the regulations must make provison[1]. These are:

1 Crofters (Scotland) Act 1955, s 26(2) (as amended); Crofters (Scotland) Act 1961, s 15(2) (as amended).

8.06 Expenses

(a) Recovery by the committee from shareholders of all expenses incurred by the committee:

(i) in maintaining the grazings and providing, maintaining or replacing any fixed equipment, and

(ii) in connection with the improvement of the grazings and fixed equipment.

Care must be taken to distinguish between expenditure on maintenance and expenditure on improvement, having regard to the statutory procedure applicable to works of improvement.

> (b) Power to the committee from time to time, in advance of expenditure, to levy on and recover from the shareholders, in such proportions as may be specified in the regulations, such sums as the committee consider necessary to meet the expenses of maintenance and improvement of the grazings and fixed equipment thereon.

8.07   The souming

> (c) The number and the kind of stock which each shareholder is entitled to put on the common grazings (the souming).

The souming is sometimes expressed in terms of a share or shares in the grazings, with each share carrying a defined entitlement to stock. Sometimes it is expressed in terms of so much stock to each pound of rent. Where the sheep stock is managed on a club system, each shareholder's share in the club is defined. The stock is owned by the club in common and the profits or losses are shared pro rata by the shareholders according to their individual interests in the club.

The Land Court considered a case[1] where the grazings regulations provided that the common grazings should be worked on the club system, that no shareholder should be permitted to keep a private pack or pet sheep and that each shareholder was bound to throw his holding open for the wintering of the club stock. The club committee declined to accept an application for membership of the club from a new tenant in the township with a share in the common grazings. He sought a remedy in the Court by way of a ruling that the grazings regulations did not prohibit him from keeping his own sheep on his inbye land. The Court ruled that the prohibition in the regulations against a private pack must apply to the inbye land as well as to the common grazings. The Court also made some general observations on the club stock system. The statutes are silent as to 'clubs' or 'club stock' although the system is widely practised in the crofting counties. Shareholding and membership of the club were so integrated in the grazings regulations that if the club committee were to have the power to exclude a shareholder from becoming a member of the club this should be specifically provided for with adequate safeguards for the shareholder. The Court concluded that there may well be a *casus omissus* in the 1955 Act as to sheep stock clubs which should be remedied. A remedy could perhaps be found by making appropriate provision in the grazings regulations.

> (d) The alteration of individual soumings where works for improvement of common grazings or fixed equipment have been carried out and all the shareholders have not contributed to the expense.

The purpose here is to restrict the benefits to shareholders who have contributed. This was later fortified by a provision[2] that the grazings regulations may:

(i) restrict the use of any part of the common grazings on which improvements have been carried out to the shareholders who contributed to the expense, and

(ii) regulate the number and kinds of stock which each contributor may put on that part and also the stock which each shareholder (whether or not a contributor) may put on the remainder of the grazings.

1 *Neish v North Talisker Grazings Committee* 1968 SLT (Land Ct) 4, 1968 SLCR App 107; see also *Crofters Commission v South Scorrybreck Grazings Committee* 1968 SLT (Land Ct) 8, 1968 SLCR App 113 and *Munro v MacLeod* 1966 SLCR App 49.
2 Crofters (Scotland) Act 1961, s 15(3).

8.08 Peats and seaweed

(e) Where appropriate, the cutting of peats and the collection of seaweed.

Seaweed was extensively used in former times as a fertiliser for the croft but is now of less importance. The cutting of peats for household fuel is still practised in some areas. The legal principles governing the right to cut peats and the respective rights of crofters and landlords in peat mosses are discussed under the relevant statutory condition which recognises the crofter's prior right in peat mosses (see para 4.16). The purpose of the regulation dealing with peat cutting is to lay down rules for the proper control of existing rights. Apart from this it is the right of the landlord to direct where a crofter may cut peats although in practice he may leave that to the grazings committee[1]. If that part of an estate over which crofters exercise peat cutting rights comes to be sold, the rights remain valid under the new proprietor. If a particular moss becomes exhausted or unavailable, the Commission may draw up a scheme regulating the use by crofters on the same estate of peat bogs and the charge for this use may be included in croft rents[2]. Prior to the 1955 Act a number of schemes were drawn up by the Land Court and the power is still there for the Commission to exercise if required. There is similar power to draw up schemes for regulating the use of seaweed or heather or grass used for thatching purposes but there is little or no call for such nowadays.

1 *Campbell v Campbell* 1955 SLCR App 230, *Parr v Maclean* (1889) 16 R 810, 26 SLR 586.
2 Crofters (Scotland) Act 1955, s 27(8).

8.09 Committee meetings and business

(f) Subject to the statutory provisions, the summoning of meetings of the committee and the procedure and conduct of business at such meetings.

The standard form of grazings regulations confirmed by the Commission provides for the appointment of a chairman of committee, the summoning of meetings, the keeping of records and the procedure and conduct of business.

8.10   Enclosure of croft

Many crofting townships are open in the sense that the township stock is allowed to graze the inbye land whenever the crop has been removed from the ground. When sowing time comes round in the spring the stock is cleared off the inbye land and the township gates are closed. Where the grazings regulations prescribe that crofts shall be available during the winter season for the grazing of stock belonging to other shareholders, any crofter may apply to the grazings committee for their consent to the exclusion of such stock from his croft or any part of it[1]. If the crofter is dissatisfied with the decision of the committee he may appeal to the Commission. Any consent given by the committee or the Commission may be given subject to conditions. A usual condition is that the crofter is required to take on to his own inbye land his stock (or a proportion of it, if only part of the croft is to be enclosed) during the time that the other crofts are open.

1 Crofters (Scotland) Act 1955, s 27(2).

8.11   Apportionment of common grazings

The provisions for apportionment of common grazings contained in the 1911 Act were re-enacted with modifications in the 1955 Act. Since then apportionment has become widely practised for the purpose of improving pasture and adding to the productive capacity of the croft. The current statutory provisions[1] provide for two kinds of apportionment, as follows:

(a) Apportionment to an individual shareholder

Any shareholder can apply to the Crofters Commission for an apportionment of part of the common grazings for his own exclusive use. The Commission, after consultation with the grazings committee, may grant an apportionment on such conditions, including fencing and drainage conditions, as they think fit.

Under the Commission's Rules of Procedure the application is brought to the notice of the committee and the other shareholders as well as the landlord. They are all given an opportunity to make representations in writing and a hearing may be required. Usual conditions attached to the granting of an apportionment include:

(i)   that the apportionment shall be enclosed by a stockproof fence and that the apportionment shall not take effect until this has been done;

(ii)   that any proposed works of improvement shall be carried out;

(iii) that the applicant's souming shall be extinguished (or reduced, if it is a partial apportionment);

(iv) that rights of access and peat cutting of other shareholders shall be preserved;

(v)   that the applicant shall continue to be liable for his share of township obligations and expenses (with right of appeal to the Commission if the Committee refuse a reasonable modification).

In certain circumstances the right to an apportionment may be lost through long delay and failure to fulfil the conditions[2].

Any apportionment of common grazing land granted to a crofter is deemed to form part of his croft. Where a shareholder who is not the tenant of a croft has obtained an apportionment he is deemed to hold the apportioned land in tenancy until it is held otherwise and the land is deemed to be a croft[3].

(b) Apportionment to a township

Where a common grazing is shared by two or more townships, any shareholders interested may apply to the Commission for apportionment of the grazing into separate parts for the exclusive use of the several townships. Application may also be made for apportionment of part of the grazing for the exclusive use of one of the townships. Such apportionment may be granted after consultation with the grazings committee and subject to such conditions, including fencing and drainage, as the Commission think fit. The Commission's Rules of Procedure prescribe a procedure following closely the procedure laid down for apportionments to individual shareholders, including publication of the application and affording an opportunity to make representations in writing and to ask for a hearing.

1 Crofters (Scotland) Act 1955, s 27(3), (4) (as amended); Crofters (Scotland) Act 1961, s 15(5).
2 *Leask v Leask* 1969 SLT (Land Ct) 5.
3 Crofters (Scotland) Act 1955, s 3(5), (6) (as substituted).

8.12   Ground game

Notwithstanding anything in the Ground Game Act 1880, the shareholders in a common grazing are entitled to appoint not more than two of their number to kill and take ground game (rabbits and hares) on the grazing[1]. Any person so appointed is deemed, for the purposes of the 1880 Act, to be the occupier of the grazing but he shall not have the right to authorise any person to kill and take ground game. The shareholders are also entitled to authorise in writing one person bona fide employed by them for reward to kill and take ground game on the grazing. Any person so authorised is deemed for the purposes of the said Act to have been authorised by the occupier of the common grazing to kill and take ground game with firearms or otherwise.

1 Crofters (Scotland) Act 1955, s 27(5).

8.13   Runrig lands

The runrig system of holding land has now practically disappeared. It refers to the practice of tenants in former times to reallocate annually the rigs comprising the arable land in their possession by drawing lots or by some other means. This periodical redivision gradually fell into abeyance and what is now regarded as runrig lands are detached rigs or blocks of land held permanently by neighbouring crofters[1].

Prior to the 1911 Act the only method, apart from agreement, whereby lands held runrig could be divided into compact holdings was for the landlord to resume possession of the land in order that individual holdings could be formed and relet. The 1911 Act authorised the Land Court to carry out apportionment and the authority is now vested in the Crofters Commission[2].

The Commission may, on the application of any landlord or crofter interested, apportion runrig lands among the holders thereof in such manner and subject to such conditions as appears to them to be just and expedient. In most cases all the tenants concur in the application and it has been the invariable practice to proceed with apportionment only where there is a concurring majority. Any apportionment of runrig lands granted to a crofter is deemed to form part of his croft[3].

1 *MacKenzie v Carloway Estates Ltd* (1940) 28 SLCR 51; see also *Walker v Forestry Commission* 1965 SLCR App 58.
2 Crofters (Scotland) Act 1955, s 27(7) (as amended).
3 Ibid, s 3(5), (6) (as substituted).

Part III   OWNERSHIP OF CROFT LAND

CONTENTS

CHAPTER 9

RIGHTS TO ACQUIRE OWNERSHIP

9.01 Options open to crofter

The Crofting Reform (Scotland) Act 1976 which came into operation on 10 June 1976, indicated a major shift towards recognition of the permanent nature of crofting tenancies. Even without proceeding to purchase, the crofter can now be regarded as part-owner of his subjects due to his interest in the permanent improvements and to his right to share in the development value[1]. But as well as entitling a crofter to share in the value of any land resumed from his tenancy, the 1976 Act conferred on a crofter the legal right to seek an owner's title to his subjects. These purchase provisions obviously pose a threat to the proprietorial rights in crofting land enjoyed by the landlord for, if his landlord refuses to sell or agreement cannot be reached, the crofter is now authorised to apply to the Land Court for the appropriate order[2].

The statutory right to purchase extends to (a) the *site of the dwelling-house* and (b) *croft land* as defined in the 1976 Act[3]. The terms of acquisition differ and are dealt with separately in the Act, giving an absolute right to the crofter to acquire the site of his croft house and the right to apply for a title to his croft land.

It is not intended that a crofter should be forced to buy his croft, for he may prefer to remain a tenant with such benefits and protections as that status implies[4]. But by enabling such purchases to take place, a crofter has now the option of obtaining the security of owning his own house and garden as well as the opportunity of more fully developing the potential of his croft land. By proceeding to decroft any subjects so acquired, the crofter can enjoy the full market potential of his dwelling-house or development, for example, by obtaining a residential mortgage or a commercial loan on normal terms against the value of his assets.

There is nothing novel about a crofter buying the site of his croft house or indeed his croft land from his landlord, but before the 1976 Act this could only be done by private agreement. Such agreements were relatively infrequent and such titles as were negotiated tended to have the superior/vassal relationship replacing that of landlord/tenant but this need no longer be the case[5]. Indeed in some cases prior to the 1976 Act the conditions of title included a feuduty greater than the annual croft rent, a consideration which need no longer be taken into account.

Where a crofter is intending to negotiate the purchase of the *site of the dwelling-house* or of his *croft land* (or part thereof) it will be of great advantage to him to understand how the Land Court have dealt with applications made to them under the 1976 Act purchase provisions.

However, it remains important to differentiate between purchases privately negotiated between parties and those ordered by the Land Court following a purchase application. Although the 1976 Act tacitly encourages such negotiations, its principal purchase provisions are available only for those transactions which take place following an order of the Land Court. Whilst it is open to parties to agree similar provisions when reaching *consensus in idem*, it is a mistake to arrange to do business 'on the terms provided by the Act'[6].

It is enacted that where a person other than the landlord is infeft in the subjects to be conveyed, that person will be involved in the procedure as required[7] and where these subjects are burdened by any heritable security and the conveyance is ordered by the Land Court, the crofter acquires them free of that security[8]. These and other such situations will therefore not prevent the conveyance taking place and will not be available as a protection against the division or depletion of the landlord's estate[9]. Similarly where the sale to the crofter or his nominee is ordered by the Land Court any right of pre-emption in the landlord's title in favour of the superior or any other person is not enforceable[10].

1 *Fulton v Noble* 1983 SLT (Land Ct) 40, 1982 SLCR 97.
2 Crofting Reform (Scotland) Act 1976, s 1(1) and (2).
3 Ibid, s 1(3) and (4).
4 *Cameron v Bank of Scotland* 1989 SLT (Land Ct) 38, 1988 SLCR 47.
5 *Fulton v Noble* supra.
6 *MacLeod's Exor v Barr's Trs* 1989 SLT 392.
7 Crofting Reform (Scotland) Act 1976, s 5(5).
8 Ibid, s 8(4).
9 Ibid, s 5(1).
10 Ibid, s 6(3).

9.02 Matters to be agreed

Because of the relatively small monetary value of most of these crofting transactions, the parties may not always resort to formal missives. Care should therefore be taken when agreeing to such terms as 'standard estate conditions' and 'reasonable legal expenses' for obvious reasons. Other matters to be considered when agreeing the terms of purchase will include the following:
(a) the price or consideration to be paid apportioned where necessary between the *site of the dwelling-house* and the *croft land*[1];
(b) the extent of the area or areas being purchased. It is always advisable to have a plan prepared differentiating where necessary between the *site of the dwelling-house* and the *croft land*;
(c) the boundaries of the subjects being acquired, which may have to be checked and agreed with neighbours;
(d) whether the landlord provided any of the fixed equipment or improvements on the subjects of purchase[2];
(e) the ownership of trees[3];
(f) the date of entry which will govern both the payment of the price and the apportioning of the rent;
(g) a new rent for the remainder of the tenanted subjects (including any share in common grazings)[4];

(h) parties' liability to each other for conveyancing and other expenses and how such expenses are to be quantified[5];

(i) whether there is to be an agreed right to 'clawback' similar to that contained in the 1976 Act purchase provisions and how such a right is to be protected, eg by standard security[6];

(j) lease-back of sporting rights (fishings/shootings) and the period and rent thereof[7];

(k) the reservations of mines, metals or minerals[8];

(l) the preservation of peat rights[9];

(m) general conditions including fencing, services and access rights[10];

(n) residual rights, such as pre-emption[10];

(o) irritancy clause in conveyance[10]; and

(p) form of conveyance[11].

1 See paras 9.05 and 9.10.
2 See para 9.05.
3 See para 9.13.
4 Crofting Reform (Scotland) Act 1976, s 7.
5 See paras 9.06 and 9.12.
6 See para 9.11.
7 See para 9.14.
8 See paras 9.04 and 9.08.
9 Crofting Reform (Scotland) Act 1976, s 6(6).
10 See para 9.05; *Campbell v Duke of Argyll's Trs* 1977 SLT (Land Ct) 22.
11 See para 9.05; *Fulton v Noble* 1983 SLT (Land Ct) 40, 1982 SLCR 97.

9.03 Application to the Land Court

Only in the event of failure to reach agreement does the 1976 Act permit the crofter to make application to the Land Court[1]. There is therefore an implied duty on the crofter first to approach his landlord and a similar duty on that landlord to respond. When considering any motions for court expenses, the Land Court will judge whether it was necessary or reasonable for the application to be lodged. To answer such a question they will require to have before them evidence of parties' actions prior to the lodging of the application, for example any correspondence between agents.

Unlike a conveyance following on a resumption order where the purpose and conditions of the order are 'integral to the conveyance',[2] it is expressly provided that even where the Land Court in their order determined the terms and conditions of acquisition, the crofter and landlord may still arrange for the conveyance to take place on any other terms and conditions they may agree[3]. The order itself remains effective for two years or such other period as may be agreed by parties or determined by the Land Court[4].

1 Crofting Reform (Scotland) Act 1976, s 1(1) and (2).
2 See ch 10; *Macdonald v Barker* 1970 SLT (Land Ct) 2.
3 Crofting Reform (Scotland) Act 1976, s 5(4).
4 Ibid, s 6(1).

(a) THE SITE OF THE DWELLING-HOUSE

9.04   Conveyance of croft house site and garden ground

A crofter has an absolute right to a conveyance of the *site of the dwelling-house* on or pertaining to his croft. Failing agreement with his landlord, he may apply to the Land Court for an order requiring the landlord to grant that conveyance[1].

The site of the dwelling-house is defined[2] as including any buildings thereon together with such garden ground as, failing agreement with the landlord, may be determined by the Land Court[3] to be appropriate for reasonable enjoyment of the dwelling-house as a residence. There is specifically excluded from the definition any right to mines, metals or minerals[4] or any possibility of claiming that more than one dwelling-house comes within this provision[5].

Where the subjects tenanted as a croft include the sites of more than one dwelling-house, the absolute right to a conveyance will extend to the site of one dwelling-house only[6] and where, after 10 June 1976, a crofter has acquired the site of that dwelling-house, the right will not extend to any further dwelling-house erected on or pertaining to the remainder of the croft after the date of that acquisition[7]. It should be noted that the Land Court have always interpreted this provision as relating solely to a habitable dwelling-house and not merely to the ruins or remains of a former croft house. This is true even where the former croft house has been utilized or adapted for other purposes, in which case the building will be regarded as a steading or other such building erected on the croft. The crofter may of course seek to acquire the site of such a building or of any additional dwelling-house as part of his *croft land*[8].

How much garden ground may be appropriate for the reasonable enjoyment of the dwelling-house as a residence will be a matter of opinion, especially where no particular area of garden ground has been fenced off from the rest of the croft[9]. It is open to the crofter to agree with the landlord the extent of the garden ground or to have it determined by the Land Court[10]. The Land Court apparently have power to determine a suitable garden area to go with the dwelling-house and to order its conveyance even when the dwelling-house pertaining to the croft is not erected on it, for example, when the dwellinghouse is on the common grazing.

Generally an area of about a quarter of an acre (0.1 hectare or thereby) is acceptable by the Land Court as the *site of the dwelling-house* to include a reasonable area of garden ground, either following parties' agreement[11] or on the suggestion of the Land Court[12]. Where there is doubt between parties and it is intended to decroft the site after acquisition, the Crofters Commission will make a direction, in advance of purchase, on the application of the crofter intending to purchase, in respect of a suitable area using the same criteria[13].

Because the 1976 Act's treatment of the *site of the dwelling-house* is so different from that of *croft land* it is wise to attach a plan to the conveyance showing clearly the boundaries of the site as agreed or determined. For example, the clawback provision applicable to *croft land*[14] does not apply to the site of the dwelling-house nor is there any authority for the landlord to be granted a lease-back of the shooting rights over or any fishing rights pertaining to the site of the dwelling-house.

A crofter acquiring the *site of the dwelling-house* after 10 June 1976 will continue to enjoy any right to cut and take peats for domestic use which was enjoyed by him immediately before the acquisition. This right will continue so long as the crofter or his spouse continues to occupy the dwelling-house[15].

1 Crofting Reform (Scotland) Act 1976, s 1(2).
2 Ibid, s 1(4).
3 Ibid, s 4(1).
4 Ibid, s 1(4)(a).
5 Ibid, s 1(4)(b), (c).
6 Ibid, s 1(4)(b).
7 Ibid, s 1(4)(c).
8 See para 9.08.
9 *MacLugash v Islay Estates Co* 1985 SLCR 99.
10 Crofting Reform (Scotland) Act 1976, s 1(4).
11 *Fraser v Noble* 1977 SLT (Land Ct) 8.
12 *MacLugash v Islay Estates Co* supra.
13 See para 10.11.
14 See para 9.11.
15 Crofting Reform (Scotland) Act 1976, s 6(6).

9.05   Conditions, price and form of conveyance

Where a crofter applies to the Land Court for an order requiring the landlord to grant a conveyance of the *site of the dwelling-house*, the Land Court will make an order laying down the boundaries of the land to be conveyed and the terms and conditions of sale so far as these have not been agreed by parties[1]. The Land Court are also instructed, failing agreement, to fix the consideration which is to be made up of two amounts being (a) the open market value of the *bare site* and (b) one-half of the open market value of the site attributable to the landlord's *fixed equipment*, if any, thereon[2]. Both amounts fall to be assessed following certain statutory assumptions:

(a) Bare site

The open market value of the *bare site* is to be determined[3] as the amount which the site, if sold on the open market by a willing seller, might be expected to realise assuming:
(i)   there were no buildings on the site;
(ii)   the site was available with vacant possession;
(iii) the site was not land subject to crofting controls; and
(iv) no planning permission exists or could be obtained for development of the site.
Obviously these statutory assumptions severely limit the open market value. The effect of this formula will be to reflect the agricultural value of the land (notwithstanding its use as the site of a dwelling-house). In some cases other factors such as location or accessibility might have a bearing in addition to the extent and agricultural worth of the site. *Bare site* prices determined by the Land Court have generally not exceeded £100 per acre pro rata and are often much less.

(b) Fixed equipment

The second amount[4] falls to be added only where the landlord has provided *fixed equipment* on the site of the dwelling-house, ie where the subjects tenanted are an equipped or partially equipped croft and part of the value of the site is attributable to such *fixed equipment*, for example where the landlord originally provided the house itself. The statutory assumptions are reduced to (ii), (iii) and (iv) in (a) above and the market value of the site as equipped, including the house itself, is determined by the Land Court as is the proportion of that value attributable to the landlord's *fixed equipment*. The amount to be added is one-half of that value so attributable[5].

In the leading case of *Campbell v Duke of Argyll's Trustees*[6], a crofter applied to the Land Court for an order requiring the landlord to grant a conveyance of the *site of the dwelling-house* and laying down the terms and conditions of title. The landlord argued in favour of the standard estate feuing conditions being inserted in the conveyance. The Full Court, however, sustained the crofter's objection to the great majority of these on the grounds that the restrictions and controls over building and land use embodied in the feuing conditions are now substantially covered by the statutory powers vested in local authorities and operated through planning procedures and building and licensing regulations. The only conditions approved by the Court were:

(i)   that the crofter should enclose the ground with a stockproof wall or fence and maintain it in good repair in all time coming;

(ii)   that the crofter should compensate the landlord for loss, injury or disturbance caused by the operation on the site; and

(iii) that in the event of the conveyance being a feu writ it might include an irritant and resolutive clause.

In that case the Land Court decided in favour of the argument for the landlord that 'conveyance' is apt to include a feu writ as well as a simple disposition.

However, in the later case of *Fulton v Noble*[7], the Land Court indicated that the time had come for the Full Court to give guidelines as to the circumstances in which either a disposition *simpliciter* or a feu disposition would be appropriate. They doubted whether in practice feu writs were needed in the crofting counties (other than in purchases from the National Trust for Scotland[8]) and since this judgment, conveyances have generally been ordered in the form of dispositions.

1 Crofting Reform (Scotland) Act 1976, s 4(1).
2 Ibid, s 4(2).
3 Ibid, s 4(2)(a).
4 Ibid, s 4(2)(b).
5 See *Galbraith v Bray's Trs* 1978 SLT (Land Ct) 3.
6 *Campbell v Duke of Argyll's Trustees* 1977 SLT (Land Ct) 22.
7 *Fulton v Noble* 1983 SLT (Land Ct) 40, 1982 SLCR 97.
8 See para 9.15.

9.06 Liability for expenses

When the Land Court make an order requiring the landlord to convey the *site of the dwelling-house* only, they may determine that any of the expenses of the conveyance and other expenses necessarily incurred by the landlord shall be borne by the crofter in whole or in part[1] but such a determination can only be made when the conveyance is not included in a deed which also conveys *croft land*[2]. Failing agreement, either party can apply to have these expenses taxed by the auditor of the Land Court, who will also decide who is to bear the expenses of taxation and in what proportion[3].

These provisions are clearly intended to avoid the situation where the expenses which would have to be borne by the landlord are out of proportion to or in excess of the price which he is to receive for *the site of the dwelling-house* and the Land Court have generally ordered the crofter to relieve the landlord of his conveyancing costs in such cases. But in some cases where the house has been provided by the landlord, or he has a substantial interest in the fixed equipment, the price payable by the crofter may be such that the landlord can be expected to meet his own costs out of the price.

1 *Ferguson v Ross Estates Co Ltd* 1977 SLT (Land Ct) 19.
2 Crofting Reform (Scotland) Act 1976, s 4(3).
3 Ibid, s 4(4).

9.07 Provisions regarding loans to crofters

Special provision is made for securing any sum due by a crofter in respect of the *site of the dwelling-house* to the Secretary of State or the Highlands and Islands Development Board following the purchase of the site by the crofter. This applies whether the acquisition follows a negotiated agreement or an order of the Land Court[1]. Questions arising can be settled by the Land Court[2] and the respective priority of each of several loans is dealt with by the 1976 Act[3].

1 Crofting Reform (Scotland) Act 1976, s 8(1).
2 Ibid, s 8(2).
3 Ibid, s 8(3).

(b) CROFT LAND

9.08 Acquisition of croft land

The 1976 Act gave the crofter a right to seek an owner's title to *croft land* tenanted by him and this will include all buildings and other improvements on the land whether provided by the landlord or the crofter. Failing agreement with the landlord regarding that acquisition, the crofter may apply to the Land Court for an order authorising him to acquire his *croft land*[1].

For the purpose of the purchase provisions *croft land* is defined[2] as including any land being part of a croft, other than:
(a) *the site of the dwelling-house* on or pertaining to the croft[3], the acquisition of which is dealt with separately under the 1976 Act[4];
(b) common grazing which has not been apportioned; or apportioned common grazing which is neither contiguous nor adjacent to any other part of the croft nor arable machair. *Croft land* therefore includes any apportionment which is adjacent or contiguous to any other part of the croft or which comprises arable machair[5].
Whereas *contiguous* means 'in actual contact' or 'touching', *adjacent* is to be viewed more flexibly as 'close' or 'neighbouring'. Each case must depend on its own merits but the Land Court have held that the 'criteria applicable to the assessment' of adjacency includes physical proximity,

access from the croft to apportioned areas and ready convenience of joint working of croft and apportioned area'[6].

Where it is intended to grant an order authorising acquisition of apportioned common grazings the Land Court must have regard to the conditions imposed by the Crofters Commission. The same applies when the land acquired is land held runrig which has been apportioned[7];

(c) any right to mines, metals or minerals or salmon fishings (not being salmon fishings in Orkney or Shetland) pertaining to the croft[8].

The Land Court may make an order authorising the crofter to acquire such *croft land* as may be specified in the order. The acquisition so ordered shall be subject to such terms and conditions as, failing agreement with the landlord, may be specified in the order[9]. The order will require the landlord to convey the *croft land* to the crofter or his nominee in accordance with those terms and conditions[10] but the crofter and the landlord may still arrange for the conveyance to take place on any other terms and conditions that they may agree[11]. The order itself remains effective for two years or such other period as may be agreed by parties or determined by the Land Court[12].

The form of conveyance has already been discussed.[13]

1 Crofting Reform (Scotland) Act 1976, s 1(1).
2 Ibid, s 1(3).
3 Ibid, s 1(3)(a).
4 See para 9.04.
5 Crofting Reform (Scotland) Act 1976, s 1(3)(b).
6 *Gillies v Countess of Sutherland's Trs* 1978 SLT (Land Ct) 2.
7 Crofting Reform (Scotland) Act 1976, s 2(5); Crofters (Scotland) Act 1955, s 27(4), (7).
8 Ibid, s 1(3)(c).
9 *Campbell v Duke of Argyll's Trs* 1977 SLT (Land Ct) 22.
10 Crofting Reform (Scotland) Act 1976, s 2(1)(a); *Robertson v Secretary of State for Scotland* 1983 SLT (Land Ct) 38.
11 Crofting Reform (Scotland) Act 1976, s 5(4).
12 Ibid, s 6(1).
13 See para 9.05.

9.09   Objections available to landlord

The Land Court may refuse the application[1] and they are directed not to make an order authorising the acquisition where the landlord has satisfied them on either or both of two grounds of objection[2]. These are:

(i) that, in all the circumstances pertaining to the landlord and having regard to the extent of land owned by him to which the 1955 Act applies, the making of an acquisition order would cause a *substantial degree of hardship to the landlord*[3];

A plea of hardship can only be successful if there are special circumstances and any hardship must be substantial and be substantiated by evidence[4]. Whatever the feelings of the landlord may be, the passing of the 1976 Act and its effect on his estate cannot be considered a sufficient hardship. The conversion of an annual rent into a capital sum will not itself imperil the landlord[5]. But where the proprietors own only a small piece of land in which they have a large financial interest, the Land Court may refuse to make an order[6]. It has been observed by the Land Court that there are more types of hardship than financial, eg social hardship where the loss of half a crofting estate might cause loss of prestige[7] or even emotional hardships where there is a long family connection with a small area of land.

(ii) that the making of an acquisition order would be *substantially detrimental to the interests of sound management* of the estate of the landlord of which the croft land forms part[8].

To succeed in this plea it would be necessary to prove that the landlord was actively engaged in estate management activities and that these would be affected in a substantial way[9]. It is not always clear what is meant by 'the estate of the landlord' although it has not been restricted to 'the extent of land owned by him to which the 1955 Act applies'.

1 Crofting Reform (Scotland) Act 1976, s 2(1)(b).
2 Ibid, s 2(2).
3 Ibid, s 2(2)(a).
4 *MacAskill v Basil Baird & Sons Ltd* 1987 SLT (Land Ct) 34, 1986 SCLR 133.
5 *Carnach Crofters v Sweeney* 1978 SLCR App 172.
6 *Geddes v Gilbertson* 1984 SLT (Land Ct) 55, 1983 SLCR 57.
7 *Geddes v Martin* 1987 SLCR 104.
8 Crofting Reform (Scotland) Act 1976, s 2(2)(b).
9 *Mackay v Barr's Trs* 1981 SLCR App 76; *Geddes v Martin* supra.

9.10 Assessment of price of croft land

For calculating the price of *croft land* there is provided a straightforward statutory formula to be applied by the Land Court[1], namely 15 times the current rent of the land to be purchased. At the landlord's request the Land Court will determine the updated fair rent which shall be deemed to be the current rent for the purpose of the calculation[2]. Where the landlord has provided fixed equipment on the croft land, the rent will normally reflect that fact.

If the landlord fails or decides not to ask for a new fair rent to be fixed, the Land Court will use the current rent for their calculation. It will be remembered that rents can be decreased as well as increased[3].

Whilst the 1976 Act excludes any right to mines, metals or minerals or salmon fishings (not being salmon fishings in Orkney and Shetland) from the definition of *croft land*[4] problems arise when there are trees belonging to the landlord growing on the land being purchased by the crofter[5].

1 Crofting Reform (Scotland) Act 1976, s 3(1).
2 Ibid, s 3(2).
3 See ch 5 regarding revision of rent.
4 Crofting Reform (Scotland) Act 1976, s 1(3)(c).
5 See para 9.13.

9.11 Five years 'clawback' provision

If the crofter who has acquired *croft land* following an application to the Land Court, or any member of the crofter's family who has obtained the title to that land, disposes of the relevant land to anyone who is not a member of the crofter's family within five years of the date of acquisition by the crofter, a claim arises in favour of the landlord[1]. This *clawback* provision applies only where the disposal is by any means other than by a lease for crofting or agricultural purposes.

The crofter or other person disposing of the relevant land is bound to pay to the landlord a sum equal to one-half of the difference between (a) the market value of the land at the date of disposal which, failing agreement, will be determined by the Land Court and (b) the consideration originally paid by the crofter to the landlord for that land[2]. The market value is fixed only after several assumptions are made[3]. An early case allowed a deduction for improvements carried out on the land but not for legal fees and outlays incurred by the crofter[4].

The Land Court may make it a condition of the original acquisition that the crofter grant a standard security in favour of the landlord to secure any sum which may become payable within the five-year clawback period[5]. They have, however, refused to put crofters to the additional expense of granting a standard security in cases where the landlord has stated no reason why such a condition was considered necessary. The crofter's assurance that there is no intention to dispose of the croft land to anyone outside his family may be accepted by the Court. In place of a standard security, the Land Court have sometimes chosen instead to require a suitable clause to be inserted in the conveyance.

Where it is made a condition of acquisition that the crofter or his nominee grants a standard security and the Land Court are satisfied that there has been a failure to execute the necessary deed within a reasonable time, the Court shall authorise their principal clerk to execute the deed[6].

'Member of the crofter's family' as used in the 1976 Act and in the foregoing paragraphs means the crofter's wife (or husband as the case may be), or son-in-law or daughter-in-law, or any of the persons who would in any circumstances have been entitled to succeed to his estate if he had died intestate[7].

If the relevant land forms part only of the croft land which was acquired, then, failing agreement of parties, the Land Court can be asked by the person disposing of the relevant land or the landlord to determine for *clawback* purposes the proportion of the amount of the consideration paid for the acquisition of the relevant land[8]. No payment of *clawback* is due where the subsequent disposal of the relevant land is in accordance with an agreement between the landlord and the person disposing of that land[9].

1 Crofting Reform (Scotland) Act 1976, s 3(3).
2 Ibid, s 3(3)(a) and (b).
3 Ibid, s 3(4).
4 *Clan Donald Lands Trust v Macdonald* 1983 SLCR 49.
5 Crofting Reform (Scotland) Act 1976, s 2(4).
6 Ibid, s 5(8).
7 Ibid, s 21(3).
8 Ibid, s 3(5).
9 Ibid, s 3(6).

9.12   Liability for expenses

The price payable for *croft land* may seem trifling particularly where the crofter is seeking to acquire a small portion only of his land, but the Land Court have ruled that they have no authority to transfer the liability for expenses from the landlord to the crofter in such a case[1]. Therefore, despite the almost compulsory nature of the sale of croft land and the low price which might be fixed in accordance with the statutory provisions, the Land Court will not order that the crofter should pay all the expenses of the conveyance of *croft land* and the landlord must bear his own.

1 *Ferguson v Ross Estates Co Ltd* 1977 SLT (Land Ct) 19.

9.13   Ownership of trees

Trees growing on croft land or grazings can give rise to several problems. One of the most obvious is where a crofter seeks to acquire his *croft land* and there are trees growing there which cannot be shown to have been planted by the crofter or his predecessors in the tenancy. When faced with such a problem, the Land Court have generally been prepared to devise a solution in keeping with the spirit of the statutory purchase provisions.

There can be no doubt that growing timber and trees on tenant *croft land* are in the ownership of the landlord. The same of course is also true of *any* permanent improvement although provided by the crofter or any of his predecessors in the tenancy, but subject always to the tenant's claim to compensation therefor on renunciation or removal[1]. The 1955 Act specifically permits a claim to compensation for 'planting trees'[2] and reserves timber and other trees planted by the crofter or his predecessors from the rights exercisable by the landlord[3]. But other growing timber belongs to the landlord and without express stipulation or contract the crofter has no right to cut and take such timber for his own use[4].

Where the *site of the dwelling-house* is purchased and there are trees growing on the site, it will be necessary to decide whether these trees belong to the landlord or are improvements provided by the crofter or by any of his predecessors in the tenancy. If they are tenant's improvements then they are included in the conveyance at no extra cost to the crofter. But if they are not tenant's improvements they will require to be dealt with as fixed equipment provided by the landlord and one-half of their value will be added to the price[5].

There is no exclusion of trees from the definition of *croft land*[6] and therefore growing timber and trees belonging to the landlord will be acquired by the crofter on purchasing his croft land unless the Land Court order the contrary, eg by allowing the landlord to retain rights for the extraction of his timber.

The method of fixing the consideration payable by the crofter for acquisition of his *croft land*[7] does not allow for any additional payment for trees unless their presence on the croft land is a factor in fixing the current rent. However, to avoid unnecessary felling of timber at the time of acquisition, the Land Court have developed a practice of fixing the market value of the trees and enabling them to be made available to the crofter at that value[8].

1 *Fraser v Carnegie* (1927) 15 SLCR 46.
2 Crofters (Scotland) Act 1955, s 14(1), Sch 5, item 7.
3 Ibid, s 3, Sch 2, cond 10(d).
4 *Gilmour v Master of Lovat* 1979 SLT (Land Ct) 2.
5 Crofting Reform (Scotland) Act 1976, s 4(2)(b).
6 Ibid, s 1(3).
7 Ibid, s 3.
8 *Gilmour v Master of Lovat* supra.

9.14 Sporting rights

Although it has been argued that a sporting lease may not be binding on singular successors of the lessor, the Land Court are bound to impose a condition that a lease be granted, on the acquisition of *croft land* by a crofter, where they are satisfied that in the absence of a lease the landlord's fishing or shooting rights would be materially affected[1]. Any such lease is to be at a nominal or token rent, eg tenpence per annum[2], for a period of not less than twenty years and subject to such other terms and conditions as the Land Court shall specify.

In one case,[3] the Land Court considered rights of fishing and observed that the right to salmon fishings (not being salmon fishings in Orkney or Shetland) is a separate feudal right excluded from the definition of *croft land*[4] and therefore no lease of salmon fishings could be ordered. They also stated that they saw no reason to ordain the crofter to grant a lease of trout fishing to the landlord, proceeding on the view[5] that the right to salmon fishing includes the right of trout fishing but the latter right is not exclusive. In other words, the landlord would continue after conveyance of the *croft land* to have the right of salmon fishing inclusive of the right to fish for trout but this would not exclude the crofter also from trout fishing *ex adverso* of the bank where the river bounded the croft land acquired by him. The Land Court also imposed a condition that the landlord should indemnify the crofter against any loss or damage arising from the exercise of the landlord's right of access to the river for fishing and ancillary purposes.

As regards the shooting rights, where the Land Court were satisfied that the loss of such rights would materially affect the landlord's rights, they made it a condition of the conveyance that the parties would enter into a lease of shooting rights in normal form for a period of twenty years, with right to the landlord to sublet and with provision for indemnity to the crofter against loss or damage to the land, the occupier or his family, arising from the exercise of the shooting rights.

Although a shooting lease has been ordered or granted, the occupier of land has a statutory[6] and inalienable right to kill and take ground game thereon, so a landlord selling to a tenant cannot by obtaining a lease exclude the former tenant's rights to kill ground game.

1 See S Scott Robinson *The Law of Game, Salmon & Freshwater Fishing in Scotland* (1990), pp 35, 36; Crofting Reform (Scotland) Act 1976, s 2(3).
2 *MacKintosh v Countess of Seafield's Trs* 1979 SLT (Land Ct) 6.
3 *Ferguson v Ross Estates Co Ltd* 1977 SLT (Land Ct) 19.
4 Crofting Reform (Scotland) Act 1976, s 1(3).
5 J H Tait *A Treatise on the Law of Scotland as applied to the Game Laws, Trout and Salmon Fishing* (2nd edn, 1928) p 105.
6 Ground Game Act 1880, s 1.

9.15 Purchases from the National Trust

Despite the land involved being held 'inalienably' by the National Trust for Scotland at 10 June 1976, there is nothing to prevent a crofter seeking to obtain an owner's title either direct from the National Trust or by application to the Land Court. The title obtained normally takes the form of a feu disposition accompanied by a conservation agreement.

Where the landlords are the National Trust the Land Court cannot order conveyance other than by a grant in feu[1]. The general requirement that the consent of the Lord Advocate be obtained to a grant in feu by the Trust exceeding 20 acres does not apply[2]. The Land Court are however instructed to have regard to the purposes of the Trust[3] and in practice this enables the Trust to obtain from the purchasing crofter a standard conservation agreement. Further provisions apply where such land as has been acquired by a crofter is later subject to compulsory purchase[4].

1 Crofting Reform (Scotland) Act 1976, s 5(7).
2 Ibid, s 5(7).
3 Ibid, s 6(4).
4 Ibid, s 6(5).

9.16   Execution of conveyance

When the Land Court order 'execution' of a deed, it is likely that they mean it to include the delivery of that deed into the hands of the party entitled thereto or that party's agent.

If, following an order, the Land Court are satisfied that the landlord has failed to execute a conveyance within a reasonable time, they have power to authorise their principal clerk to execute such deeds or deed as adjusted at his sight as may be necessary to give effect to the order[1]. A similar provision applies where the crofter or his nominee has failed to execute a standard security in favour of the landlord in compliance with a condition imposed by the Land Court in such an order[2] to protect the landlord's potential claim to clawback.

In several cases, the landlord has adjusted and even subscribed the conveyance but has refused to deliver it in accordance with the order, whilst insisting variously on the settlement of a debt by the crofter or the execution of a standard security or of a shooting lease (none of which had previously been requested and which may not have been competent or allowed by the Land Court). The Land Court have taken the view that a standard security or shooting lease must be requested prior to the order so that the request can be dealt with in the order. Whereas the Land Court have generally dealt with such cases by issuing a further order and thus extending the period for delivery of the conveyance, it would not be inappropriate for the principal clerk to be authorised to execute the deed in such circumstances.

1 Crofting Reform (Scotland) Act 1976, s 5(2).
2 Ibid, s 2(4).

APPLICATION TO THE LAND COURT

9.17   Form of application

The application form (general), which should be used by a crofter seeking to purchase all or part of his *croft land* or the *site of the dwelling-house* is obtainable from the Land Court. Where the crofter wishes to acquire the *croft land* and *the site of the dwelling-house*, he should state separate craves, (1) for an order authorising him to acquire the *croft land*; and (2) for an order requiring the landlord to grant a conveyance of the *site of the dwelling-house*.

The statement of facts attached to the application should contain particulars of the croft, ie its area (arable and outrun), the extent of the common grazings, if any, and the share therein, any apportionment and the current rent. The applicant should state whether he claims that all the permanent improvements on the croft have been provided by himself or his predecessors in the tenancy or whether all or any have been provided by the landlord as fixed equipment or otherwise. It will also be useful to provide a plan of the subjects which the crofter seeks to purchase and to explain what attempts, if any, have been made at negotiating the sale of the subjects with the landlord. It will be remembered that such negotiations (or lack thereof) may have an important bearing on the award of court expenses.

FOLLOWING ACQUISITION

9.18   Effect of ownership

By becoming the owner of his croft, the crofter does not alter the status of the land which remains subject to the controls of the Crofters Acts. However, the tenancy is extinguished by *confusio* and the new owner becomes the owner (and perhaps the owner occupier) of a vacant croft[1].

As the expression 'crofter' means the tenant of a croft[2] the protective provisions of the Crofters Acts do not apply to an owner occupier of a croft[3]. So long as the former crofter or a member of his family continues to occupy and work the croft and fulfil any township obligations, it is the policy of the Crofters Commission not to seek re-letting proposals. Failing this, however, the Commission may decide to call on the owner to let the croft to a suitably qualified person. Alternatively the owner occupier may seek an appropriate decrofting direction.

If a crofter becomes owner of part only of his croft, he will normally continue as tenant of the remainder. Where the whole of the croft land is purchased, a crofter may remain the tenant of rights in common grazings which will be deemed to be a croft for the purposes of the Crofters Acts[4]. The crofter or his landlord may ask the Land Court to adjust a new fair rent for the remainder, notwithstanding that it is less than seven years since the term at which the existing rent for the croft first became payable[5].

A crofter acquiring his croft (or part thereof) is required within one month to intimate that fact to the Crofters Commission[6]. For seven years following the acquisition of the *site of the dwellinghouse*, the crofter (or a member of his family) can seek housing grant and loan, whilst an owner–occupier of a croft (or similar holding in the crofting counties) may at any time apply for financial assistance (see paras 3.13 and 3.14)[7].

1 *Sutherland v Sutherland* 1986 SLT (Land Ct) 22, 1984 SLCR 94.
2 Crofters (Scotland) Act 1955, s 3(2).
3 *Cameron v Bank of Scotland* 1989 SLT (Land Ct) 38, 1988 SLCR 47.
4 Crofters (Scotland) Act 1955, s 3(6).
5 Crofting Reform (Scotland) Act 1976, s 7.
6 Ibid, s 6(7).
7 Crofters (Scotland) Act 1955, ss 22, 23, 31; Crofting Reform (Scotland) Act 1976, s 12.

CHAPTER 10

RELEASE FROM CROFTING CONTROLS

10.01 Crofting as interference with landownership

Any land which comes under crofting controls may be severely restricted in the use to which it can be put by its proprietor. *Rankine* considered that the Crofters Acts 'in their general scope and in almost every detail are a material interference with freedom of contract and ownership'[1]. The Land Court have always recognised that these Acts have been 'expressly framed for the purpose of making material changes in the powers and rights of landlords for the benefit of tenants'[2]. How then can a landowner rid his land of these restrictions and in what circumstances is this possible?

One of the objects of the Crofters Acts is to ensure that croft land will not be lost to crofting when an individual tenancy comes to an end[3] but that it will continue to be available for letting to crofters should they desire it. Although the proprietor of croft land may wish to have his land released from crofting controls, the Acts have conferred upon that land *even when vacant* (ie free of any tenant) certain attributes of which it cannot be deprived except by the due observance of the statutory requirements of relief[4]. In certain circumstances, land which has been removed from crofting controls can be recalled into crofting if the reason for, or conditions of, removal are not fulfilled.

There are two main methods of removing croft land from crofting. These are:

(1) *Resumption* by order of the Scottish Land Court, and
(2) *Decrofting* by direction of the Crofters Commission.

In each case the application is made by the landowner or proprietor, although there is provision for a tenant crofter to seek a decrofting direction whilst intending to purchase his croft or part of it.

Which of the two procedures should be pursued depends on whether there is a tenant crofter with the tenancy of the croft. If there is a tenant the correct procedure is *resumption*. The lack of a tenant on croft land merely leaves the land vacant and available for a further tenant[5] and does not affect the crofting status of the land itself. If there is no tenant the land requires to be *decrofted*. Land may also be removed from crofting by acquisition under the compulsory purchase code.

1 J Rankine *The Law of Leases in Scotland* (3rd edn, 1916) p 607.
2 *MacAlpin v Duke of Hamilton's Trs* (1914) 2 SLCR 74.
3 *Watson v Maclennan* 1972 SLT (Land Ct) 2.
4 *Whyte v Garden's Trs* (1925) 13 SLCR 99.
5 See para 6.02.

(1) RESUMPTION

10.02   The protection of the Land Court

Although the Crofters Holdings (Scotland) Act 1886 granted crofters security of tenure (subject only to the threat of removal for non-payment of rent or the breach of one or more of the statutory conditions), the Act did allow the landlord to apply to resume any croft or part thereof for a reasonable purpose[1]. Of course, the removal of the crofting tenant is only one effect of resumption. The other is that it restores the land to the landlord's control free from the constraints of the Crofters Acts. In a crofting context such restoration is frequently fictional, for it applies even where the land has been from time immemorial possessed by the crofter and his forebears and where there is no evidence that the land has ever been in the natural possession of its owner[2].

The Crofters (Scotland) Act 1955 enables the Land Court to grant a resumption order when persuaded to do so on the application of a landlord and on fixing the compensation due to the crofter on his losing the use of his land[3]. The Crofting Reform (Scotland) Act 1976 whilst giving recognition to the quasi-dual ownership in crofting subjects not only enabled the crofter to purchase his subjects, but also entitled him to share in the development value of any land being removed from his tenancy by resumption[4]. Since 1976, developments in fish farming and forestry have meant that large sums of money are often involved. The Court therefore have been given a protective duty to ensure the crofter receives his fair share of the value of land taken from him. However, the procedure is protective in other ways and there are sound reasons for this:

(1) The crofting tenant has a substantial security of tenure and this has to be safeguarded. Refusals are therefore common where the purpose is clearly outwith the scope of the statutory provisions or seen as an unfair attempt to encroach upon a tenure which has become a kind of special property[5].

(2) There is a scarcity of land available for crofting and so the Court will seek to ensure that not too much is being resumed for the purpose given[6].

(3) A good reason is necessary for resuming croft land and the Court's order will be effectual only for the reason given in the order.

(4) It is recognised that once land passes out of crofting it is unlikely to be returned to it.

1 Crofters Holdings (Scotland) Act 1886, s 2.
2 J Rankine *The Law of Leases in Scotland* (3rd edn, 1916) p 647.
3 Crofters (Scotland) Act 1955, s 12.
4 Crofting Reform (Scotland) Act 1976, s 9.
5 *Rankine* p 648.
6 *Cameron v Corpach Common Graziers* 1984 SLT (Land Ct) 41; *Beardsell v Bell* 1975 SLT (Land Ct) 2.

10.03   Application to be made by landlord

An application for resumption, which may be in respect of the croft or any part thereof, croft land or common grazing, requires to be made by the landlord[1] to the Land Court on the appropriate form. 'Landlord' means any person for the time being entitled to receive the rents and profits or to take possession, of a croft[2]. The right of a landlord to resume part of tenanted subjects during the currency of a lease is normally a matter of contract but in crofting any provisions permitting resumption in a written lease have generally been held to be void so far as inconsistent with the statutes[3]. The applicant's interest in the land should be an immediate right of property as landlord in respect of the area of land involved in the application[4]. On the death of a landlord, who had obtained a resumption order but only under certain conditions, his legatees were allowed to continue with his appeal against its terms[5].

In cases where resumption seems appropriate, for instance where the landlord is himself making use of croft land for non-agricultural purposes, it may be necessary for a crofter to find a way of forcing the landlord to seek resumption, for example by raising an action of interdict where the use being made of the land conflicts with his own lease[6]. Where there is doubt as to whether resumption is appropriate in the circumstances, it would appear possible to ask the Court to decide the point[7] but an application by crofters seeking an order requiring the landlord to resume has been held to be incompetent[8].

The need for resumption may become apparent while the landlord is entering into an agreement to sell the land to a third party for development, or where the land has already been developed and has not been available for crofting use for some time[9], or where there is a concluded contract of sale which is conditional on resumption being ordered by the Court. In some cases the prospective purchaser of the land to be developed may, in addition to having agreed a price with the selling landlord, be committed to satisfying the conditions and payments ordered by the Court on resumption being granted. The interest of that prospective purchaser may coincide with or differ from that of the landlord and so the Court has recognised the right of a third party to be represented at the hearing of a resumption application and to bring evidence to the Court regarding the reasonableness of the purpose and the value of the land sought to be resumed[10]. Where the sale has been completed before resumption has been granted or even applied for, the duty of pursuing the application will fall on the purchaser who, having already completed his title, has thus become the landlord.

To facilitate the working of the Court and the practical problems relating to the development of land, the Court have recently shown themselves prepared to consider the question of resumption as being prior to and separate from the necessity of valuing the land should resumption be granted.

1 Crofters (Scotland) Act 1955, s 12(1).
2 Ibid, s 37(1).
3 Ibid, s 3(4); see *Smith v Marquis of Aberdeen's Trs* (1917) 5 SLCR 30 at 39; *Whyte v Garden's Trs* (1925) 13 SLCR 99; *Marquess of Bute v Baxter* 1966 SLT (Land Ct) 9.
4 *Steele v Ballantyne* (1925) 13 SLCR 3.
5 *Whyte v Stewart* 1914 SC 675, 1914 1 SLT 451, 51 SLR 596, sub nom *Stewart v Whyte* (1914) 2 SLCR 101.
6 *Wester Ross Salmon Ltd v Maclean* 1986 SLT (Land Ct) 11, 1985 SLCR 124.
7 Crofters (Scotland) Act 1961, s 4(1).
8 *Keil Common Graziers v MacColl* 1986 SLCR 142.
9 *Highland Regional Council v Kylesku Common Graziers* 1985 SLT (Land Ct) 21, 1984 SLCR 70; *Shetland Islands Council v Jamieson* 1988 SLCR 97.
10 *Applecross Trust Trs v Cameron* 1988 SLCR 113.

10.04 Reasonable purpose

The Land Court may authorise resumption for some reasonable purpose[1] which has to be approved by them as having relation:
(a) to the good of the croft,
(b) to the good of the estate or
(c) to the public interest.

   It is sufficient if the landlord establishes reasonable cause on the basis of any one of these propositions[2]. However it is the duty of the Court to consider the facts in each case and to balance all three interests:

(a)   The good of the croft

It is the crofting unit which is to be examined and not the crofter and his present way of working it. Amongst the questions that the Court will consider are whether the remainder of the croft will be workable and whether the crofting status of the land is seriously under attack by the applicant for no good reason[3]. Whilst it has been argued that a reduction in the size of a croft would be in the interest of easier working[4], it will not be considered that the resumption of a whole croft is for the good of the croft[5].

(b)   The good of the estate

This is the reason mostly pursued by the landlord/applicant because the removal of a tenant can generally be shown to be for the benefit of the landlord and his estate in one way or another although his financial benefit alone is not a sufficient ground for resumption[6]. Care should be taken when trying to define 'estate'. Some developers have required to become applicants because they have completed their purchases of land without its having been resumed. In such cases it seems that the croft land owned by the developer is the 'estate' referred to in the Act. But where the applicant is infeft in widespread properties the Court will have to decide the meaning of 'estate' in the particular circumstances of the application.

(c)   The public interest

A variety of arguments can be put forward under this heading: that there is a need for employment opportunities (eg in fish farming or forestry) or that there is a public need for housing or a school or a community centre or indeed for any of the purposes set down in the statute[7]. The 1955 Act indicates that a government department which is also a landlord will be treated as any other landlord[8] and an argument by a private landlord, that public monies would be saved if resumption were to be granted, has been rejected[9].

The statute instructs that the expression 'reasonable purpose' is to include the using, letting or feuing of the land proposed to be resumed for the building of dwellings, or for small allotments, or for harbours, piers, boat shelters or other like buildings, or for churches or other places of religious worship, or for schools, or for halls or community centres, or for planting, or for roads practicable for vehicular traffic from the croft or township to the public road or to the seashore and any other purpose likely to provide employment for crofters and others in the community, and the protection of an ancient monument or other object of historical or archaeological interest from injury or destruction[10].

It is considered that this specification of particular purposes has been enacted to show types of reasonable purposes to which the legislature referred, and therefore to aid the construction of 'reasonable purpose'[11]. The Court have accepted many and various non-agricultural proposals as reasonable purposes for resumption including the construction of a missile base[12], holiday homes[13] and the grazing and training of horses[14]. However the fact that the purpose for which the landlord desires to resume is one listed in the Act does not necessarily mean that it is a reasonable purpose in all the circumstances and that therefore resumption must be granted automatically[15].

It is thought that the legislative intention is to permit resumption only to enable land to be taken from crofting tenure *and* away from agricultural use altogether. The landlord's wish to resume any croft land for agricultural purposes is unreasonable and inconsistent with the security of tenure attached to the *croft land* itself. If the land is to be relet as an agricultural tenancy then the present tenancy can be terminated only by removal of the crofter or by obtaining his renunciation[16] to be followed by decrofting.

1   Crofters (Scotland) Act 1955, s 12(1).
2   *Libberton Proprietors Ltd v Mackay* 1973 SLT (Land Ct) 13.
3   *Watson v Maclennan* 1972 SLT (Land Ct) 2.
4   *Mackays' Trs v Colthart* (1959) 47 SLCR 43.
5   *Lochiel Estates v Campbell* 1968 SLT (Land Ct) 2; *Lord Burton v MacDonald* 1978 SLCR App 92.
6   *Buckworth v Ross* (1925) 13 SLCR 94 at 98.
7   Crofters (Scotland) Act 1955, s 12(2).
8   Ibid, s 38(1).
9   *Dunbeath Estate Ltd v Gunn* 1988 SLCR 52.
10 Crofters (Scotland) Act 1955, s 12(2).
11 *Duncan v Buttar* (1915) 3 SLCR 32.
12 *Andreae v Mackay* (1958) 47 SLCR 30.
13 *Bray v MacAuslane* 1961 SLCR App 105.
14 *Sumburgh Co v Mail* 1975 SLT (Land Ct) 9.
15 *Portman Trs v MacRae* 1971 SLT (Land Ct) 6, 1970 SLCR App 146.
16 *Crichton Stuart v Ogilvie* 1914 SC 888, 1914 2 SLT 116, 51 SLR 761; *Board of Agriculture v Maclean* (1929) 17 SLCR 71.

10.05   Proof of specific proposals required

The intention to resume therefore must be supplemented by a relevant purpose in the statutory sense. The landlord, to have his application fully considered by the Court, must furnish the Court with specific proposals for the intended use of the resumed land. Such proposals should be supported by evidence, both documentary and otherwise of the forward planning which has already taken place and by the production of planning permissions etc already obtained. Even where the landlord has obtained the agreement of the crofter to the resumption and is acting in good faith, the Court may hold that without sufficient proof the purpose stated by the landlord is not a reasonable purpose in terms of the Act and dismiss the application[1]. A principal factor is the prospect of benefit to the land itself, ie the croft or the estate, for it is the land which is of importance, not simply the intentions or desires of the interested parties. In one situation it is stipulated that the Land Court have no discretion but to grant resumption[2]. This is where an application to resume part of a common grazings is made for the purpose of tree planting with the consent of a majority of the persons sharing in the grazings along with the approval of the Crofters Commission. However, even when such consent and approval are obtained and submitted along with the application, the Court will consider closely the terms of that approval[3].

1 *Murray's Trs v Ross* 1964 SLT (Land Ct) 9.
2 Crofters (Scotland) Act 1955, s 12(3).
3 *Fountain Forestry Ltd v Ross* 1985 SLCR 115.

10.06   Consent and participation of crofters

Similar scrutiny can be expected from the Court where a crofting tenant has 'consented' in writing in exchange for a consideration. Although the application takes the form of a legal process, it is not sufficient for the applicant simply to obtain the consent of the tenant to the proposed resumption. Where a crofter had accepted a sum of 'compensation' and granted his consent, the Court held that the word 'compensation' should be given its statutory meaning[1] and therefore it did not include any payment to the crofter as a share in value of the land resumed[2]. Simple consent to the loss of his croft land by a crofter can never therefore be sufficient to allow resumption to take place and a hearing is normally required on the questions of (1) reasonable purpose and (2) valuation. Although either may be agreed by parties it is for the Court to decide how best to deal with each application for it is the function of the Court not only to determine whether croft land is to be resumed but, if so, its value. It is also for the Court to fix the conditions of resumption as well as any compensation and further payments to be made. The Court have pointed out that all parties should be prepared to bring expert evidence to assist the Court in their findings and that legal aid is available for this purpose[3].

Mention should also be made here of the principle that the expenses of the resumption application should fall solely on the landlord/applicant, no matter the outcome of the application. It is the landlord who initiates the move to alter the *status quo* and it is he who should pay its cost, both to himself and to the crofters affected[4]. This is a point which is not always taken by crofters and their representatives who are too often ready to concede their expenses in exchange for a cash settlement which may or may not match the sum to which they are entitled. Unlike civil disputes, it is unlikely that an attempt to preclude the Court's valuation by submitting a formal tender would avoid the landlord's liability for expenses.

1 Crofters (Scotland) Act 1955, s 12(1).
2 *Galson Estate Ltd v Saunders* 1984 SLCR 74.
3 *Wester Ross Salmon Ltd v Maclean* 1986 SLT (Land Ct) 11 at 16, 1985 SLCR 124.
4 *Duke of Hamiltons Trs v Fullarton* (1922) 10 SLCR 29; *Crombie v Kennedy* (1924) 12 SLCR 28.

10.07   Compensations and conditions

If the Court are satisfied that the application has passed the test of reasonable purpose then the Court are bound to order resumption on the date stated in the application or forthwith or otherwise at the earliest date reasonably possible[1]. This may require surrender by the crofter at the next suitable term date (either Whitsunday (28 May) or Martinmas (28 November))[2]. The Land Court will keep in mind general agricultural considerations where necessary[3]. It is not open to the Court to postpone resumption to a distant future date or until the fulfilment of conditions or the payment of the crofter's compensation or share of value.

The Court are allowed wide discretion to order resumption upon such terms and conditions as they think fit[4]. These terms and conditions may be best seen as an attempt to minimise the effect on the tenant of the loss of his land[5] and the landlord and his successors will normally be required to accept conditions placed on the resumed area for the benefit of any remaining croft land. A usual condition is that the resumed land will be fenced with gates and/or cattle grids which will be maintained thereafter by the proprietors of the resumed land. Often conditions are peculiar to the particular case in an effort to cause the least possible disturbance by the removal of the land from the tenancy.

The Court can order the crofter to surrender the land on adequate financial compensation being made to him for improvements belonging to him on that land and the landlord may also be required to compensate the crofter either by letting to him other land of equivalent value in the neighbourhood *or* by compensation in money *or* by way of adjustment in rent *or* in such other manner as the Court may determine in respect of the land itself. The wording of the 1955 Act seems to contemplate some compensation more than just for unexhausted improvements and a payment may be ordered in view of the compulsory termination of a tenure which was practically permanent in character[6]. The compensation is primarily the responsibility of the landlord applicant and cannot be simply passed on to a subsequent purchaser[7]. But where the subjects are being acquired by an authority possessing compulsory purchase powers, the crofter may elect to have his compensation assessed under that code (see para 10.14).

Although these compensation provisions can be important in many cases they are now virtually neglected in favour of the more substantial payment under the 1976 Act. In any event, it is unlikely that the landlord will admit to having other land in the vicinity suitable for taking into crofting tenure and the compensation payment or adjustment of rent would normally involve minimal amounts. The Court can award interest on sums awarded for compensation for land resumed[8].

1 *Whyte v Stewart* 1914 SC 675, 1914 1 SLT 451, 51 SLR 596, sub nom *Stewart v Whyte* (1914) 2 SLCR 101.
2 *Hourston v Robertson* (1921) 9 SLCR 27.
3 *Crombie v Kennedy* (1924) 12 SLCR 28.
4 Crofters (Scotland) Act 1955, s 12(1).
5 *Secretary of State for Scotland v Ramage* (1961) 49 SLCR 35.
6 *Hay v Scollay* (1932) 20 SLCR 27.
7 *Enessy Co SA v Shareholders in Tarbert Common Grazings* 1983 SLCR 54, 1984 SLT (Land Ct) 7.
8 Crofters (Scotland) Act 1955, s 12(1A).

10.08 Share of development value

As already explained, the 1976 Act recognised the quasi dual ownership in crofting subjects that already existed. One manifestation of this is that if his land is valuable, the crofter is entitled to share in that value should his land be taken from him by resumption[1].

The provisions of the 1976 Act relating to the crofter's share of the value of land being resumed are somewhat complicated and close attention should be paid to their wording[2]. In addition to any compensation payment which the crofter may be awarded (see para 10.07), he will also be entitled to receive from the landlord a share in the value of the land resumed. This share is one-half of the difference between the market value of the land at the date of resumption (less the compensation payments) and the crofting value. The land requires to be valued (a) free from the crofter's interests, (b) free from the constraints of crofting legislation and (c) assuming vacant possession. For obvious reasons the term 'development value' is often used. The crofting value in relation to the land resumed has the same meaning as it has when the Court are required to determine the consideration payable for croft land on acquisition, ie 15 times the annual rent for that land. In fact, because development value is so high and the crofting value generally so low, it is normal for parties to agree that the crofting value for the purpose of the calculation is zero and this certainly simplifies parties' thinking.

The 1976 Act directs that the market value in which the crofter is to share will be determined by the Land Court and to do this the Court will require evidence to satisfy themselves. No matter what development has taken place on the ground prior to the resumption order, it is usually the market value of the bare land which requires to be determined and that as at the date on which the resumption is authorised even when the development took place some years previously[3]. Where any development has been carried out by any person other than the crofter or any of his predecessors in the tenancy then there shall be deducted from the market value such amount as, in the opinion of the Court, is attributable to that development[4]. Recent cases give some guidance as to the Court's method of calculating the market value[5].

Two different methods of finding the market value are provided by the 1976 Act. Where the development has been or is to be carried out either by the landlord or by any person not being an authority possessing compulsory purchase powers, the market value is the amount which the land might realise if sold on the open market by a willing seller[6]. But where the development has been or is to be carried out by such an authority (not being the landlord) on the acquisition by them of the land resumed, the market value is fixed by reference to the compensation payable by the authority to the landlord on acquisition[7]. In the latter case, the Land Court have no jurisdiction in fixing the crofter's share where the compensation payable is still to be agreed[8]. If there is an unresolved dispute on the compensation payable there is no mechanism within the 1976 Act for resolving it, but a reference can be made to the Lands Tribunal[9]. Where the payment relates to more than the resumed land the Court must determine that part of the payment which relates to the land resumed[10]. By use of the words 'compensation payable' what is apparently contemplated is a situation where the crofter is not a party to any agreement, the Court are excluded from the valuation process and the landlord accepts a figure as the open market value from an authority that need not even be a party to the resumption application. It would then be unfair if the landlord was thereafter required to pay to the crofter approximately half of a different sum than he actually received[11].

Where the land resumed is common grazing, the part share of the value of that land payable to the crofters is apportioned among such crofters according to their several rights in the grazing[12]. Interest can be awarded in the event of late payment of a share in value[13].

---

1 Crofting Reform (Scotland) Act 1976, s 9(1).

2 Ibid, s 9.
3 *Highland Regional Council v Kylesku Common Graziers* 1985 SLT (Land Ct) 21, 1984 SLCR 70.
4 Crofting Reform (Scotland) Act 1976, s 9(5).
5 *Wester Ross Salmon Ltd v Maclean* 1986 SLT (Land Ct) 11, 1985 SLCR 124; *Vestey v Blunt* 1988 SLT (Land Ct) 34, 1986 SLCR 150; *Kershaw v MacKenzie* 1988 SLT (Land Ct) 41, 1987 SLCR 127; *MacLennan Salmon Co Ltd v Macdonald* 1989 SLT (Land Ct) 21, 1988 SLCR 89; *Trs of the Tenth Duke of Argyll v MacCormick* 1989 SLT (Land Ct) 58, 1988 SLCR 123 (under appeal).
6 Crofting Reform (Scotland) Act 1976, s 9(2).
7 Ibid, s 9(3).
8 *Maclean v Secretary of State for Scotland* 1980 SLT (Land Ct) 18.
9 Lands Tribunal Act 1949, s 1(5).
10 Crofting Reform (Scotland) Act 1976, s 9(3).
11 *Hilleary v Macdonald*, 1989 SLT (Land Ct) 70 1988 SLCR 80.
12 Crofting Reform (Scotland) Act 1976, s 9(4).
13 Ibid, s 9(5A).

10.09   Following resumption

Where the Court have authorised resumption of croft land and the land has been surrendered and the stated purpose fulfilled, the provisions of the Crofting Acts cease to apply to the resumed land although such land may be later made available for the subsequent enlargement of existing crofts[1]. The Court may recall a resumption order where they consider that the purpose for which it was granted was never fulfilled or where the land had never in fact been surrendered. It is a firm and necessary principle that the security of crofting tenure continues to attach to croft land which the Land Court have authorised to be resumed for a specific purpose and subject to the conditions imposed until the purpose and conditions have been implemented[2]. A rehearing of a resumption application may be sought to recall an order as the land is taken out of crofting only 'on its being resumed'. Whether actual resumption has or has not occurred is a matter of evidence[3].

If a resumption order is granted then it is proper that a copy of that order is kept with the title deeds of the land involved. Copies of such orders may be obtained from the Court. Indeed it may be considered wise for the Order of Court to be referred to in any subsequent conveyance. This will be useful when the land is sold at which time it may be necessary to prove that it is no longer subject to crofting tenure. Such orders should be scrutinised by purchasers for conditions not appearing in the title deeds. Many conditions it will be remembered are for the benefit of neighbouring croft land which has been given a higher degree of protection, eg by fencing conditions, by order of the Court. In addition, if the reason for resumption has never been fulfilled, the crofting restrictions may be reinstated and a purchaser would be well-advised to give special attention to the history of the land involved and to the details of the resumption order.

1 Crofters (Scotland) Act 1955, s 12(4).
2 *Macdonald v Barker* 1970 SLT (Land Ct) 2.
3 *Secretary of State for Scotland v Shareholders of Lealt and Culnacnock Common Grazings* 1982 SLT (Land Ct) 20.

10.10   Application forms

The relevant application forms are obtainable from the Court. There are separate forms for the resumption of croft land (form 6) and the resumption of grazings (form 7). In addition to the completion of the details on the face of the application, the applicant is required to set forth a statement of facts. This should include a description of not only the area which is sought to be resumed but also of the whole croft or common grazing involved, the crofter or crofters affected and the rent or rents currently paid, together with details of the applicant and his property or 'estate'. The statement of facts should also specify the reason for and purpose of the resumption and the market value of the area sought to be resumed. It should be remembered that the rule is that resumption is granted for the express purpose stated in the application and for none other. If it were otherwise, the scrutiny of the application by the Court would be rendered pointless.

(2) DECROFTING

10.11   Procedures of the Crofters Commission

Decrofting is the non–statutory term now in general use for the power given by section 16(9) and (13) of the 1955 Act to the Crofters Commission to release untenanted croft land from crofting controls. Whereas the process was first made available to a landlord where resumption was denied him for lack of a tenant, decrofting is now appropriate in all cases where the landlord/tenant relationship has ended. It can be sought by a landlord with a vacant croft, by a crofter who has purchased his croft (and had become an owner/occupier[1]) or even provisionally by a crofter intending to purchase. The same rules apply to crofting landlords as to their former tenants who acquired their land and the same application form is required to be completed (obtainable from the Crofters Commission).

The application is made by lodging the completed form with the Crofters Commission and this can be done at any time by the owner of a vacant croft. It will be noted that this description includes the owner/occupier of a croft, for a croft purchased by the crofter has no tenant and is therefore technically 'vacant'[2]. A crofter who is proposing to purchase his croft or part of it can apply for a provisional direction, which will not have effect until the land to which it relates has been acquired and that within five years of the date of the direction[3]. This procedure enables a crofter to be sure that land which he intends to purchase can indeed be removed from crofting controls.

The Commission's procedures are conveniently modified when considering only the decrofting of a croft house site and garden ground. The Commission are required to make a decrofting direction if they are satisfied that the extent of the garden ground sought is appropriate for the reasonable enjoyment of the dwelling-house. This coincides with the crofter's right to purchase his croft house[4] and therefore ensures that the same subjects can be both purchased and decrofted if so required[5]. Where a crofter intends to negotiate the purchase of his house site, decrofting in advance will provide useful guidance as to an appropriate area of garden ground. Normally an area of one-quarter acre will be permitted, although a larger area may be decrofted where boundaries are dictated by the terrain or suggested by the position of the dwelling-house on the croft.

Decrofting is also to be granted if the Commission are satisfied that the vacant croft land is to be used for or in connection with some reasonable purpose which would have permitted the land to be resumed had it been tenanted, provided the extent of the land is not excessive[6]. However, the Commission are required to have regard (i) to the general interest of the crofting community in the district in which the croft is situated and in particular (ii) to the demand, if any, for a tenancy of the croft from persons who might reasonably be expected to obtain that tenancy if the croft were offered for letting on the open market[7]. The Land Court have interpreted this statutory guideline to mean that the interests of the local crofting community are paramount[8].

Subject to the same considerations, a decrofting direction may be given on the application of the landlord where the croft is merely vacant and this would appear to allow decrofting for any purpose within the discretion of the Commission[9]. Where a croft has become vacant in consequence of an order made by the Commission in respect of an absentee tenant[10] and the croft remains unlet for six months, the landlord can obtain a decrofting direction by applying during the following three months[11].

1 See *Laird, Applicant* 1973 SLT (Land Ct) 4.
2 Crofters (Scotland) Act 1955, s 16(11), (11A).
3 Ibid, s 16A(4).
4 Crofters (Scotland) Act 1955, s 1(2); see para 9.04.
5 Ibid, s 16A(1)(b).
6 Ibid, s 16A(1)(a).
7 Ibid, s 16A(2).
8 *Gray v Crofters Commission* 1980 SLT (Land Ct) 2.
9 Crofters (Scotland) Act 1955, s 16(9): see *Gray v Crofters Commission* supra; Rules of Procedure 31(3).
10 Ibid, s 17(1).
11 Ibid, s 16(7).

10.12 Consideration of application

Once received, each decrofting application is considered on its individual merit with reference to the statutory requirements. As previously explained, there is a simplified procedure for croft house sites. All other applications have to be advertised in one or more newspapers circulating in the district where the croft is situated. Such representations as are received are then intimated to the applicant while the Commission investigate the purpose of the application and the extent of the land sought to be decrofted. The Commission have power to impose conditions in the decrofting direction to ensure that the land is used for the proposed purpose[1] and they may modify the application as they think fit and offer to grant a modified direction[2].

Once their initial investigation is complete, the Commission issue to the applicant their preliminary decision specifying the nature of and the reason for that decision. The applicant is then invited to lodge written representations and to decide whether he wishes a hearing to be fixed. Such a hearing might also be afforded by the Commission if requested by some other involved party[3]. Thereafter the Commission give notice of their proposed final decision including, if the application has succeeded, the wording of the proposed direction modified as required and containing such conditions as they consider necessary. An explanation of the reason for the proposed final decision must be given[4]. The applicant may then within 21 days appeal against the proposed decision on fact or law to the Land Court who may hear or consider such evidence as they think fit in order to enable them to dispose of the appeal[5]. While given this power of review, the Court nevertheless consider that they should be slow to disturb a decision of the Commission if made in accordance with law and with adequate reason to support it[6]. The Commission have in the past taken the view that as they act in a quasi-judicial capacity whilst coming to the decision being appealed, it would be inappropriate for them to appear as parties to the appeal[7].

1 Crofters (Scotland) Act 1955, s 16A(3).
2 Ibid, s 16A(5).
3 Ibid, s 16A(6).
4 Ibid, s 16A(7).
5 Ibid, s 16A(8).
6 *Stevens v Crofters Commission* 1984 SLCR 30 at 38.
7 *MacColl v Crofters Commission* 1986 SLT (Land Ct) 4, 1985 SLCR 142; see para 2.01.

10.13 Conditional directions

Where the Commission have exercised their power to impose conditions (for the purpose of securing that the land decrofted is used for the proposed use) several problems arise. If at any time the Commission are satisfied that there has been a breach of any such condition they may make a further direction that the land be brought back under crofting controls and that it shall be a vacant croft[1].

It is important therefore that a subsequent acquirer of that land should be aware that the land was once in crofting and that its decrofting was conditional. At present there is no simple way of discovering if this is the case.

Such conditions as are imposed will attach to the land and will normally be intended to protect the local community interest. The continuing enforcement of these conditions is a duty which rests uneasily with the Commission whose resources do not stretch to the constant checking of land otherwise removed from crofting controls.

Where a party owns land which has been conditionally decrofted, he may wish to seek a modification of the decrofting direction allowing unnecessary or expired conditions to be adjusted or deleted. Although a hearing might be appropriate in a complex case, there would appear to be no express power to the Commission to grant a further direction (other than in the case of a breach of conditions as already described). Nevertheless the Commission have shown themselves willing to reconsider such conditions in the light of changing circumstances.

1 Crofters (Scotland) Act 1955, s 16A(3), Rules of Procedure 35, 36.

10.14 Compulsory purchase: powers and options

A crofter, being a tenant, can have no greater right to occupy his croft than can be provided by his landlord[1]. An authority possessing compulsory purchase powers may therefore acquire and take possession of tenanted croft land without the necessity of obtaining a resumption order from the Land Court. Special provisions apply where such an authority is involved either in the resumption process[2] or by compulsory purchase[3].

Where a croft or part thereof is compulsorily acquired, the crofter is entitled to:

(a) compensation under the compulsory purchase code[4] and he may also qualify for certain other benefits available to persons displaced from land[5]; such compensation and benefits might be referred, in the event of dispute, to the Lands Tribunal for determination; and

(b) a share in the development value of the land acquired[6] being one-half of the difference between the market value as determined by the Land Court less any compensation payable as above and less the value of any development carried out by any person other than the crofter or his predecessors in the tenancy[7] and the crofting value[8]. Again the land requires to be valued as land free from the constraints of crofting legislation.

Where the land compulsorily acquired is common grazing, the share of value is apportioned among the crofters according to their several rights in the grazing[9].

Where a croft or part of a croft is being *resumed* prior to acquisition from the landlord for a non-agricultural purpose by an authority possessing compulsory purchase powers, the crofter may elect to have his compensation fixed under the compulsory purchase code[10] and by the Lands Tribunal in the event of a dispute[11]. If only part of his croft is being resumed, the crofter may seek to require the authority to take the remainder of his croft as well and to compensate him accordingly[12].

1 *McLean v Inverness-shire County Council* 1949 SC 69.
2 Crofting Reform (Scotland) Act 1976, s 9(3).
3 Ibid, s 10.
4 Land Clauses Consolidation (Scotland) Act 1845, s 114; Land Compensation (Scotland) Act 1973, s 45; see *Anderson v Moray District Council* 1978 SLT (Lands Tr) 37; *MacLean v Secretary of State for Scotland* 1980 SLT (Land Ct) 18.
5 Land Compensation (Scotland) Act 1973, Pt III.
6 Crofting Reform (Scotland) Act 1976, s 10(1).
7 Ibid, s 10(2), (4).
8 Ibid, s 10(5).
9 Ibid, s 10(3).
10 Land Compensation (Scotland) Act 1973, s 56.
11 Land Compensation (Scotland) Act 1963, s 8.
12 Land Compensation (Scotland) Act 1973, s 58.

10.15   Planning blight[1]

Where a proposed development is having a depressing effect on the value of a crofter's subjects, his interest may be protected against planning blight in the same way as an owner's interest. The procedure to secure this protection involves the Lands Tribunal, is extremely complicated and is outwith the scheme of this text. If successful, the crofter can insist on his interest being acquired by the authority responsible for the proposed development and claim compensation.

1 Crofting Reform (Scotland) Act 1976, s 11; Town and Country Planning (Scotland) Act 1972, ss 181–196; Land Compensation (Scotland) Act 1973, ss 64–77.

Part IV COTTARS

CONTENTS

CHAPTER 11

COTTARS' RIGHTS

11.01 Introduction

A cottar is the occupier of a dwelling-house situated in the crofting counties with or without land who pays no rent to the landowner but whose presence and status as occupier have been acknowledged by the landowner; or the tenant from year to year of a dwelling-house situated as aforesaid who resides therein and who pays therefor to the landlord an annual rent not exceeding six pounds, whether with or without garden ground but without arable or pasture land[1].

Cottars were first defined by the Crofters Holdings (Scotland) Act 1886[2], then by the Crofters (Scotland) Act 1955. The anomalous position of cottars in the crofting counties was again recognised in the Crofting Reform (Scotland) Act 1976. It was clearly thought desirable that they should be dealt with at the same time and in a similar fashion to crofters. However, unlike crofters, the tenancies of cottars in no way depend on the situation as at the passing of the 1886 Act or any other date[3]. There is no register of cottars and they are required to identify themselves. Nor is there any power given to the Land Court or any other independent body to fix the rent of a cottar's subject. The jurisdiction of ordinary courts is excluded[4]. It is usual for a cottar to occupy only a house and garden. The house may have been provided by himself or it may belong to the landlord. In most cases the dwelling-house is the only subject tenanted by the cottar but temporary use of it or the use of part of it as a shop or for summer letting to visitors, may not disqualify him from being declared a cottar[5].

1 Crofters (Scotland) Act 1955, s 28(4).
2 Crofters Holdings (Scotland) Act 1886, s 34..
3 M'Alister v Gray (1938) 26 SLCR 3.
4 M'dougall v M'Alister (1890) 17 R 555, 27 SLR 445.
5 M'Alister v Gray supra.

11.02 Two classes

The dropping of the words '*to the landlord*' which appeared in the original 1886 definition (after the mention of rent) from the 1955 definition does not appear to have affected the persons who are entitled to recognition as cottars. Two classes of cottars are recognised, the rent paying and the non-rent paying. Neither class has security of tenure under the Crofters Acts.

(a) The non-rent paying cottar

The non-rent paying cottar is defined simply as 'the occupier of a dwelling-house situated in the crofting counties with or without land who pays no rent'. The landowner must know of and consent to the occupation of such cottar, for such knowledge and consent of the proprietor is the only title this type of cottar can have to the occupancy of the subjects[1].

(b) The rent paying cottar

The rent paying cottar is defined as 'the tenant from year to year of a dwelling-house situated in the crofting counties who resides therein and who pays therefor an annual rent not exceeding £6 in money, whether with or without garden ground but without arable or pasture land'.

These definitions take no account of the time or method of acquiring possession, but only deal with the attributes or qualities of the subsequent occupation. The continued existence of persons legally recognizable as cottars is often considered so unlikely that it may be necessary for an individual to seek a declarator in the Land Court as to his status. He should also seek to establish the boundaries of his subject and would be well-advised to consider seeking a conveyance of it as allowed by the 1976 Act[2] without delay. As there is no fixity of tenure nor any right to apply for a fair or equitable rent, a cottar's status must be regarded as highly vulnerable for it seems he runs the risk of losing his interest if he incurs the displeasure of his landlord. There is also the risk of losing his status as cottar should he be required to pay a rent in excess of £6 per annum.

Occupation without the knowledge and consent of the landowner is not sufficient to qualify a person as a cottar. A cottar must hold directly from the landlord and will be excluded if he is a subtenant[3]. In distinguishing cottars from crofters it is to be noted that for a cottar the principal subject is the dwelling-house, whereas for a crofter it is the land[4].

1 *Duke of Argyll's Trs v MacNeill* 1983 SLT (Land Ct) 35, 1982 SLCR 67.
2 Crofting Reform (Scotland) Act 1976, s 1(2).
3 *Macinnes v Lady Strathcona* (1926) 14 SLCR 39.
4 *Wylie v Marquis of Zetland* (1914) 2 SLCR 53.

11.03 No right of succession

There is no right of succession to a cottar's subject. The executor of a cottar has no claim against either the landowner or the landlord. Any person who obtains the occupancy of a cottar subject, following upon the death of an existing cottar, must do so by the permision of the landowner or landlord, which permission that proprietor may withhold if he chooses. The fact that the new occupier may be the intestate successor or legatee of the deceased cottar is immaterial. He requires to obtain either an acknowledgement of his status from the proprietor or a new tenancy of the subject.

11.04 Compensation for improvements

The rent paying cottar is entitled to compensation for permanent improvements if he renounces his tenancy or is removed. The non-rent paying cottar is entitled to compensation only if he is removed from his dwelling and any land or building occupied by him in connection with his dwelling[1]. Any right to compensation is for an improvement suitable to the cottar's subject[2] that has been executed or paid for by the cottar or any of his predecessors in the same family[3] (ie the wife or husband of the cottar and any person to whom the cottar or the wife or husband could possibly have succeeded in case of intestacy[4]). The non-rent paying cottar has no claim when he chooses voluntarily to quit his subject.

It is also necessary that such an improvement was not one which the cottar was bound to execute by written agreement nor one for which he had already received fair consideration, either by reduction of rent or otherwise[5]. Failing agreement, the amount of compensation can be fixed by the Land Court in the same way as for crofters[6].

1 Crofters (Scotland) Act 1955, s 28(1).
2 Ibid, s 28(1)(a).
3 Ibid, s 28(1)(b).
4 Ibid, s 28(4).
5 Ibid, s 28(1)(c).
6 Ibid, s 28(2).

11.05   Acquisition of cottar's subjects

Like a crofter, a cottar has an absolute right to acquire an owner's title to the site of his dwelling-house and the buildings thereon together with the garden ground. The cottar and the landlord or owner[1] of the cottar's subject can by agreement fix the terms and conditions of sale, including price and extent of garden ground. Failing agreement the cottar can apply to the Court for an order requiring the landlord or owner to grant a conveyance to the cottar or his nominee[2]. The Court will deal with the application in the same way as they would deal with a similar application by a crofter[3]. Given the risk of loss of tenancy or occupancy a cottar would normally be well-advised to seek an owner's title to his subject without delay.

1 Crofting Reform (Scotland) Act 1976, s 21(2).
2 Ibid, s 1(2).
3 Ibid, s 4.

11.06   Assistance to cottars, etc

The Secretary of State can provide assistance to cottars in the same manner as to crofters by way of grant and loan for the erection, improvement or rebuilding of dwelling-houses and other buildings[1]. This assistance so far as it relates to dwelling-houses will continue to be available for a period of seven years after the date of acquisition to a cottar who, after 10 June 1976, acquires his house site and garden ground[2]. It will not, however, be available to a member of the cottar's family for as already explained there is no statutory right of succession to a cottar's subject. The provision made for security by means of a heritable security over the house for the amount outstanding on an existing loan applies to a cottar who has purchased his dwelling-house as it applies to a crofter[3].

A cottar's interests are afforded protection against planning blight in the same way as a crofter's interests are protected[4]. The 'non-entitled spouse' of a cottar is not entitled to seek, in respect of the dwelling-house on the cottar's subjects, an order transferring to that spouse the tenancy of the dwelling-house[5].

1 Crofters (Scotland) Act 1955, s 28(3).
2 Crofting Reform (Scotland) Act 1976, s 12(1)(d).
3 Ibid, s 12(3).
4 Ibid, s 11.
5 Matrimonial Homes (Family Protection) (Scotland) Act 1981, s 13(3).

11.07 Squatters

The word 'squatter' is confined to persons occupying subjects (which may be land or a house) without legal right and in the face of the landowner. These are generally people who, with the approval of the local crofters, or at least without objection, have built their houses on the common grazing and perhaps enclosed some land. In some cases the squatter may have squatted on the inbye land of a croft.

Such people are not recognized as cottars because they have no direct relationship with the landowner.

Appendices

A (1) Crofters (Scotland) Act 1955 (c 21)
  (2) Crofters (Scotland) Act 1961 (c 58)
  (3) Crofting Reform (Scotland) Act 1976 (c 21)
  (4) Succession (Scotland) Act 1964 (c 41), s 16

B (1) Rules of the Scottish Land Court
  (2) Forms available from the Land Court

C (1) Rules of procedure of the Crofters Commission
  (2) Forms available from the Crofters Commission

D Availability of legal aid

Crofters (Scotland) Act 1955 (3 and 4 Eliz 2 (c 21))

ARRANGEMENT OF SECTIONS

Establishment of Crofters Commission

1. Constitution and general functions of Crofters Commission

(1) There shall be constituted a Commission to be called 'the Crofters Commission' (hereafter in this Act referred to as 'the Commission') which shall have the functions of reorganising, developing and regulating crofting in the crofting counties of Scotland, of promoting the interests of crofters there and of keeping under review matters relating to crofting, and such other functions as are conferred on them by or under this Act [¹and the Crofting Reform (Scotland) Act 1976].

(2) The Commission shall carry out their functions in accordance with such directions of a general character as may be given by the Secretary of State and in carrying out their functions shall have regard to local circumstances and conditions.

(3) The Commission shall consist of not more than [²nine] members appointed by the Secretary of State, and of the members one shall be appointed by the Secretary of State to be chairman of the Commission.

(4) The Commission shall include members with knowledge of crofting conditions and at least one member who can speak the Gaelic language.

(5) The provisions contained in the First Schedule to this Act shall have effect in relation to the Commission.

[1]

Notes.—1 Words in sub-s (1) added by Crofting Reform (Scotland) Act 1976 (c 21), Sch 2, para 4.
2 Word in sub-s (3) substituted by Crofters (Scotland) Act 1961 (c 58), s 1.

2. Particular powers and duties of the Commission

(1) In the exercise of their general functions of reorganising, developing and regulating crofting, it shall be the duty of the Commission:—
  (a) to keep under general review all matters relating to crofts and crofting conditions, including, without prejudice to the foregoing generality, land settlement, the improvement of land and livestock, the planting of trees, the supply of agricultural equipment and requisites, the marketing of agricultural produce, experimental work on crofting methods, the provision of demonstration crofts, the needs of the crofting communities for public services of all kinds, the provision of social amenities and the need for industries to provide supplementary occupations for crofters or work for their families; and to make such recommendations as they may think fit on any of the matters aforesaid;

(b) to collaborate so far as their powers and duties permit with any body or person in the carrying out of any measures for the economic development and social improvement of the crofting counties;

(c) to advise the Secretary of State on any matter relating to crofts and crofting conditions which he may refer to them, or on which they may think fit to submit advice to him;

(d) to exercise the powers conferred on them by this Act [¹and the Crofting Reform (Scotland) Act 1976] in such manner as may seem to them in each case desirable.

(2) For the purpose of assisting them in the local execution of their functions under this Act, the Commission shall have power to appoint a panel of suitable persons resident in the crofting counties to act as assessors, when required by the Commission so to act, and may make to such assessors in respect of any loss of earnings they would otherwise have made or any additional expenses (including travelling and subsistence expenses) to which they would not otherwise have been subject, being loss or expenses necesssarily suffered or incurred by them for the purpose of enabling them to perform duties as such assessors, such payments as the Secretary of State may, with the approval of the Treasury, determine.

(3) The Commission shall send to the [²principal clerk of the Land Court] to be recorded in the Crofters Holdings Book every order, determination, consent, authorisation or other proceeding of theirs which they may think proper to be recorded therein; . . .³

(4) The Commission shall make an annual report to the Secretary of State on the exercise and performance by them of their functions under this Act [⁴and the Crofting Reform (Scotland) Act 1976], and the Secretary of State shall lay a copy of the report before each House of Parliament, together with such comments as he may think fit to make.

[2]

Notes.—1 Words in sub-s (1) inserted by Crofting Reform (Scotland) Act 1976 (c 21), Sch 2, para 5(a).
2 Words in sub-s (3) substituted by Crofting Reform (Scotland) Act 1976 (c 21), Sch 2, para 5(b).
3 Words in sub-s (3) repealed by Crofting Reform (Scotland) Act 1976 (c 21), Sch 3.
4 Words in sub-s (4) inserted by Crofting Reform (Scotland) Act 1976 (c 21), Sch 2, para 5(c).

Crofting Tenure

3. Definition of 'croft' and 'crofter', and conditions of tenure of crofter

(1) In this Act the expression 'croft' means—

(a) as from the commencement of this Act, every holding (whether occupied by a landholder or not) situate in the crofting counties which was, immediately before the commencement of this Act, a holding to which any of the provisions of the Landholders Acts relating to landholders applied;

(b) as from the commencement of this Act, every holding situate as aforesaid which was, immediately before the commencement of this Act, a holding to which the provisions of the Landholders Acts, relating to statutory small tenants applied;

(c) as from the date of registration, every holding situate as aforesaid which [¹was before the commencement of the Crofters (Scotland) Act 1961,] constituted a croft by the registration of the tenant thereof as a crofter under section four of this Act.

[² (d) as from the date of the direction, every holding situated as aforesaid as to which the Secretary of State has directed under subsection (1) of section two of the Crofters (Scotland) Act 1961, that it shall be a croft.]

(2) In this Act the expression 'crofter' means the tenant of a croft.

(3) A crofter shall not be subject to be removed from the croft of which he is tenant except—

- (a) where one year's rent of the croft is unpaid;
- (b) in consequence of the breach of one or more of the conditions set out in the Second Schedule to this Act (in this Act referred to as 'the statutory conditions'), other than the condition as to payment of rent; or
- (c) in pursuance of any enactment, including any enactment contained in this Act.

(4) Any contract or agreement made by a crofter by virtue of which he is deprived of any right conferred on him by any provision of this Act shall to that extent be void unless the contract or agreement is approved by the Land Court.

[³(5) For the purposes of this Act, the Crofters (Scotland) Act 1961 and the Crofting Reform (Scotland) Act 1976, any right in pasture or grazing land held or to be held by the tenant of a croft, whether alone or in common with others, and any land comprising any part of a common grazing which has been apportioned for the exclusive use of a crofter under section 27(4) of this Act and any land held runrig which has been apportioned under section 27(7) of this Act, shall be deemed to form part of the croft.

(6) For the purposes of the aforesaid Acts, where—

- (a) a crofter has acquired his entire croft other than any such right or land as is referred to in subsection (5) above, or
- (b) any person, not being a crofter, has obtained an apportionment of any land under the said section 27,

then the person referred to in paragraph (a) or (b) above shall be deemed to hold the right or land referred to therein in tenancy until held otherwise and that right or land shall be deemed to be a croft.]

[3]

Notes.—1 Words in sub-s (1)(c) substituted by Crofters (Scotland) Act 1961 (c 58), Sch 1, Pt II, para 9.

2 Para 3(1)(d) added by Crofters (Scotland) Act 1961 (c 58), Sch 1, Pt II, para 9.

3 Section 3(5)(6) substituted for s 3(5) by Crofting Reform (Scotland) Act 1976 (c 21), s 14.

---

4. [*Repealed by Crofters (Scotland) Act 1961 (c 58), Sch 3.*]

[4]

5. Rent

(1) The rent payable by a crofter as one of the statutory conditions shall be the yearly rent, including money and any prestations other than money, payable for the year current at the commencement of this Act or, in the case of a croft let after the commencement of this Act, fixed at the date of the letting, unless and until that rent is altered in accordance with the provisions of this Act.

(2) The rent may be altered by agreement in writing between the landlord and the crofter to such amount and for such period as may be so agreed; and thereupon the rent so agreed shall be the rent payable by the crofter so long as the agreement subsists and thereafter so long as—

- (a) no new agreement between the landlord and the crofter shall have been made; or
- (b) no different rent shall have been fixed by the Land Court under this Act.

(3) The Land Court may, on the application of the crofter or the landlord, determine what is a fair rent to be paid by the crofter to the landlord for the croft, and may pronounce an order accordingly; and the rent so fixed by the Land Court shall be the rent payable by the crofter as from the first term of Whitsunday or Martinmas next succeeding the decision of the Land Court:

Provided that[1]—
(a) where the rent payable for the croft has been fixed by the Land Court it shall not be altered, except by mutual agreement between the crofter and the landlord, for a period of seven years from the term at which it first became payable; and
(b) where a croft is let after the commencement of this Act, the rent shall not be altered by the Land Court for a period of seven years from the term at which it first became payable or for such longer period as may have been agreed upon between the crofter and the landlord.

(4) Before determining what is a fair rent for a croft, the Land Court shall hear the parties and shall take into consideration all the circumstances of the case, of the croft and of the district, and in particular shall take into consideration any permanent or unexhausted improvements on the croft and suitable thereto which have been executed or paid for by the crofter or his predecessors in the tenancy.

[5]

Note.—1 Section 5(3) provisos excluded by Crofting Reform (Scotland) Act 1976 (c 21), s 7.

---

6. Record of croft

(1) The Land Court shall, on the application of the landlord or the crofter, make a record of the condition of the cultivation of a croft and of the buildings and other permanent improvements thereon, and by whom the permanent improvements have been executed or paid for.

(2) Any application under this section shall be intimated by the Land Court to the other party concerned and each party shall be given an opportunity of being heard on any matter affecting the record of the croft.

[6]

7. Renunciation of tenancy

(1) A crofter shall be entitled, on one year's notice in writing to the landlord, to renounce his tenancy as at any term of Whitsunday or Martinmas.

(2) If a crofter renounces his tenancy the landlord shall be entitled to set off all rent due or to become due against any sum found to be due [1by the landlord] to the crofter or to the Secretary of State by way of compensation for permanent improvements made on the croft.

[7]

Note.—1 Words inserted by Crofters (Scotland) Act 1961 (c 58), Sch 1, Pt I, para 1.

---

8. Assignation of croft

[1(1) A crofter shall not assign his croft—
(a) to a member of his family unless he obtains the consent in writing of his landlord or, failing such consent, the consent in writing of the Commission on an application made to them;
(b) to a person other than a member of his family unless he obtains the consent in writing of the Commission on an application made to them.

(2) A landlord who has given his consent in pursuance of subsection (1)(a) above shall notify the Commission of the assignation and the name of the assignee.]

(3) The Commission shall give notice to the landlord of any application made to them for their consent to the assignation of a croft and before [2deciding whether to give or to withhold] their consent shall afford to the crofter and to the landlord an opportunity of making representations to them.

(4) In considering any application made as aforesaid the Commission shall take into

account the family and other circumstances of the crofter and of the proposed assignee of the croft and the general interests of the township in which the croft is situated, . . .[3]

(5) Where a crofter assigns his croft otherwise than with the consent in writing of the Commission [[4]in a case where he is required to obtain such consent in pursuance of subsection (1) above], . . .[5] such assignation and any deed purporting so to assign the croft shall be null and void and the Commission may declare the croft to be vacant.

[[6](6) An assignation to which the Commission have given their consent under this section shall take effect at the term of Whitsunday on Martinmas first occurring not less than two months after the date on which such consent was intimated to the crofter, unless before the said term of Whitsunday or Martinmas, as the case may be, the crofter or his [[7]executor] or legatee and the assignee jointly give to the Commission notice in writing that they do not intend to proceed with the assignation.]

[[8](7) Any reference in this section to a croft shall include a reference to a part of a croft, being a part consisting of any right in pasture or grazing land deemed by virtue of section 3(5) of this Act to form part of a croft.

(8) In this section 'member of his family', in relation to a crofter, has the same meaning as 'member of the crofter's family' has in section 10(7) of this Act[9].]

[8]

Notes.—1 Section 8(1)(2) substituted by Crofting Reform (Scotland) Act 1976 (c 21), Sch 2, para 6(a).
2 Words in sub-s (3) substituted by Crofters (Scotland) Act 1961 (c 58), Sch 1, Pt II, para 10.
3 Words in sub-s (4) repealed by Crofters (Scotland) Act 1961 (c 58), Sch 3.
4 Words in sub-s (5) inserted by Crofting Reform (Scotland) Act 1976 (c 21), Sch 2, para 6(b).
5 Words in sub-s (5) repealed by Crofters (Scotland) Act 1961 (c 58), Sch 3.
6 Section 8(6) added by Crofters (Scotland) Act 1961 (c 58), Sch 1, Pt II, para 10.
7 Word in sub-s (6) substituted by Law Reform (Miscellaneous Provisions) (Scotland) Act 1968 (c 70), Sch 2, Pt I, para 1.
8 Section 8(7), (8) added by Crofting Reform (Scotland) Act 1976 (c 21), Sch 2, para 6(c).
9 Section 8 extended by Crofting Reform (Scotland) Act 1976 (c 21), s 15.

9. Subdivision of croft

A crofter shall not, except with the consent in writing of the landlord and of the Commission, subdivide his croft, and any subdivision of a croft otherwise than with such consent shall be null and void.

[9]

10. Bequest of croft

(1) A crofter may, by will or other testamentary writing, bequeath the tenancy of his croft to any one person; but where the power conferred by this subsection is exercised in favour of a person not being a member of the crofter's family, the bequest shall be null and void unless the Commission, on application made to them by the legatee, otherwise determine.

(2) A person to whom the tenancy of a croft is bequeathed as aforesaid (in this section referred to as 'the legatee') shall, if he accepts the bequest, give notice of the bequest to the landlord within two months after the death of the crofter, unless he is prevented by some unavoidable cause from giving such notice within that time, and in that event he shall give such notice within a further period of four months. If no such notice is given in accordance with the provisions of this subsection the bequest shall become null and void.

The giving of such notice shall import acceptance of the bequest and, unless the landlord intimates objection to the Commission under the next following subsection, the legatee shall come into the place of the deceased crofter in the croft as from the date of the death of the deceased crofter, and the landlord shall notify the Commission accordingly.

(3) Where notice has been given as aforesaid to the landlord he may within one month after the giving of the notice intimate to the legatee and to the Commission that he objects to receive the legatee as tenant of the croft and shall state the grounds of his objection.

(4) If, after affording to the legatee and to the landlord an opportunity of making representations to them, the Commission are satisfied that the objection is reasonable, they shall declare the bequest to be null and void, and shall notify the landlord and the legatee accordingly. If they are not so satisfied they shall notify the landlord and the legatee to that effect, and the legatee shall thereupon come into the place of the deceased crofter in the croft as from the date of the death of the deceased crofter.

(5) If the bequest becomes null and void under this section, the right to the croft shall [¹be treated as intestate estate of the deceased crofter in accordance with Part I of the Succession (Scotland) Act 1964.]

(6) Subject to the foregoing provisions of this section, any question arising with respect to the validity or effect of the bequest shall be determined by any court having jurisdiction to determine the validity and effect of the whole testamentary writings of the deceased crofter.

(7) In this section the expression 'member of the crofter's family' means the wife or husband of the crofter or his son-in-law or daughter-in-law [²or any one of the persons who would be, or would in any circumstances have been, entitled to succeed to the estate on intestacy by virtue of the Succession (Scotland) Act 1964.]

[10]

Notes.—1 Words in sub-s (5) substituted by Law Reform (Miscellaneous Provisions) (Scotland) Act 1968 (c 70), Sch 2, Pt I, para 2.
2 Words in sub-s (7) substituted by Law Reform (Miscellaneous Provisions) (Scotland) Act 1968 (c 70), Sch 2, Pt I, para 3.

## [¹11.	Succession to croft

(1) Where, owing to the failure of a crofter to bequeath the tenancy of his croft or of such a bequest to receive effect, the right to the tenancy of the croft falls to be treated as intestate estate of the deceased crofter in accordance with Part I of the Succession (Scotland) Act 1964, and the tenancy is transferred in pursuance of section 16(2) of that Act, the executor of the deceased crofter shall as soon as may be furnish particulars of the transferee to the landlord, who shall accept the transferee as tenant; and the landlord shall notify the Commission accordingly.

(3) If at the expiry of three months from the relevant date, that is to say—
  (a) where the deceased crofter has exercised his power to bequeath the tenancy of the croft in favour of a person not being a member of the deceased crofter's family and the Commission, on application made to them by the legatee, have refused to determine that the bequest shall not be null and void, from the date of the Commission's refusal;
  (b) where the deceased crofter has otherwise failed to bequeath the tenancy, from the date of death of the deceased crofter;
  (c) where the deceased crofter has bequeathed the tenancy and the bequest has become null and void under section 10(2) of this Act, from the date on which the bequest became null and void as aforesaid;
  (d) where the deceased crofter has bequeathed the tenancy and the Commission have declared the bequest to be null and void under section 10(4) of this Act,

from the date on which the Commission notified the landlord and the legatee to
that effect,
the executor has not furnished to the landlord particulars of any transferee in
accordance with subsection (1) of this section, the landlord shall forthwith notify the
Commission to that effect.

(4) If at the expiry of the three months aforesaid it appears to the Commission,
whether from a notification under subsection (3) of this section or otherwise, that the
executor has not furnished to the landlord particulars of any transferee in accordance
with subsection (1) of this section, the Commission may give notice in such manner as
they may think proper, whether by advertisement or otherwise, to persons who may
claim to be entitled—
  (a) to succeed to the intestate estate of the deceased crofter, or
  (b) to claim legal rights or the prior rights of a surviving spouse out of that estate,
requiring them if they desire to have the tenancy of the croft transferred to them in or
towards satisfaction of their entitlement or claim to give intimation accordingly to the
Commission before such date as may be specified in the notice, being a date not earlier
than six months after the relevant date within the meaning of subsection (3) of this
section; and the Commission may, subject to the provisions of subsection (4A) of this
section, nominate as successor to the tenancy any one of the persons who have so
given intimation.

(4A) The Commission shall, before nominating any person as successor to the
tenancy of the croft in pursuance of subsection (4) of this section, consult with the
executor (if any) of the deceased crofter, and the Commission shall not nominate any
person as successor unless it appears to them—
  (a) that that person is a person entitled to succeed to the intestate estate of the
      deceased crofter, or to claim legal rights or the prior rights of a surviving spouse
      out of that estate, and
  (b) that adequate provision is being, or will be, made for the settlement of the
      entitlement or claim in the said intestate estate of any other person who is
      known to them to be entitled to succeed to, or to claim any such rights out of,
      that estate.

(4B) The Commission shall give notice to the landlord of any person nominated by
them in pursuance of subsection (4) of this section, and the landlord shall accept that
person as successor to the tenancy of the croft.

(4C) The nomination by the Commission, in pursuance of subsection (4) of this
section, of any person as successor to the tenancy of the croft shall transfer the interest
of the tenant under that tenancy to that person, and such transfer shall be in or towards
satisfaction of that person's entitlement or claim in the intestate estate of the deceased
crofter.

(5) If at the expiry of one month from the end of the period referred to in section
16(3)(b) of the Succession (Scotland) Act 1964 the executor has not furnished to the
landlord particulars of any transferee in accordance with subsection (1) of this section
and the Commission have not nominated any person as successor under subsection (4)
thereof, the Commission may declare the croft to be vacant and, if they do so, shall
notify the landlord accordingly.

(6) Where the Commission have under the foregoing provisions of this section
nominated a person as successor to the tenancy or, as the case may be, have declared
the croft to be vacant, any right of any person (other than the person so nominated)
in, or in relation to, the tenancy shall be extinguished.

(7) Where a croft has been declared under subsection (5) of this section to be vacant,
the landlord shall be liable—
  (a) if the deceased crofter was at the date of his death under any liability to the
      Secretary of State in respect of any loan, to pay to the Secretary of State the
      whole or so much of the value of the improvements on the croft as will

discharge the liability of the deceased crofter, and to pay to the executor of the deceased crofter, if a claim is made in that behalf not later than twelve months after the date on which the croft was declared to be vacant, any balance of the value aforesaid;

(b) if at the date of his death the deceased crofter was not under any such liability to the Secretary of State and a claim is made in that behalf as aforesaid, to pay to the executor of the deceased crofter the value of the improvements on the croft.

In this subsection the expression 'the value of the improvements on the croft' means such sum as may be agreed, or as, failing agreement, may be determined by the Land Court, to be the sum which would have been due by the landlord by way of compensation for permanent improvements if the deceased crofter had immediately before his death renounced his tenancy.

(7A) [2]Where a croft has been declared under subsection (5) of this section to be vacant consequent on the death after the commencement of the Crofters (Scotland) Act 1961, of a crofter who immediately before his death was qualified as mentioned in the next following subsection, and the value of the improvements on the croft is determined by the Land Court under the last foregoing subsection, the executor of the crofter may request the Land Court to determine what would have been the value of the improvements on the croft if the said Act had not been passed, and if the value last mentioned is greater than the value determined by the Land Court under the last foregoing subsection, the difference between the two said values shall be payable to the executor by the Secretary of State:

Provided that the Secretary of State shall be entitled to set off any amount due to him by the crofter at the date of his death in respect of a loan made under subsection (2) or (3) of section twenty-two of this Act or subsection (7) of section seven or section nine of the Act of 1911 against any sum payable to the executor by the Secretary of State under this subsection

(7B) The reference in the last foregoing subsection to a crofter who immediately before his death was qualified is a reference to a crofter—

(a) whose tenancy of the croft in question began before the commencement of the Crofters (Scotland) Act 1961, or

(b) who held the tenancy of such croft as statutory successor to his immediate predecessor in the tenancy and each of whose predecessors (being in each case a person whose tenancy of the croft began after the commencement of the said Act) held such tenancy as statutory successor to his immediate predecessor.]

[11]

Notes.—1 Section 11 substituted by virtue of Law Reform (Miscellaneous Provisions) (Scotland) Act 1968 (c 70), s 8, Sch 2, Pt II in relation to the estate of any person dying after 25 November 1968.
2 Section 11(7A) modified by Highlands and Islands Development (Scotland) Act 1965 (c 46), s 8(3)(b).

12. Resumption of croft or part of croft by landlord

(1) The Land Court may, on the application of the landlord and on being satisfied that he desires to resume the croft, or part of thereof, for some reasonable purpose having relation to the good of the croft or of the estate or to the public interest, authorise the resumption thereof by the landlord upon such terms and conditions as they may think fit, and may require the crofter to surrender his croft, in whole or in part, to the landlord accordingly, upon the landlord making adequate compensation to the crofter either by letting to him other land of equivalent value in the neighbourhood or by compensation in money or by way of an adjustment of rent or in such other manner as the Land Court may determine.

[(1A) A sum awarded as compensation under subsection (1) above shall, if the Land Court so determine, carry interest as from the date when such sum is payable at the same rate as would apply (in the absence of any such statement as is provided for in Rule 66 of the Act of Sederunt (Rules of Court, consolidation and amendment) 1965) in the case of decree or extract in an action commenced on that date in the Court of Session if interest were included in or exigible under that decree or extract;

Provided that this subsection shall not affect any case in which the hearing has begun before the coming into force of section 30 of the Law Reform (Miscellaneous Provisions) (Scotland) Act 1985.[1]]

(2) For the purposes of the foregoing subsection the expression 'reasonable purpose' shall include the using, letting or feuing of the land proposed to be resumed for the building of dwellings, or for small allotments, or for harbours, piers, boat shelters or other like buildings, or for churches or other places of religious worship, or for schools, or for halls or community centres, or for planting, or for roads practicable for vehicular traffic from the croft or township to the public road or to the seashore [[2]or for any other purpose likely to provide employment for crofters and others in the locality], and the protection of an ancient monument or other object of historical or archaeological interest from injury or destruction.

(3) Where an application is made, with the consent of a majority of the persons sharing in a common grazing and with the approval of the Commission, for authority to resume any land forming part of the common grazing for the purpose of using, letting or otherwise disposing of it for the planting of trees, the Land Court shall not withhold their authority for such resumption.

[[3](4) The provisions of the Crofters (Scotland) Acts 1955 and 1961, shall cease to apply to any land on its being resumed in pursuance of an order authorising its resumption made under this section by the Land Court, without prejudice, however, to the subsequent exercise of any powers conferred by any enactment for . . .[4] the enlargement of existing crofts.]

[12]

Notes.—1 Section 12(1A) added by the Law Reform (Miscellaneous Provisions) (Scotland) Act 1985 (c 73), s 30(1).
2 Words in sub-s (2) inserted by Crofters (Scotland) Act 1961 (c 58), Sch 1, Pt II, para 11.
3 Section 12(4) added by Crofters (Scotland) Act 1961 (c 58), Sch 1, Pt II, para 11.
4 Words in sub-s (4) repealed by Crofting Reform (Scotland) Act 1976 (c 21), Sch 3.

---

13. Provisions as to removal of crofter

(1) When—
    (a) one year's rent of a croft is unpaid, or
    (b) a crofter has broken one or more of the statutory conditions (other than the condition as to payment of rent),
the Land Court may, on the application of the landlord and after considering any objections stated by the crofter, make an order for the removal of the crofter.

(2) When a crofter whose rights to compensation for permanent improvements have been transferred in whole or in part to the Secretary of State under section twenty-three of this Act—
    (a) has abandoned his croft; or
    (b) has broken any of the statutory conditions (other than the condition as to payment of rent); or
    (c) has broken any of the conditions of repayment of a loan contained in the agreement for the loan;

the Land Court may, on the application of the Secretary of State and after considering any objections stated by the crofter or the landlord, make an order for the removal of the crofter.

(3) If a crofter is removed from his croft, the landlord shall be entitled to set off all rent due or to become due against any sum found to be due [¹by the landlord] to the crofter or to the Secretary of State for permanent improvements made on the croft.

[13]

Note.—1 Words in sub-s (3) inserted by Crofters (Scotland) Act 1961 (c 58), Sch 1, Pt I, para 3.

¹14. Compensation for improvements and compensation for deterioration or damage

(1) Where—
  (i) a crofter renounces his tenancy or is removed from his croft, or
  (ii) the tenancy of a croft, being a tenancy the interest of the tenant under which is comprised in the estate of a deceased crofter, is terminated in pursuance of section 16(3) of the Succession (Scotland) Act, 1964,
the crofter or, as the case may be, the executor of the deceased crofter shall, subject to the provisions of this Act, be entitled to compensation for any permanent improvement made on the croft if—
  (a) ²the improvement is suitable to the croft; and
  (b) the improvement was executed or paid for by the crofter or, as the case may be, the deceased crofter, or any of the predecessors of the crofter or of the deceased crofter in the tenancy; and
  (c) either the improvement was executed otherwise than in pursuance of a specific agreement in writing under which the crofter or, as the case may be, the deceased crofter was bound to execute the improvement or, if the improvement was executed in pursuance of such an agreement, the crofter has not received or, as the case may be, the deceased crofter did not receive and his executor has not received, by way of reduction of rent or otherwise, fair consideration for the improvement.

(2) Where—
  (a) a person on becoming the tenant of a croft has with the consent of the landlord paid to the outgoing tenant any compensation due to him in respect of any permanent improvement and has agreed with the Secretary of State to assume any outstanding liability to the Secretary of State of the outgoing tenant in respect of any loan made to him; or
  (b) on a person becoming the tenant of a croft the Secretary of State on his behalf has paid to the landlord a sum representing the value to such person of an existing improvement on the croft;
such person shall for the purposes of the foregoing subsection be deemed to have executed or paid for the improvement.

For the purposes of paragraph (a) of this subsection a landlord who has not paid the compensation due either to the outgoing tenant or to the Secretary of State and has not applied to the Secretary of State to determine under subsection (4) of section twenty-three of this Act that any amount due by him to the Secretary of State by virtue of subsection (3) of that section shall be deemed to be a loan by the Secretary of State to him shall be deemed to have given his consent.

(3) The provisions of subsection (1) of this section shall not apply to any buildings erected by a crofter in contravention of any interdict or other judicial order.

(6) ³Where—
  (a) a crofter renounces his tenancy or is removed from his croft, or

(b) the tenancy of a croft, being a tenancy the interest of the tenant under which is comprised in the estate of a deceased crofter, is terminated in pursuance of section 16(3) of the Succession (Scotland) Act 1964,

the landlord shall be entitled to recover from the crofter or, as the case may be, from the executor of the deceased crofter compensation for any deterioration of, or damage to, any fixed equipment provided by the landlord committed or permitted by the crofter or, as the case may be, by the deceased crofter or his executor.

(7) The amount of the compensation payable under the last foregoing subsection shall be the cost, as at the date of the crofter's quitting the croft or, as the case may be, of the termination of the tenancy, of making good the deterioration or damage; and the landlord shall be entitled to set off the amount so payable against any compensation payable by him in respect of permanent improvements.

(8) The amount of the compensation payable under subsection (1) or subsection (6) of this section shall, failing agreement, be fixed by the Land Court.

(9) Where—
(a) a crofter has given notice of renunciation of his tenancy, or
(b) the landlord of the croft either gives to the executor of a deceased crofter, or receives from such an executor, notice terminating the tenancy of the croft in pursuance of section 16(3) of the Succession (Scotland) Act 1964,

the Land Court may on the joint application of the crofter or, as the case may be, the executor of the deceased crofter and the landlord or, where the crofter's rights to compensation for permanent improvements have been transferred in whole or in part under section twenty-three of this Act to the Secretary of State, on the joint application of the Secretary of State and the landlord, assess prior to the renunciation or, as the case may be, the termination the amounts which will on renunciation or termination become due under this section by the landlord by way of compensation for permanent improvements and by the crofter or executor by way of compensation for deterioration or damage; and the amounts so assessed shall, on renunciation or, as the case may be, termination, become due accordingly.

(10) Nothing in this Act shall affect the provisions of the Agricultural Holdings (Scotland) Act 1949, with respect to the payment to outgoing tenants of compensation for improvements:
Provided that—
(a) where any improvements are valued under that Act with a view to the payment of compensation to a crofter or to the executor of a deceased crofter, the valuation shall, unless the landlord and the crofter or executor otherwise agree in writing, be made by the Land Court; and
(b) compensation shall not be payable under that Act for an improvement for which compensation is payable under this Act.

(11) Notwithstanding anything in this section—
(a) a crofter who immediately before the commencement of this Act was a statutory small tenant, or
(b) the statutory successor of such a crofter, or
(c) the executor of such a crofter or of such a statutory successor,

shall not be entitled, in respect of any permanent improvement made or begun before the commencement of this Act, to any compensation to which he would not have been entitled if his tenancy had expired immediately before the commencement of this Act.

[14]

Notes.—1 Section 14 substituted by virtue of Law Reform (Miscellaneous Provisions) (Scotland) Act 1968 (c 70), s 8, Sch 2, Pt II in relation to the estate of any person dying

after 25 November 1968. Section 14(1) amended by Crofters (Scotland) Act 1961 (c 58), s 6(1); excluded by Crofting Reform (Scotland) Act 1976 (c 21), s 6(2)(a).
2 Section 14(1)(a) extended by Crofters (Scotland) Act 1961 (c 58), s 5(2)(3).
3 Section 14(6) excluded by Crofting Reform (Scotland) Act 1976 (c 21), s 6(2)(b).

Administration of Crofts

15. Commission to obtain information and to compile register of crofts

(1) The Commission may by notice served on the owner or the occupier of any holding require him to furnish them with such information as may be specified in the notice with regard to the [¹extent], the rent and the tenure of the holding and with regard to such other matters relating to the ownership or the occupation of the holding as the Commission may reasonably require for the execution of their functions under this Act [²and the Crofting Reform (Scotland) Act 1976].

(2)–(4) [*Repealed by Crofters (Scotland) Act 1961 (c 58), s 3(4), Sch 3.*]

(5) If any owner or occupier on whom a notice has been served under subsection (1) of this section—

(a) fails without reasonable cause or neglects to furnish to the Commission within three months after the service of the notice the information specified in the notice; or

(b) in furnishing such information as aforesaid knowingly or recklessly furnishes any information which is false in a material particular,

he shall be liable on summary conviction to a fine not exceeding ten pounds.

[15]

Notes.—1 Word in sub-s (1) substituted by Crofting Reform (Scotland) Act 1976 (c 21), Sch 2, para 7(a).
2 Words in sub-s (1) added by Crofting Reform (Scotland) Act 1976 (c 21), Sch 2, para 7(b).

16. Vacant crofts

(1) Where—

(a) the landlord of a croft receives from the crofter a notice of renunciation of his tenancy or obtains from the Land Court an order for the removal of the crofter; or

[¹(aa) the landlord of the croft either gives to the executor of a deceased crofter, or receives from such an executor, notice terminating the tenancy of the croft in pursuance of section 16(3) of the Succession (Scotland) Act 1964; or]

(b) for any other reason the croft has become vacant;

the landlord shall within one month [²from—

(i)   the receipt of the notice of renunciation of the tenancy, or

(ii) the date on which the Land Court made the order, or

(iii) the date on which the landlord gave or received notice terminating the tenancy, or

(iv) the date on which the vacancy came to the landlord's knowledge,

as the case may be,] give notice thereof to the Commission.

(2) [*Repealed by Crofting Reform (Scotland) Act 1976 (c 21), Sch 3.*]

(3) The Landlord of a croft shall not, except with the consent in writing of the Commission, or, if the Commission withhold their consent, with the consent of the Secretary of State, let the croft or any part thereof to any person; and any letting of the croft otherwise than with such consent shall be null and void.

[³(3A) Where any person is in occupation of a croft under a letting which is null and void by virtue of the last foregoing subsection, the Commission may serve on him a notice in writing requiring him to give up his occupation of such croft on or before such day as may be specified in the notice, being a day not less than one month from the date of the service of the notice; and if he fails to give up his occupation of the croft on or before that day, subsection (3) of the next following section shall, subject to any necessary modifications, apply as it applies where a crofter fails to give up the occupation of a croft as mentioned in that subsection.]

(4) Where a croft is vacant the Commission may—
  (a) [*Repealed by Crofting Reform (Scotland) Act 1976 (c 21), Sch 3*]
  (b) . . .[4], at any time after the expiry of one month from the occurrence of the vacancy;
give notice to the landlord requiring him to submit to them his proposals for re-letting the croft, whether as a separate croft or as an enlargement of another croft, and if, within a period of two months from the giving of such notice, no such proposals are submitted or such proposals are submitted but the Commission refuse to approve them, the Commission may, if they think fit, themselves let the croft to such person or persons and on such terms and conditions (including conditions as to rent) as may be fixed by the Commission after consultation with the landlord; and such let shall have effect in all respects as if it had been granted by the landlord:

  Provided that the Commission shall not themselves let the croft while [[5]the Secretary of State is considering an application made to him under subsection (3) above for consent to let, or the Commission are considering an application made to them under subsection (9) below for a direction that the croft shall cease to be a croft].

(5) Where a croft has been let on terms and conditions fixed by the Commission, the landlord may within one month from the date of the letting apply to the Land Court for a variation of the terms and conditions so fixed, and any variation made in pursuance of such application shall have effect as from the date of the letting.

(6) [6]Where the Commission have under subsection (4) of this section let a vacant croft as an enlargement of another croft, and any of the buildings on the vacant croft thereby cease to be required in connection with the occupation of the croft, the Commission shall give notice to that effect to the landlord, and thereupon—
  (a) the buildings shall cease to form part of the croft; and
  (b) the landlord may, at any time within six months after the giving of such notice, give notice to the Secretary of State requiring him to purchase the buildings.

[[7](7) Where a croft has, in consequence of the making of an order under section 17(1) of this Act, become vacant and has remained unlet for a period of six months beginning with the date on which the croft so became vacant, the Commission shall, if the landlord at any time within three months after the expiry of the period aforesaid, gives notice to the Commission requiring them to do so, direct that the croft shall cease to be a croft; and if the landlord within one month after the issuing of such a direction gives notice to the Secretary of State requiring him to purchase the buildings on the croft, the Secretary of State shall purchase such buildings.]

(8) [8]Where a notice has been duly given under paragraph (b) of subsection (6) of this section or [[9]by the landlord to the Secretary of State] under the last foregoing subsection, the Secretary of State shall be deemed to be authorised to purchase the buildings compulsorily and to have served notice to treat in respect thereof on the date on which the notice aforesaid was given:

  Provided that the consideration payable by the Secretary of State in respect of the purchase of the buildings shall be such sum as may be agreed by the Secretary of State and the landlord, or, failing agreement, as may be determined by the Land Court to be equal to the amount which an out-going tenant who had erected or paid for the erection of the buildings would have been entitled to receive [[10]from the landlord] by way of compensation for permanent improvements in respect of the buildings as at the date on which notice was given as aforesaid to the Secretary of State requiring him to purchase the buildings.

[^{11}(9) Where a croft is vacant, the Commission may, on the application of the landlord, direct that the croft shall cease to be a croft or refuse to grant the application; and if the Commission direct under this subsection or under subsection (7) above that a croft shall cease to be a croft, the provisions of this Act and, subject to subsection (9A) below, the Crofters (Scotland) Act 1961 shall cease to apply to the croft, without prejudice, however, to the subsequent exercise of any powers conferred by any enactment for the enlargement of existing crofts.

(9A) The coming into effect of a direction given by the Commission by virtue of section 16A(4) of this Act shall not affect the powers contained in the proviso to section 13(3) of the said Act of 1961 (subleases).]

(10) Any person who, being the landlord of a croft, fails to comply with the requirements of subsection (1) or subsection (2) of this section shall be liable on summary conviction to a fine not exceeding ten pounds.

(11) For the purposes of this section a croft shall be taken to be vacant at the commencement of this Act notwithstanding that it is occupied, if it is occupied otherwise than by a crofter and the consent of the Secretary of State to such occupation has not been obtained.

[^{12}(11A) For the purposes of this section [^{13}and section 16A of this Act] a croft shall be taken to be vacant notwithstanding that it is occupied, if it is occupied otherwise than by the tenant of the croft.]

(12) The provisions of subsections (1) and (10) of this section shall not apply to a croft which the Commission have in the exercise of any power conferred on them by this Act declared to be vacant.

[^{14}(13) The provisions of this section shall have effect in relation to a part of a croft as they have effect in relation to a croft.]

[^{15}(14) For the avoidance of doubt it is hereby declared that this section has effect (and shall be deemed always to have had effect since 27th August 1961) as if—
  (a) a person who has become the owner-occupier of a croft were required under subsection (1) above within one month of the date on which he became such owner-occupier to give notice thereof to the Commission; and
  (b) any reference in the section other than in subsection (1) above to a landlord included a reference to an owner-occupier.]

[16]

Notes.—1 Section 16(1)(aa) inserted by Law Reform (Miscellaneous Provisions) (Scotland) Act 1968 (c 70), Sch 2, Pt I, para 17.
2 Words in sub-s (1) substituted by Law Reform (Miscellaneous Provisions) (Scotland) Act 1968 (c 70), Sch 2, Pt I, para 17.
3 Section 16(3A) inserted by Crofters (Scotland) Act 1961 (c 58), Sch 1, Pt II, para 12(a).
4 Words in sub-s (4)(b) repealed by Crofting Reform (Scotland) Act 1976 (c 21), Sch 3.
5 Words in proviso to sub-s (4) substituted by Crofting Reform (Scotland) Act 1976 (c 21), Sch 2, para 8(a).
6 Section 16(6) applied by Crofters (Scotland) Act 1961 (c 58), s 9(7).
7 Section 16(7) substituted by Crofting Reform (Scotland) Act 1976 (c 21), s 13(1).
8 Section s 16(8) applied by Crofters (Scotland) Act 1961 (c 58), s 9(7).
9 Words in sub-s (8) inserted by Crofting Reform (Scotland) Act 1976 (c 21), Sch 2, para 8(b).
10 Words in proviso to sub-s (8) inserted by Crofters (Scotland) Act 1961 (c 58), Sch 1, Pt I, para 5.
11 Section 16(9)(9A) substituted for s 16(9) by Crofting Reform (Scotland) Act 1976 (c 21), s 13(2).
12 Section 16(11A) inserted by Crofters (Scotland) Act 1961 (c 58), Sch 1, Pt II, para 12(c).
13 Words in sub-s (11A) inserted by Crofting Reform (Scotland) Act 1976 (c 21), Sch 2, para 8(c).
14 Section 16(13) inserted by Crofters (Scotland) Act 1961 (c 58), Sch 1, Pt II, para 12(d).
15 Section 16(14) added by Crofting Reform (Scotland) Act 1976 (c 21), Sch 2, para 8(d).

[¹16A.   Provisions supplementary to s 16(9)

(1) The Commission shall give a direction under section 16(9) of this Act that a croft shall cease to be a croft if—

   (a) subject to subsection (2) below, they are satisfied that the applicant has applied for the direction in order that the croft may be used for or in connection with some reasonable purpose within the meaning of section 12(2) of this Act and that the extent of the land to which the application relates is not excessive in relation to that purpose; or

   (b) the application is made in respect of a part of a croft, which consists only of the site of the dwelling-house on or pertaining to the croft and in respect of which a crofter is entitled at the time of the application, or has been entitled, to a conveyance by virtue of section 1(2) of the Crofting Reform (Scotland) Act 1976, and they are satisfied that the extent of garden ground included in that part is appropriate for the reasonable enjoyment of the dwelling-house as a residence.

(2) Without prejudice to subsection (1)(b) above, the Commission, in determining whether or not to give such a direction, shall have regard to the general interest of the crofting community in the district in which the croft is situated and in particular to the demand, if any, for a tenancy of the croft from persons who might reasonably be expected to obtain that tenancy if the croft were offered for letting on the open market on the date when they are considering the application.

(3) Where the Commission give such a direction on being satisfied as mentioned in subsection (1)(a) above, they may in the direction impose such conditions as appear to them requisite for securing that the land to which the direction relates is used for the proposed use; and if at any time they are satisfied that there has been a breach of any such condition, they may make a further direction that the land in respect of which there has been such a breach shall be a vacant croft.

(4) The Commission may, on the application of a crofter who is proposing to acquire croft land or the site of the dwelling-house on or pertaining to his croft, give a direction under the said section 16(9) as if the land were a vacant croft and the application were made by the landlord, that in the event of such acquisition of the land it shall cease to be a croft, or refuse the application; but such a direction shall not have effect until the land to which it relates has been acquired by the crofter or his nominee and unless the acquisition is made within five years of the date of the giving of the direction.

(5) A direction under the said section 16(9) may be given taking account of such modification of the application in relation to which the direction is given as the Commission consider appropriate.

(6) The Commission shall advertise all applications under the said section 16(9) or subsection (4) above (except an application made in respect of a part of a croft consisting only of the site of the dwelling-house on or pertaining to the croft) in one or more newspapers circulating in the district in which the croft to which the application relates is situated, and before disposing of such an application shall, if requested by the applicant, afford a hearing to the applicant and to such other person as they think fit.

(7) The Commission shall give notice in writing to the applicant of their proposed decision on an application made to them under the said section 16(9) or subsection (4) above, specifying the nature of and the reasons for such decision.

(8) The applicant may within 21 days of receipt of the notice under subsection (7) above, and the owner of land to which a further direction under subsection (3) above relates may within 21 days of the making of that further direction, appeal against the proposed decision or further direction to the Land Court who may hear or consider such evidence as they think fit in order to enable them to dispose of the appeal.

(9) The Commission shall give effect to the determination of the Land Court on an appeal under subsection (8) above.]

[17]

_____

Note.—1 Section 16A inserted by Crofting Reform (Scotland) Act 1976 (c 21), s 13(3).

_____

17.   Absentee crofters

(1) If the Commission determine in relation to a croft—
-   (a) that the crofter is not ordinarily resident on, or within [¹sixteen kilometres] of, the croft; and
-   (b) that it is in the general interest of the crofting community in the district in which the croft is situate that the tenancy of the crofter should be terminated and the croft let to some other person or persons;

then, subject to the provisions of this section, they shall have power to make an order terminating the tenancy of the crofter and requiring him to give up his occupation of the croft at a term of Whitsunday or Martinmas not earlier than three months after the making of such order.

(2) Before making an order under the foregoing subsection the Commission shall take into consideration all the circumstances of the case, including the extent, if any, to which the croft is being worked and, where the croft is being worked by a member of the crofter's family, the nature of the arrangement under which it is being so worked, and shall give to the crofter and to the landlord, not less than six months before the term at which the proposed order will take effect, notice that they propose to make such an order and shall afford to the crofter and the landlord an opportunity of making representations to them against the making of the proposed order.

Where the Commission make such an order, they shall, not less than three months before the term at which the order takes effect, give notice to the crofter and to the landlord of the making of the order.

(3) Where an order has been made under subsection (1) of this section and the crofter has failed to give up his occupation of the croft on or before the day on which the order takes effect, the sheriff on the application of the Commission shall, except on cause shown to the contrary, grant warrant for ejection of the crofter. The Commission may recover from the crofter the expenses incurred by them in any application under this subsection and in the execution of any warrant granted thereon.

(4)–(8) [*Repealed by Crofting Reform (Scotland) Act 1976 (c 21), Sch 3.*]

(9) . . .², a crofter shall, on the termination of his tenancy by an order made under subsection (1) of this section, be entitled to the like rights to, and subject to the like liabilities in respect of, compensation as if he had renounced his tenancy at the term at which the order takes effect.

(10) [*Repealed by Crofting Reform (Scotland) Act 1976 (c 21), Sch 3.*]

[18]

_____

Notes.—1 Words in sub-s (1)(a) substituted by Crofting Reform (Scotland) Act 1976 (c 21), Sch 2, para 9.
2 Words repealed by Crofting Reform (Scotland) Act 1976 (c 21), s 22(3), Sch 3.

_____

18.   [*Repealed by Crofting Reform (Scotland) Act 1976 (c 21), Sch 3.*]

[19]

19–21.   [*Repealed by Crofters (Scotland) Act 1961 (c 58), Sch 3.*]

[20]

22. Power of Secretary of State to give financial assistance to crofters

(1) [1]For the purpose of aiding and developing agricultural production on crofts the Secretary of State may, after consultation with the Commission and with the approval of the Treasury, make schemes for providing grants and loans to crofters, and any such schemes may provide for the administration of such grants and loans through the agency of the Commission.

Any scheme under this subsection shall be embodied in a statutory instrument which shall be laid before Parliament after being made.

(2) [2]The Secretary of State may, in accordance with arrangements made by him with the approval of the Treasury, provide assistance by way of grants or loans or by the supply for payment in cash of building or other materials towards the erection or improvement or rebuilding of dwelling-houses and other buildings for crofters.

(3) The Secretary of State may, in accordance with arrangements made by him with the approval of the Treasury, provide assistance by way of loan to the incoming tenant of a croft to enable him to pay to the outgoing tenant of the croft or to the landlord thereof the compensation for permanent improvements due to such outgoing tenant.

(4) Regulations shall be made by the Secretary of State—
   (a) for securing that, where a grant has been made towards the erection, improvement or rebuilding of a dwelling-house or other building, conditions with respect to the occupation and maintenance thereof shall apply thereto for such period from the completion of the work (not being longer than forty years) as may be specified in the regulations;
   (b) for securing that in the event of a breach of any of the conditions the Secretary of State may recover from such person as may be specified in the regulations a sum bearing the same proportion to the grant made as the period between the date of the breach of the condition and the expiration of the period specified under paragraph (a) of this subsection bears to the last mentioned period, together with interest on such sum from the date on which the grant was made at such rate as may be specified in the regulations;
   (c) for providing that the conditions applied by the regulations to a dwelling-house or building shall cease to apply on payment to the Secretary of State by such person as may be specified in the regulations of such amount as may be so specified;
   (d) [*Repealed by Crofting Reform (Scotland) Act 1976 (c 21), Sch 3.*]
   (e) [3]for securing that, where any conditions apply to a dwelling-house or building by virtue of the regulations, the Secretary of State shall cause to be recorded in the appropriate Register of Sasines a notice in a form prescribed by the regulations specifying the conditions which by virtue of the regulations apply to the dwelling-house or building; and that, where such conditions cease to apply, [by virtue of such a payment to the Secretary of State as is referred to in paragraph (c) above,] the Secretary of State shall cause to be so recorded a notice in a form prescribed as aforesaid stating that the conditions no longer apply to the dwelling-house or building;
   (f) for such other incidental and supplementary matters as appear to the Secretary of State to be requisite or expedient for the purposes aforesaid.

(5) No assistance by way of grant shall be given under subsection (2) of this section towards the erection, improvement or rebuilding of any dwelling-house or other building [4or towards the provision or improvement of roads, or water or electricity or gas supplies] if assistance out of public moneys by way of grant or subsidy has been given under any other enactment towards [5the works in question].

(6) For the purposes of subsection (2) of this section the occupier of a holding constituted under the Congested Districts (Scotland) Act 1897, on land acquired by

the Congested Districts (Scotland) Commissioners, who is also the owner of the holding, shall be deemed to be a crofter.

(7) A person shall not be disqualified for receiving assistance under subsection (2) of this section by reason only that after he has applied for and the Secretary of State has undertaken to provide such assistance he has become the owner of the croft in respect of which the application was made.

(8) [*Repealed by Crofting Reform (Scotland) Act 1976 (c 21), Sch 3.*]

Notes.—1 Section 22(1) extended by Crofters (Scotland) Act 1961 (c 58), s 14 and Crofting Reform (Scotland) Act 1976 (c 21), s 12(5). See the Crofting Counties Agricultural Grants (Scotland) Scheme 1988, SI 1988/559.
2 Section 22(2) extended by Crofting Reform (Scotland) Act 1976 (c 21), s 12(1)(2).
3 Section 22(4)(e) words inserted by the Law Reform (Miscellaneous Provisions) (Scotland) Act 1985 (c 73), s 31.
4 Words in sub-s (5) inserted by Crofting Reform (Scotland) Act 1976 (c 21), Sch 2, para 10.
5 Words in sub-s (5) substituted by Crofting Reform (Scotland) Act 1976 (c 21), Sch 2, para 10.

23. Supplementary provisions as to loans

(1) Where assistance is given under subsection (2) or subsection (3) of the last foregoing section by way of loan, the following provisions of this section shall have effect.

(2) The Secretary of State shall give notice to the landlord of the giving of any such assistance as aforesaid.

(3) [1]The agreement for the loan shall be recorded in the Crofters Holdings Book and as recorded shall have the effect of transferring to the Secretary of State all rights of the crofter and his statutory successors to compensation for permanent improvements up to the amount of any outstanding liability to the Secretary of State.

(4) Any amount due by virtue of subsection (3) of this section to the Secretary of State by the landlord may, if the Secretary of State on the application of the landlord so determines, be deemed to be a loan by the Secretary of State to the landlord, and the provisions of the Third Schedule to this Act shall apply in relation thereto.

(5) Where the outgoing tenant of a croft is under any liability to the Secretary of State in respect of a loan made to him, the Secretary of State and the incoming tenant may agree that the latter shall assume such liability, and if they so agree the amount thereof shall be deemed to be a loan made to the incoming tenant under subsection (3) of the last foregoing section, and this section shall have effect accordingly.

(6) The provision of the Third Schedule to this Act shall apply in relation to any loan made by virtue of subsection (6) of subsection (7) of the last foregoing section.

[22]

Note.—1 Section 23(3) amended by Coal-Mining (Subsidence) Act 1957 (c 59), s 10(7).

Common Grazings

24. Appointment, etc, of grazings committee or grazings constable

(1) [1]The crofters who share in a common grazing may from time to time, at a public meeting called in accordance with the next following subsection, appoint a grazings committee of such number as the meeting shall decide.

(2) Notice of a meeting for the appointment of a grazings committee may be given by any two crofters interested in the common grazing and shall be given by notice published in each of two successive weeks in one or more newspapers circulating in the district in which the township is situate or by notice posted for two successive

weeks [²in such public place or places in that district as may be approved by the Commission].

(3) If the crofters who share in a common grazing fail at any time to appoint a grazings committee, the Commission may, after making such inquiry, if any, as they may deem necessary, appoint a grazings committee, or may appoint a person to be grazings constable; and a committee or constable so appointed shall have the like powers and duties as a grazings committee appointed under subsection (1) of this section.

(4) The term of office of the members of a grazings committee appointed under this section shall be three years, and at the expiry of that period a new grazings committee shall be appointed as aforesaid. A retiring member of a committee shall be eligible for re-election.

(5) A majority of the members of a grazings committee shall be a quorum; and any vacancy occurring in the membership of a grazings committee by reason of the death or resignation of a member shall be filled by nomination of the remaining members.

(6) A grazings committee appointed under subsection (1) of this section, or in the case of a grazings committee appointed under subsection (3) thereof the Commission, shall appoint some person, whether a member of the committee or not, to be the clerk of the committee.

(7) The term of office of a grazings constable appointed by the Commission under subsection (3) of this section shall be such as may be specified in the instrument by which he is appointed, and he shall receive such annual remuneration as the Commission may determine; and such remuneration shall be defrayed by an assessment levied in such manner as the Commission may deem reasonable on the crofters who share in the common grazing.

(8) If the Commission are satisfied, after making such inquiry, if any, as they may deem necessary, that any or all of the members or the clerk of a grazings committee (however appointed under this section) are not properly carrying out the duties imposed on them under this Act, the Commission may remove from office any or all such members or such clerk and may appoint or provide for the appointment of other persons (whether crofters or not) in their or his place.

[³(9) A grazings committee shall pay such annual remuneration to the clerk appointed under subsection (6) or (8) of this section as they may determine; and they may recover from the crofters sharing in the common grazings all expenditure incurred by them in paying such remuneration.]

[23]

Notes.—1 Section 24(1) amended by Crofters (Scotland) Act 1961 (c 58), s 15(1).
2 Words in sub-s (2) substituted by Crofters (Scotland) Act 1961 (c 58), Sch 1, Pt II, para 13.
3 Section 24(9) added by Crofting Reform (Scotland) Act 1976 (c 21), s 16(1).

25. Powers and duties of grazings committees²

(1) It shall be the duty of a grazings committee—
   (a) ¹to maintain the common grazings and [²to provide, maintain and, if necessary, replace] the fixed equipment required in connection therewith;
   (b) ³to carry out works for the improvement of such grazings and equipment;
   (c) to make and administer, with a view to their due observance, regulations (in this Act referred to as 'common grazings regulations') with respect to the management and use of the common grazings:
[*Proviso to s 25(1) repealed by Crofting Reform (Scotland) Act 1976 (c 21), Sch 3.*]

[⁴(1a) The grazings committee shall give notice to each crofter sharing in the common grazings of any proposals to carry out works in pursuance of the duty imposed by subsection (1)(b) above and the proposed allocation of the expenditure to be incurred in respect of those works among such crofters; and any such crofter may within one month of the date of such notice make representations in respect of the proposals or the proposed allocation to the Commission who may approve the proposals or proposed allocation with or without modifications or reject them.

(1B) Notwithstanding section 13(2) of the Act of 1961 (which provides that where a right in common grazings is sublet the subtenant comes in place of the crofter in relation to any matter which concerns such right), subsection (1A) above shall have effect in a case where such a right is sublet as if any reference to a crofter included a reference to a crofter in whose place a subtenant has come; but no liability to meet expenditure incurred by a grazings committee in the performance of the duties imposed on them by subsection (1)(b) above shall be imposed on such a crofter in respect of any period during which such a subtenancy subsists.]

(2) A person appointed by the Commission shall have power to summon and to attend any meeting of a grazings committee for the purpose of advising them and otherwise assisting them in the performance of their duties.

[24]

Notes.—1 Section 25(1)(a) explained by Crofting Reform (Scotland) Act 1976 (c 21), s 16(2).
2 Words in sub-s (1)(a) inserted by Crofters (Scotland) Act 1961 (c 58), Sch 1, Pt II, para 14.
3 Section 25(1)(b) explained by Crofting Reform (Scotland) Act 1976 (c 21), s 16(2).
4 Section 25(1A)(1B) inserted by Crofting Reform (Scotland) Act 1976 (c 21), s 16(3).

---

26. Common grazings regulations

(1) Every grazings committee shall, as soon as may be after the commencement of this Act, and in any event within six months after being required by the Commission so to do, make and submit to the Commission new common grazings regulations.
(2) [1]Without prejudice to the generality of the power conferred on a grazings committee by paragraph (c) of subsection (1) of the last foregoing section, common grazings regulations shall make provision with respect to the following matters:—
  (a) the recovery by the grazings committee from the crofters sharing in the common grazings of all expenses incurred by the committee in maintaining the common grazings and in [2providing] maintaining or replacing any fixed equipment required in connection therewith;
  [3(b) the recovery by the grazings committee from such crofters of all expenses incurred by the committee in the performance of the duties imposed on them by section 25(1)(b) of this Act according to the proposed allocation of expenditure referred to in subsection (1A) of the said section 25 or, as the case may be, that allocation as approved or modified by the Commission under that subsection;]
  (c) the number and the kind of stock which each crofter is entitled to put on the common grazings;
  (d) the alteration of individual soumings where works for the improvement of the common grazings or the fixed equipment required in connection therewith have been carried out and all the crofters have not contributed to the expenses incurred in carrying out such works;
  (e) where appropriate, the cutting of peats and the collection of seaweed;
  (f) subject to the provisions of this Act, the summoning of meetings of the grazings committee and the procedure and conduct of business at such meetings.

(3) Common grazings regulations made by a grazings committee shall be of no effect unless confirmed by the Commission. The Commission may confirm with or without modification or refuse to confirm any common grazings regulations submitted to them for confirmation, and may fix the date on which the regulations

are to come into operation; and if no date is so fixed, the regulations shall come into operation at the expiration of one month from the date of their confirmation.

(4) If a grazings committee fail within the time limited by subsection (1) of this section to make and submit to the Commission common grazings regulations or to make and submit to the Commission common grazings regulations which in the opinion of the Commission are sufficient and satisfactory, the Commission may themselves make such common grazings regulations, which shall have the like force and effect as if they had been made by the grazings committee and confirmed by the Commission.

(5) A grazings committee may from time to time, and, if so required by the Commission, shall within the time limited by such requirement, make further regulations amending the common grazings regulations for the time being in force, and the provisions of the last two foregoing subsections shall apply to any such amending regulations subject to any necessary modifications.

(6) Before confirming, making or amending regulations in accordance with the foregoing provisions of this section, the Commission shall consult the landlord of the common grazings to which the regulations relate; and the Commission shall send a copy of any regulations so confirmed, made or amended to the landlord and to the grazings committee.

(7) Common grazings regulations for the time being in force under this section shall have effect notwithstanding anything contrary thereto or inconsistent therewith contained in any lease or other agreement, whether entered into before or after the coming into force of such regulations.

[25]

Notes.—1 Section 26(2) amended by Crofters (Scotland) Act 1961 (c 58), s 15(2).
2 Word in sub-s (2)(a) inserted by Crofters (Scotland) Act 1961 (c 58), Sch 1, Pt II, para 15.
3 Section 26(2)(b) substituted by Crofting Reform (Scotland) Act 1976 (c 21), s 16(4).

---

27. Miscellaneous provisions as to common grazings, as to lands held runrig, and as to use by crofters of peat bogs, etc

(1) Any person who contravenes or fails to comply with any common grazings regulations for the time being in force under the last foregoing section of this Act shall be guilty of an offence and shall be liable on summary conviction to a fine not exceeding [¹£10], and in the case of a continuing offence to a further fine not exceeding [¹50 pence] for each day on which the offence is continued after the grazings committee or the Commission have served notice on him warning him of the offence.

(2) Where it is prescribed by the common grazings regulations applicable to the common grazings of a township that the right of a crofter to share in such grazings shall be conditional on his making his croft available during the winter season for the accommodation of any stock belonging to other persons sharing in such grazings, any crofter may apply to the grazings committee for their consent to the exclusion of such stock from his croft or from part thereof, and if he is dissatisfied with the decision of the committee on such application he may appeal therefrom to the Commission.

Any consent given under this subsection by a grazings committee or, on appeal, by the Commission may be given subject to such conditions, if any, as the committee or the Commission, as the case may be, may think proper.

(3) ²The Commission may, on the application of any crofters interested, after consultation with the grazings committee, apportion a common grazing shared by two or more townships into separate parts for the exclusive use of the several townships [³or may apportion a part of such grazing for the exclusive use of one of the townships.]

(4) [4]The Commission may, on the application of any crofter interested, after consultation with the grazings committee, apportion a part of a common grazing for the exclusive use of the crofter so applying.

(5) Notwithstanding anything in the Ground Game Act 1980, it shall be lawful for the crofters interested in a common grazing or in a part of a common grazing apportioned under subsection (3) of this section—

(a) to appoint not more than two of their number; and

(b) to authorise in writing one person bona fide employed by them for reward,

to kill and take ground game on the common grazing or the part thereof, as the case may be; and for the purposes of the said Act of 1880 any person appointed as aforesaid shall be deemed to be the occupier of the common grazing or the part thereof, but shall not have the right to authorise any other person to kill and take ground game, and any person authorised as aforesaid shall be deemed to have been authorised by the occupier of the common grazing or the part thereof to kill and take ground game with firearms or otherwise.

(6) [*Repealed by Crofters (Scotland) Act 1961 (c 58), Sch 3.*]

(7) The Commission may, on the application of any landlord or crofter interested, apportion lands held runrig among the holders thereof in such manner [[5]and subject to such conditions] as appears to the Commission in the circumstances of the case to be just and expedient.

(8) The Commission may draw up a scheme regulating the use by crofters on the same estate of peat bogs, or of seaweed for the reasonable purposes of their crofts, or of heather or grass used for thatching purposes, and the charge for the use of all or any of these may be included in the rents fixed for the crofts.

[26]

Notes.—1 Words in sub-s (1) substituted by Crofting Reform (Scotland) Act 1976 (c 21), Sch 2, para 11.

2 Section 27(3) amended by Crofters (Scotland) Act 1961 (c 58), s 15(5).

3 Words in sub-s (3) added by ibid, s 15(4).

4 Section 27(4) amended by ibid, s 15(5).

5 Words in sub-s (7) inserted by Crofting Reform (Scotland) Act 1976 (c 21), s 16(5).

Cottars

28. Provisions as to cottars

(1) [1]When a cottar if not paying rent is removed from his dwelling and any land or building occupied by him in connection therewith, or if paying rent renounces his tenancy or is removed, he shall be entitled to compensation for any permanent improvement if—

(a) the improvement is suitable to the subject; and

(b) the improvement was executed or paid for by the cottar or any of his predecessors in the same family; and

(c) either the improvement was executed otherwise than in pursuance of a specific agreement in writing under which the cottar was bound to execute the improvement, or, if the improvement was executed in pursuance of such an agreement, the cottar has not received, by way of reduction of rent or otherwise, fair consideration for the improvement.

[[2](2) The amount of the compensation payable under the foregoing subsection shall, failing agreement, be fixed by the Land Court, and—

(a) where the cottar renounced his tenancy or was removed from his subject before the commencement of the Crofters (Scotland) Act 1961, the provisions of subsections (3), (4) and (5) of section fourteen of this Act (which relates to compensation to crofters for improvements) shall apply in relation to such cottar as they apply in relation to a crofter whose tenancy was terminated before the said commencement;

(b) where the cottar renounces his tenancy or is removed from his subject after the commencement of the said Act of 1961, the provisions of subsection (3) of section fourteen of this Act and of subsections (1) and (2) of section six of the said Act of 1961 (which relate to compensation to crofters for improvements) shall apply in relation to such cottar as they apply in relation to crofters.

(2A) Where compensation falls to be assessed under subsections (1) and (2) of section six of the said Act of 1961, as applied by paragraph (b) of the last foregoing subsection, in respect of any permanent improvement and the amount of such compensation is fixed by the Land Court under the last foregoing subsection, then if the cottar is qualified as mentioned in the next following subsection he may request the Land Court to determine the amount which would have been payable by way of compensation in respect of that improvement if the said Act of 1961 had not been passed and if the amount last mentioned is greater than the amount fixed by the Land Court as aforesaid, the difference between the two said amounts shall be payable to the cottar by the Secretary of State:

Provided that—

(a) the Secretary of State shall be entitled to set off any amount due to him by the cottar in respect of a loan made under subsection (2) of section twenty-two of this Act or section nine of the Act of 1911 against any sum payable to the cottar by the Secretary of State under this subsection; and

(b) this subsection shall not apply where compensation in respect of the improvement in question has on a previous occasion fallen to be assessed under subsections (1) and (2) of section six of the said Act of 1961, as applied as aforesaid.

(2B) The reference in the last foregoing subsection to a cottar who is qualified is a reference to a cottar—

(a) whose occupation of the subject in question began before the commencement of the said Act of 1961, or

(b) who occupies such subject as heir-at-law, legatee or assignee of his immediate predecessor as occupier of the subject, and each of whose predecessors (being in each case a person whose occupation of the subject began after the commencement of the said Act of 1961) occupied the subject as heir-in-law, legatee or assignee of his immediate predecessor.]

(3) The Secretary of State shall have the like powers to provide assistance by way of loan, grant and the supply of building or other materials for the erection, improvement or rebuilding of dwelling-houses and other buildings for cottars as he has to provide assistance for the erection, improvement or rebuilding of dwelling-houses and other buildings for crofters, and subsections (2), (4), (5) and (7) of section twenty-two of this Act shall apply accordingly.

(4) In this section—

'cottar' means the occupier of a dwelling-house situate in the crofting counties with or without land who pays no rent, or the tenant from year to year of a dwelling-house situate as aforesaid who resides therein and who pays therefor an annual rent not exceeding six pounds in money, whether with or without garden ground but without arable or pasture land.

'predecessors in the same family' means in relation to a cottar the wife or husband of the cottar and any person to whom the cottar or the wife or husband of the cottar might, failing nearer heirs, have succeeded in case of intestacy.

[27]

Notes.—1 Section 28(1) excluded by Crofting Reform (Scotland) Act 1976 (c 21), s 6(2)(c).

2 Section 28(2), (2A), (2B), substituted for s 28(2) by Crofters (Scotland) Act 1961 (c 58), Sch 1, Pt I, para 7.

Miscellaneous and General Provisions

29. Service of notices

(1) Any notice of the purposes of this Act shall be in writing, and any notice or other document required or authorised by or under this Act to be given to or served on any person shall be duly given or served if it is delivered to him or left at his proper address or sent to him by post.

(2) Where any notice or other document is to be given to or served on a person as being the person having any interest in land and it is not practicable after reasonable inquiry to ascertain his name or address, the notice or document may be given or served by addressing it to him by the description of the person having that interest in the land (naming it) and delivering the notice or document to some responsible person on the land or by affixing it, or a copy of it, to some conspicuous object on the land.

[28]

30. Provisions as to entry and inspection

(1) Any person authorised by the Secretary of State or the Commission in that behalf shall have power at all reasonable times to enter on and inspect any land for the purpose of determining whether, and if so in what manner, any of the powers conferred on the Secretary of State or the Commission by this Act are to be exercised in relation to the land, or whether, and if so in what manner, any direction given under any such power has been complied with.

(2) Any person authorised as aforesaid who proposes to exercise any power of entry or inspection conferred by this Act shall if so required produce some duly authenticated document showing his authority to exercise the power.

(3) Admission to any land shall not be demanded as of right in the exercise of any such power as aforesaid unless in the case of land being used for residential purposes seven days, or in the case of any other land twenty-four hours, notice of the intended entry has been given to the occupier of the land.

(4) Any person who obstructs any person authorised by the Secretary of State or the Commission exercising any such power as aforesaid shall be guilty of an offence and shall be liable on summary conviction to a fine not exceeding [¹£10] in the case of a first offence of twenty pounds in the case of a second or any subsequent offence.

[29]

Note.—1 Word in sub-s (4) substituted by Crofting Reform (Scotland) Act 1976 (c 21), Sch 2, para 13.

31. Building grants and loans to owner-occupiers of like economic status as crofters

(1) ¹The Secretary of State shall have the like powers to provide assistance by way of loan, grant and the supply of building or other materials for the erection, improvement or rebuilding of buildings other than dwelling-houses for owners of holdings to which this section applies as he has to provide assistance for the erection, improvement or rebuilding of such buildings for crofters; and subsections (2), (4) and (5) of section twenty-two of this Act shall apply accordingly.

(2) This section applies to any holding which—
    (a) is situate in the crofting counties; and
    [²(b) is either—
          (i) a holding of which the area does not exceed 30 hectares, or
          (ii) a holding of which the annual rent, if it were a croft let to a crofter under this Act and the Crofters (Scotland) Act 1961, would not in the opinion of the Secretary of State exceed £100, or

    (iii) a holding which exceeds 30 hectares and of which the annual rent if it were a croft so let would in the opinion of the Secretary of State exceed £100, but which in the opinion of the Secretary of State is not substantially larger than 30 hectares or is capable of being let as a croft at an annual rent not substantially in excess of £100;] and

(c) is owned by a person who in the opinion of the Secretary of State is of substantially the same economic status as a crofter; and

(d) is occupied by the owner thereof.

(3) The provisions of the Third Schedule to this Act shall apply in relation to any loan made to the owner of a holding under this section.

[30]

Notes.—1 Section 31(1) extended by Crofting Reform (Scotland) Act 1976 (c 21), s 12(2).
2 Section 31(2)(b) substituted by Crofting Reform (Scotland) Act 1976 (c 21), Sch 2, para 13.

32. Provisions as to compulsory purchase of land and as to management of land

(1) Where by virtue of any provision of this Act the Secretary of State is deemed to be authorised to purchase land compulsorily, then in relation to any such compulsory purchase the Lands Clauses Acts and other enactments mentioned in Part I of the Second Schedule to the Acquisition of Land (Authorisation Procedure) (Scotland) Act 1947, shall be incorporated in accordance with the provisions of the said Part I as if the Secretary of State had been authorised under section one of that Act to purchase the land compulsorily; and [¹the Land Compensation (Scotland) Act 1963], shall have effect in relation to any such compulsory purchase subject to the provisions of Part II of that Schedule, of the proviso to subsection (8) of section sixteen of this Act and of the next following subsection.

(2) The power conferred by [²section 39 of the Land Compensation (Scotland) Act 1963], to withdraw a notice to treat shall not be exercisable in the case of a notice to treat which is deemed to have been served by virtue of subsection (8) of section sixteen of this Act or of [³subsection (9) or (10) of section nine of the Crofters (Scotland) Act 1961.]

(3) The Secretary of State may manage, farm, sell, let or otherwise deal with or dispose of land acquired by him under this Act in such manner as appears to him expedient for the purpose for which it was acquired.

[31]

Notes.—1 Words in sub-s (1) substituted by virtue of Land Compensation (Scotland) Act 1963 (c 51), s 47(1).
2 Words in sub-s (2) substituted by virtue of Land Compensation (Scotland) Act 1963 (c 51), s 47(2).
3 Words in sub-s (2) substituted by Crofters (Scotland) Act 1961 (c 58), Sch 1, Pt II, para 16.

33. Provisions as to representations

(1) Any enactment in this Act providing, in relation to the taking of any action by the Secretary of State, for his taking the action after affording to a person an opportunity of making representations to the Secretary of State shall be construed as a provision that the Secretary of State shall comply with the following requirements.

(2) The Secretary of State shall give notice to the said person specifying the matter under consideration and informing him of the effect of the next following subsection.

(3) A person to whom notice is given as aforesaid may within the time specified in the notice make representations to the Secretary of State in writing, and, whether or not representations are made to the Secretary of State in writing, may within the time so specified require that an opportunity be afforded to him of being heard by a person

appointed by the Secretary of State for the purpose; and, if he so requires, such an opportunity shall be afforded to him and, on the same occasion, to any other person to whom under the enactment referred to in subsection (1) of this section the Secretary of State is required to afford such an opportunity, and the Secretary of State shall not take action in relation to the matter until he has considered any representations made as aforesaid.

(4) Where any enactment in this Act provides in relation to the taking of any action by the Commission for their taking the action after affording to a person an opportunity of making representations to them, the provisions of this section shall have effect in relation thereto with the substitution for references to the Secretary of State of references to the Commission.

[32]

34. Determination of disputes, etc

(1) The provisions of the Landholders Acts with regard to the Land Court shall, with any necessary modifications, apply for the determination of any matter which they [¹have jurisdiction] under this Act [²or the Crofting Reform (Scotland) Act 1976] to determine, in like manner as those provisions apply for the determination by the Land Court of matters referred to them under those Acts.

(2) [*Repealed by Crofters (Scotland) Act 1961 (c 58), Sch 3.*]

[33]

Notes.—1 Words in sub-s (1) substituted by Crofters (Scotland) Act 1961 (c 58), Sch 1, Pt II, para 17.
2 Words in sub-s (1) inserted by Crofting Reform (Scotland) Act 1976 (c 21), Sch 2, para 14.

35. Financial provisions

(1) The expenses of the Commission shall be defrayed by the Secretary of State.

(2) All expenses incurred by the Secretary of State under the provisions of this Act shall be defrayed out of moneys provided by Parliament.

(3) All sums received by the Secretary of State under the provisions of this Act shall be paid into the Exchequer.

[34]

36. Regulations

Any regulations made by the Secretary of State under this Act shall be embodied in a statutory instrument which shall be subject to annulment in pursuance of a resolution of either House of Parliament.

[35]

37. Interpretation

(1) In this Act, unless the context otherwise requires, the following expressions have the meanings respectively assigned to them—
'the Act of 1886' means the Crofters Holdings (Scotland) Act 1886;
'the Act of 1911' means the Small Landholders (Scotland) Act 1911;
'croft' and 'crofter' have the meanings assigned to them respectively by section three of this Act;
'the Crofters Holdings Book' has the meaning assigned to it by section thirty-nine of this Act;
'crofting counties' means the [¹former] counties of Argyll, Caithness, Inverness, Orkney, Ross and Cromarty, Sutherland and Zetland;

'fixed equipment' has the like meaning as in the Agricultural Holdings (Scotland) Act 1949;

'functions' includes powers and duties;

'Land Court' means the Scottish Land Court;

'the Landholders Acts' means the Small Landholders (Scotland) Acts 1886 to 1931;

'landlord' means any person for the time being entitled to receive the rents and profits, or to take possession, of a croft;

'permanent improvement' means any of the improvements specified in the Fifth Schedule to this Act; [2Provided that no building or other structure erected on a croft shall be held to be a permanent improvement on the croft unless it is a fixture on the land;]

'prescribed' means prescribed by regulations made by the Secretary of State;

'predecessors in the tenancy' means in relation to a crofter the persons who before him have been tenants of the croft since it was last vacant;

'statutory successor' means any person who under this Act has succeeded or may succeed to a croft whether as [3a person to whom the tenancy of the croft has been transferred in pursuance of section 16(2) of the Succession (Scotland) Act 1964 or as the executor,] heir-at-law, legatee or assignee of his immediate predecessor being a crofter in occupation of the croft;

'Whitsunday' and 'Martinmas' mean respectively the twenty-eighth day of May and the twenty-eighth day of November.

(2) [*Repealed by Crofters (Scotland) Act 1961 (c 58), Sch 3.*]

(3) References in this Act to any enactment shall, unless the context otherwise requires, be construed as references to that enactment as amended by or under any other enactment, including this Act.

[36]

Notes.—1 Word inserted by Local Government (Scotland) Act 1973 (c 65), Sch 27, Pt II, para 120.

2 Proviso added by Crofters (Scotland) Act 1961 (c 58), Sch 1, Pt II, para 18.

3 Words inserted by Law Reform (Miscellaneous Provisions) (Scotland) Act 1968 (c 70), Sch 2, Pt I, para 18.

---

38. Application of Act and modification of enactments in relation to the crofting counties

(1) This Act shall apply to land an interest in which belongs to Her Majesty in right of the Crown and land an interest in which belongs to a government department or is held in trust for Her Majesty for the purposes of a government department; but in its application to any land an interest in which belongs or is held as aforesaid this Act shall have effect subject to such modifications as may be prescribed.

(2) Subject to the provisions of the two next following subsections, references in any enactment (other than [1section twenty-five of the Act of 1911 and] this Act) or in any investment to a landholder or statutory small tenant and to a holding within the meaning of the Landholders Acts and to the Landholders Acts shall, unless the context otherwise requires, be construed in the application of that enactment to the crofting counties respectively as references to a crofter and to a croft within the meaning of this Act, and as including a reference to this Act.

(3) The enactments specified in Part I of the Sixth Schedule to this Act shall cease to apply to the crofting counties to the extent specified in the second column of the said Part I.

(4) The enactments specified in Part II of the Sixth Schedule to this Act shall in their application to the crofting counties have effect subject to the modifications specified in the second column of the said Part II.

[37]

39. Transitional provisions and savings

(1) The tenancy of a crofter under this Act shall, in the case of every person who at the commencement of this Act became a crofter, be deemed, so far as is consistent with the provisions of this Act, to be a continuance of his tenancy as a landholder or a statutory small tenant, and all contracts and other instruments shall be read and construed accordingly.

(2) The book (heretofore called the 'Landholders Holdings Book') kept in pursuance of section twenty-seven of the Act of 1886, shall in the crofting counties be called the 'Crofters Holdings Book'.

(3) Where the rent payable for a croft which was immediately before the commencement of this Act a holding to which the provisions of the Landholders Acts relating to statutory small tenants applied was last fixed by the Land Court before the commencement of this Act, it may, notwithstanding anything in the proviso to subsection (3) of section five of this Act, be altered by the Land Court at any time after the commencement of this Act.

(4) Notwithstanding anything in this Act, the right of any person to succeed to the tenancy of a holding, whether by virtue of a bequest made by the tenant thereof or by virtue of the right to the tenancy having devolved upon the heir-at-law of the tenant, shall, if the tenant died before the commencement of this Act, be determined as if this Act had not passed.

(5) Save as expressly provided in this Act, nothing in this Act shall affect any order, rule, regulation, record, application, reference, appointment, loan, agreement, finding or award made, approval, consent or direction given, decree or instrument granted, proceeding taken, notice served or given, condition imposed, rent or amount of compensation fixed, or thing done in the crofting counties or in relation to land therein, under any enactment relating to landholders, statutory small tenants or cottars which by virtue of this Act has ceased to apply to the crofting counties or to any land therein, but any such order, rule, regulation, record, application, reference, appointment, loan, agreement, finding, award, approval, consent, direction, decree, instrument, proceeding, notice, condition, rent or amount of compensation or thing which is in force at the commencement of this Act shall continue in force and, so far as it could have been made, given, granted, taken, served, imposed, fixed or done under the corresponding provision of this Act, shall have effect as if it had been made, given, granted, taken, served, imposed, fixed or done under that corresponding provision.

[38]

40. Citation and commencement

(1) This Act may be cited as the Crofters (Scotland) Act 1955.

(2) [1]This Act shall come into operation on such date as Her Majesty may by Order in Council appoint; and an Order under this subsection may appoint different dates in relation to different provisions of this Act.

[39]

Note.—1 By virtue of SI 1955/1201 the date appointed under s 40(2) was 1 October 1955.

SCHEDULES

FIRST SCHEDULE

PROVISIONS AS TO THE CROFTERS COMMISSION

Constitution of the Commission

1. The Commission shall be a body corporate and shall have a common seal.

2. Every member of the Commission shall hold and vacate office in accordance with the terms of the instrument under which he is appointed; but notwithstanding anything in such an instrument any member of the Commission may resign his office by a notice given under his hand to the Secretary of State, and a member of the Commission who ceases to hold office shall be eligible for re-appointment to the Commission.

3. [*Repealed by House of Commons Disqualification Act 1957 (c 20), Sch 4, Pt I.*]

4. The Secretary of State shall pay to the members of the Commission such remuneration and such allowances as he may, with the approval of the Treasury, determine.

[¹4A. The Secretary of State shall, in the case of any member of the Commission to whom he may with the approval of the Minister for the Civil Service determine that this paragraph applies, pay such pension, allowance or gratuity to or in respect of the member on his retirement or death, or make such payments towards the provision of such a pension, allowance or gratuity, as he may, with the like approval, determine.

4B. If a person ceases to be a member of the Commission and it appears to the Secretary of State that there are special circumstances which make it right that that person should receive compensation he may, with the approval of the said Minister, pay to that person a sum of such amount as he may, with the like approval, determine.]

Note.—1 Paras 4A, 4B, inserted by Crofting Reform (Scotland) Act 1976 (c 21), s 18.

Meetings and Proceedings of the Commission

5. The quorum of the Commission shall be three or such larger number as the Commission may from time to time determine.

6. The proceedings of the Commission shall not be invalidated by any vacancy in the membership of the Commission or by any defect in the appointment of any member thereof.

7. If at any meeting of the Commission the votes are equally divided on any question, the person acting as chairman of the meeting shall have a second or casting vote.

8. The Commission shall refer to one or more of their number for report and recommendation such matters as may be determined by the Commission and shall delegate to one or more of their number such of the functions conferred on the Commission by this Act, to such extent and subject to such conditions or restrictions, as may with the approval of the Secretary of State be so determined.

9. In any application or other proceeding coming before them the Commission may order that the evidence shall be taken on oath.

10. Subject to the foregoing provisions of this Schedule, the Commission shall have power to regulate their own procedure.

Office, Officers and Servants

11. The Commission shall have an office in the crofting counties at which communications and notices will at all times be received.

12. The Secretary of State may provide the services of such officers and servants as the Commission may require.

Instruments executed or issued by the Commission

13. The application of the seal of the Commission to any document shall be attested by at least one member of the Commission and by the person for the time being acting as secretary to the Commission.

14. Every document purporting to be an instrument issued by the Commission and to be sealed and attested as aforesaid or to be duly signed on behalf of the Commission shall be received in evidence and shall be deemed to be such an instrument without further proof unless the contrary is shown.

[40]

SECOND SCHEDULE

THE STATUTORY CONDITIONS

1. The crofter shall pay his rent at the terms at which it is due and payable.

2. The crofter shall not, except in accordance with the provisions of this Act, execute any deed purporting to assign his tenancy.

3. The crofter shall, by himself or his family, with or without hired labour, cultivate his croft, without prejudice to the right hereby conferred on him to make such use thereof for subsidiary or auxiliary occupations as, in case of dispute [[1]the Land Court] may find to be reasonable and not inconsistent with the cultivation of the croft.

Note.—1 Words in statutory condition 3 substituted by Crofters (Scotland) Act 1961 (c 58), Sch 1, Pt II, para 20.

[[1]3A The crofter shall provide such fixed equipment on his croft as may be necessary to enable him to cultivate the croft.]

Note.—1 Para 3A added by Crofters (Scotland) Act 1961 (c 58), Sch 1, Pt II, para 20.

4. The crofter shall not, to the prejudice of the interest of the landlord, persistently injure the croft by the dilapidation of buildings or, after notice in writing has been given by the landlord to the crofter not to commit, or to desist from, the particular injury specified in the notice, by the deterioration of the soil.

[[1]5. A crofter shall not sublet his croft or any part thereof otherwise than with the consent in writing of the Commission and in accordance with such conditions (which shall not include conditions relating to rent) as the Commission in giving their consent may impose:
   Provided that nothing in this paragraph shall be construed as debarring a crofter from subletting any dwelling-house or other building forming part of his croft to holiday visitors.]

Note.—1 Para 5 substituted by Crofters (Scotland) Act 1961 (c 58), Sch 1, Pt II, para 20.

6. The crofter shall not, except in accordance with the provisions of this Act, subdivide his croft.

7. The crofter shall not, without the consent in writing of the landlord, erect or suffer to be erected on the croft any dwelling-house otherwise than in substitution for a dwelling-house which at the commencement of this Act was already on the croft:

Provided that, if at the commencement of this Act there was no dwelling-house on the croft, the crofter may erect one dwelling-house thereon.

8. The crofter shall not persistently violate any written condition signed by him for the protection of the interest of the landlord or of neighbouring crofters which is legally applicable to the croft and which the Land Court shall find to be reasonable.

9. The crofter shall not do any act whereby he becomes notour bankrupt within the meaning of the Bankruptcy (Scotland) Act 1913, and shall not execute a trust deed for creditors.

10. The crofter shall permit the landlord or any person authorised by the landlord in that behalf to enter upon the croft for the purpose of exercising (subject always to the payment of such compensation as in case of dispute the Land Court may find to be reasonable in respect of any damage done or occasioned thereby) any of the following rights, and shall not obstruct the landlord or any person authorised as aforesaid in the exercise of any of such rights, that is to say—
   (a) mining or taking minerals, or digging or searching for minerals;
   (b) quarrying or taking stone, marble, gravel, sand, clay, slate or other workable mineral;
   (c) using for any estate purpose any springs of water rising on the croft and not required for the use thereof;
   (d) cutting or taking timber or peats, excepting timber and other trees planted by the crofter or any of his predecessors in the tenancy, or which may be necessary for ornament or shelter, and excepting also such peats as may be required for the use of the croft;
   (e) opening or making roads, fences, drains and water-courses;
   (f) passing and re-passing to and from the shore of the sea or any loch with or without vehicles for the purpose of exercising any right of property or other right belonging to the landlord;
   (g) viewing or examining at reasonable times the state of the croft and all buildings or improvements thereon;
   (h) hunting, shooting, fishing or taking game or fish, wild birds or vermin;
but nothing in this paragraph shall be held to preclude the crofter from recovering any compensation for damage by game which is recoverable under section fifteen of the Agricultural Holdings (Scotland) Act 1949, by a tenant, and that section shall apply accordingly, with the substitution, however, of the Land Court for arbitration.

11. The crofter shall not on his croft, without the consent in writing of the landlord, open any house for the sale of intoxicating liquors.

12. In this Schedule—
   the expression 'cultivate' includes the use of a croft for horticulture or for any purpose of husbandry, including the keeping or breeding of livestock, poultry or bees, and the growing of fruit, vegetables and the like;
   the expression 'game' means deer, hares, rabbits, pheasants, partridges, grouse, blackgame, capercailzie, ptarmigan, woodcock, snipe, wild duck, widgeon and teal.

[41]

THIRD SCHEDULE

PROVISIONS AS TO SECURITY, ETC, OF LOANS

1. The loan shall be secured by a [¹heritable security over] the land in favour of the Secretary of State.

Note.—1 Words in para 1 substituted by Crofting Reform (Scotland) Act 1976 (c 21), Sch 2, para 15(a).

2. The loan shall either be repaid by half-yearly instalments of principal with such interest and within such period (not exceeding such period as may be fixed by the Treasury) from the date of the loan, or at such date thereafter not exceeding eighteen months as may be agreed on, or shall be repaid with such interest and within such period by a terminable annuity payable by half-yearly instalments.

3. The amount for the time being unpaid may at any time be discharged, and any such terminable annuity may at any time be redeemed in accordance with tables fixed by the Secretary of State.

4. A certificate by the Secretary of State that the whole of the loan has been repaid or that such terminable annuity has been redeemed shall, without any other instrument, operate as a discharge of the loan or extinction of the terminable annuity, as the case may be, and the recording of such certificate in the . . .[1] Register of Sasines shall be equivalent to the recording of a discharge of the said [[2]heritable security.]

Notes.—1 Word in para 4 repealed by Crofting Reform (Scotland) Act 1976 (c 21), Sch 3.
2 Words in para 4 substituted by Crofting Reform (Scotland) Act 1976 (c 21), Sch 2, para 15(b).

---

5. The Secretary of State shall cause to be prepared and duly recorded all deeds, writs and instruments necessary for securing the payment of any loan over land made by him, and shall include in the loan the cost so incurred, or to be incurred, in accordance with scales set forth in tables fixed by the Secretary of State.

[42]

FOURTH SCHEDULE

[Repealed by Crofters (Scotland) Act 1961 (c 58), Sch 3.]

[43]

FIFTH SCHEDULE

Permanent Improvements

1. Dwelling-house.

[[1]1A. Improvement works carried out in compliance with a notice of a final resolution served under Part II of the Housing (Scotland) Act 1974.]

2. Farm offices.

3. Subsoil and other drains.

4. Walls and fences.

5. Deep trenching.

6. Clearing the ground.

7. Planting trees.

8. Making piers or landing stages.

9. Roads practicable for vehicles from the croft to the public road or the sea shore.

10. All other improvements which, in the judgment of the Land Court, will add to the value of the croft [[2]as an agricultural subject.]

[[3]11. Buildings or other structures erected under section five of the Crofters (Scotland) Act 1961, being buildings or structures which are fixtures on the land; or works executed under the said section five.]

Notes.—1 Para 1A substituted by Housing (Scotland) Act 1974 (c 45), s 25(3).
2 Words in para 10 substituted by Crofters (Scotland) Act 1961 (c 58), Sch 1, Pt II, para 21.
3 Para 11 added by Crofters (Scotland) Act 1961 (c 58), Sch 1, Pt II, para 21.

[44]

SIXTH SCHEDULE

APPLICATION OF ENACTMENTS TO CROFTING COUNTIES
PART I

Enactments ceasing to have effect

Enactment	Provisions ceasing to have effect in crofting counties
The Crofters Holdings (Scotland) Act 1886 (49 & 50 Vict c 29)	Sections one to ten. In section twelve the words from 'It shall be competent for the Crofters Commission to draw up a scheme' to the end of the section. Section sixteen. Sections nineteen and twenty. Sections thirty-one and thirty-four. The Schedule.
The Crofters Holdings (Scotland) Act 1887 (50 & 51 Vict c 24)	The whole Act.
The Crofters Common Grazings Regulation Act 1891 (54 & 55 Vict c 41)	The whole Act.
The Crofters Common Grazings Regulation Act 1908 (8 Edw 7 c 50)	The whole Act.
The Small Landholders (Scotland) Act 1911 (1 & 2 Geo 5 c 49)	Sections one and two. Sections eight to ten. Sections twelve to fifteen. Sections seventeen to twenty-three. Section twenty-four except paragraph (b) of subsection (5). Section twenty-seven. Sections thirty-two and thirty-three.
The Land Settlement (Scotland) Act 1919 (9 & 10 Geo 5 c 97)	Sections twelve and thirteen. Section fourteen except in relation to paragraph (b) of the subsection substituted for subsection (5) of section twenty-four of the Act of 1911. Section seventeen and the Second Schedule in so far as they amend subsection (6) of section seven and section twenty-four of the Act of 1911.
The Small Landholders (Scotland) Act 1931 (21 & 22 Geo 5 c 44)	Section one. Sections three, five and six. Sections eight to fourteen. Section eighteen. Sections twenty-two to twenty-five.
The Agriculture (Scotland) Act 1948 (11 & 12 Geo 6 c 45)	Part II and the Fifth and Sixth Schedules in so far as they apply to any land being or forming part of a croft within the meaning of this Act. Sections sixty-six and seventy-seven.

PART II

Modification of Enactments

Enactment	Modification of enactments in application to crofting counties
The Small Landholders (Scotland) Act 1911 (1 & 2 Geo 5 c 49)	In section seven, subsections (1) and (6) and in paragraph (f) of subsection (11) the words from 'and it may be a term' to the end of the paragraph shall be omitted. In section twenty-six, subsection (1), in subsection (2) the words from 'and shall not' to the end of the subsection, and subsections (3), (6), (9) and (10) shall be omitted; and in subsection (7) for the words from the beginning of the subsection to 'nothing in that section' there shall be substituted the words 'Nothing in section thirty-three of the Act of 1886'. In section thirty-one, in subsection (1) the definitions of 'Act of 1887', 'Act of 1891', 'Act of 1908' and 'statutory successor', and subsection (4) shall be omitted.

[45]

Crofters (Scotland) Act 1961 (9 and 10 Eliz 2 (c 58))

ARRANGEMENT OF SECTIONS

1. [*Amends Crofters (Scotland) Act 1955 (c 21), s 1(3).*]

[46]

2. Provisions as to new crofts and enlarged crofts and common grazings

(1) [*Repealed by Crofting Reform (Scotland) Act 1976 (c 21), Sch 3.*]

(2) Where the owner of any land which is not itself a croft and which does not form part of a croft agrees to grant a tenancy of such land to any crofter, then—
   (a) except in such a case as is mentioned in paragraph (b) of this subsection, if the owner of the said land and the crofter agree that such land will form part of any croft of which the crofter is tenant, the land shall, as from the date of entry under the said tenancy, form part of such croft, and the Act of 1955 [1this Act and the Crofting Reform (Scotland) Act 1976] shall apply accordingly to the croft as so enlarged;
   (b) in a case where the area of the croft (exclusive of any common pasture or grazing held therewith) together with the area of the land exceeds [230 hectares]

and the rent of the croft together with the rent under the said tenancy exceeds [²£100], the [²Commission] may, on an application in that behalf made to [²them] jointly by the owner of the land and the crofter, direct that the land shall form part of the croft and, if [²they make] such direction, then as from the date of the direction or the date of entry under the said tenancy, whichever is the later, the land shall form part of the croft, and the Act of 1955 [³this Act and the Crofting Reform (Scotland) Act 1976] shall apply accordingly to the croft as so enlarged.

[⁴(2A) The Commission shall make a direction under subsection (2) above only if they are satisfied that such a direction—

(a) would be of benefit to the croft; and
(b) would not result in the croft as enlarged by the land referred to in that subsection being substantially larger than 30 hectares or capable of being let as a croft at an annual rent substantially in excess of £100.]

(3) Where any such land as is mentioned in paragraph (a) of subsection (3) of section eight of this Act is included in a reorganisation scheme made under that section and confirmed by the Secretary of State, then as from the date on which the scheme is put into effect the Act of 1955 [⁵this Act and the Crofting Reform (Scotland) Act 1976] shall apply to such land.

(4) Where the owner of any land to which the Act of 1955 and this Act do not apply agrees to grant rights in any pasture or grazing land to the crofters sharing in any common grazing and the said owner and crofters agree that such land will form part of the said common grazing, then as from the date on which such rights are first exercisable by the crofters, the land shall form part of the common grazing, and the said Acts shall apply accordingly to the common grazing as so enlarged.

(5) . . .⁶ the owner of any land which becomes part of a croft or of a common grazing by virtue of paragraph (a) of subsection (2) of this section or, as the case may be, the last foregoing subsection, shall give notice to the Commission of the enlargement of such croft or common grazing.

(6) In the application to the crofting counties of section four of the Small Landholders and Agricultural Holdings (Scotland) Act 1931 (which amongst other things confers power on the Land Court in certain circumstances to cancel the registration of a person as a crofter) the words from 'and where a person' to the end of the section shall cease to have effect. . . .⁷

(7) [*Repealed by Crofting Reform (Scotland) Act 1976 (c 21), Sch 3.*]

[47]

Notes.—1 Words in sub-s (1(a) substituted by Crofting Reform (Scotland) Act 1976 (c 21), Sch 2, para 17(b).
2 Words in sub-s 2(b) substituted by ibid, s 17(c).
3 Words in sub-s 2(b) substituted by ibid, s 17(b).
4 Section 2(2A) inserted by Crofting Reform (Scotland) Act 1976 (c 21), Sch 2, para 17(d).
5 Words in sub-s (3) substituted by Crofting Reform (Scotland) Act 1976 (c 21), Sch 2, para 17(b).
6 Words in sub-s (5) repealed by Crofting Reform (Scotland) Act 1976 (c 21), Sch 3.
7 Words in sub-s (6) repealed by Statute Law (Repeals) Act 1974 (c 22), Sch, Pt V.

---

3. Commission to maintain Register of Crofts

(1) It shall be the duty of the Commission to compile and maintain a register of crofts (in this Act referred to as 'the Register of Crofts').

(2) There shall be entered in the Register of Crofts—

(a) the name, location, rent and extent of every croft;
(b) the name of the tenant and the landlord of each croft; and
(c) such other matters relating to each croft as the Commission may, with the approval of the Secretary of State, decide are proper to be entered in the Register;

and the Commission shall from time to time insert new entries in the Register or alter or omit existing entries so far as may be necessary to ensure the accuracy of the Register and shall send a copy of any new entry inserted by them after the commencement of this Act, or of any entry altered by them after such commencement, to the landlord and the tenant of the croft concerned, and shall intimate the omission of any entry to the owner and the tenant (if any) of the land concerned.

[[1]Provided that the Commission shall not be required under this subsection to send a copy of any new entry or of any entry altered by them or to intimate the omission of any entry to any person who has to any extent assisted the Commission in the performance of their duties of inserting or, as the case may be, altering or omitting an entry by the furnishing of information to them.]

(3) The Commission shall, on a request for an extract of any entry in the Register of Crofts being made to them by a person who, in their opinion, has good reason for desiring an extract of the said entry, furnish that person with such extract certified by the person for the time being acting as secretary to the Commission; and a document purporting to be an extract of an entry in the Register and to be certified as aforesaid shall be sufficient evidence that the Register contains such an entry.

(4) Subsections (2) to (4) of section fifteen of the Act of 1955 (which relate to the compilation by the Commission of a register of crofts) shall cease to have effect, but the register of crofts compiled by the Commission under the said subsection (2) shall, so far as it contains particulars which are required by or under subsection (2) of this section to be entered in the Register of Crofts, be deemed to have been compiled by the Commission in pursuance of subsection (1) of this section.

[48]

Note.—1 Proviso to sub-s (2) added by Crofting Reform (Scotland) Act 1976 (c 21), Sch 2, para 18.

---

4. Determination of questions by Land Court

(1) Without prejudice to any jurisdiction exercisable by them under any enactment, the Land Court shall have power to determine, either on the application of any person having an interest or on a reference made to them by the Commission, any question of fact or law arising under the Act of 1955 or this Act [[1]or the Crofting Reform (Scotland) Act 1976], whether such question arises before or after the commencement of this Act, and including, without prejudice to the said generality,—

(a) the question whether any holding is a croft;
(b) the question who is the tenant of any croft;
(c) any question as to the boundaries of a croft or of any pasture or grazing land a right in which forms part of a croft;
(d) the question whether any land is or forms part of a common pasture or grazing to which the Act of 1955 and this Act [[1]and the Crofting Reform (Scotland) Act 1976] apply:
    Provided that the Land Court shall not have power under this subsection to determine—
(i) any question of a kind reserved by the Act of 1955 or this Act [[1]or the Crofting Reform (Scotland) Act 1976] to a court other than the Land Court; or
(ii) any question (other than a question of law) decided by the Secretary of State or the Commission in the discharge of any of his or their functions under the Act of 1955 or this Act [[1]or the Crofting Reform (Scotland) Act 1976].

(2) The Land Court shall cause intimation to be made to the Commission of their determination on any question coming before them under the Landholders Acts (in their application to the crofting counties) or the Act of 1955 or this Act [[1]or the Crofting Reform (Scotland) Act 1976].

(3) So much of subsection (2) of section twenty-five of the Act of 1911 as provides for the stating by the Land Court of a special case for the opinion of the Court of Session on any question of law arising in proceedings in the Land Court under the Landholders Acts shall apply in relation to proceedings in the Land Court under any other enactment as it applies in relation to the first-mentioned proceedings.

(4) [*Repealed by Statute Law (Repeals) Act 1974 (c 22), Sch, Pt V*].

[49]

Note.—1 Words in sub-ss (1), (2) inserted by Crofting Reform (Scotland) Act 1976 (c 21), Sch 2, para 19.

---

5.   Permanent improvements made on crofts for purposes of subsidiary or auxiliary occupations

(1) A crofter may erect any buildings or other structures, or execute any works, on his croft which—
  (a) are reasonably required to enable him to make use of the croft for any subsidiary or auxiliary occupation in accordance with paragraph 3 of the Second Schedule to the Act of 1955, and
  (b) will not interfere substantially with the use of the croft as an agricultural subject.

(2) Any buildings or other structures erected, or any works executed, under the foregoing subsection on any croft shall, if in the case of any such buildings or structures they are fixtures on the land, be permanent improvements on that croft and shall be deemed to be suitable to the croft for the purposes of paragraph (a) of subsection (1) of section fourteen of the Act of 1955.

(3) The provisions of the last foregoing subsection shall apply in relation to buildings or other structures erected, or works executed, on any croft before the commencement of this Act if such buildings, structures or works could have been erected or executed under subsection (1) of this section had the said subsection (1) then been in force:
    Provided that nothing in this subsection shall authorise the payment of compensation under section fourteen of the Act of 1955 in respect of any such buildings, structures or works as are mentioned in this subsection where the crofter has renounced his tenancy or has been removed from his croft before the commencement of this Act.   [50]

6.   Assessment of compensation for improvements

(1) The amount of any compensation payable under subsection (1) of section fourteen of the Act of 1955 to a crofter who renounces his tenancy or is removed from his croft after the commencement of this Act [[1], or to the executor of a deceased crofter,] in respect of a permanent improvement [[2]on the croft] shall be a sum equal to—
  [(a) the value of that improvement as at the date when—
      (i)   the crofter renounced his tenancy, or
      (ii)   the crofter was removed from the croft, or
      (iii) the tenancy of the croft was terminated in pursuance of section 16(3) of the Succession (Scotland) Act 1964,
    as the case may be,] calculated in accordance with the provisions of the next following subsection, less
  (b) the value of any assistance or consideration which may be proved to have been given by the landlord of the croft or any of his predecessors in title in respect of the improvement.

(2) For the purposes of the foregoing subsection, the value of an improvement on any croft shall be taken to be the amount, if any, which, having regard to the location of the croft and any other circumstances which might affect the demand for the tenancy thereof, the landlord might reasonably be expected to receive in respect of the

improvement from a person who might reasonably be expected to obtain the tenancy of the croft if the croft were offered on the open market for letting . . .[3] with entry on the date referred to in paragraph (a) of the foregoing subsection.

(3) [3]Where compensation falls to be assessed under the two foregoing subsections in respect of any permanent improvement on a croft and the amount of such compensation is fixed or assessed by the Land Court under subsection (8) of section fourteen of the Act of 1955 . . .[4] or paragraph (a) of subsection (3) of section nine of this Act, then if the crofter [[6]or, as the case may be, the executor of the deceased crofter] is qualified as mentioned in the next following subsection he may request the Land Court to determine the amount which would have been payable by way of compensation in respect of that improvement if this Act had not been passed, and if the amount last mentioned is greater than the amount fixed or assessed by the Land Court as aforesaid, the difference between the two said amounts shall be payable to the crofter [[6]or executor] by the Secretary of State:

Provided that—
(a) the Secretary of State shall be entitled to set off any amount due to him by the crofter [[6]or, as the case may be, the executor of the deceased crofter] in respect of a loan made under subsection (2) or (3) of section twenty-two of the Act of 1955 or subsection (7) of section seven or section nine of the Act of 1911 against any sum payable to the crofter [[6]or executor] by the Secretary of State under this subsection; and
(b) this subsection shall not apply where compensation in respect of the improvement in question has on a previous occasion fallen to be assessed under the two foregoing subsections.

(4) The reference in the last foregoing subsection to a crofter who is qualified is a reference to a crofter—
(a) whose tenancy of the croft in question began before the commencement of this Act, or
(b) who holds the tenancy of such croft as statutory successor to his immediate predecessor in the tenancy and each of whose predecessors (being in each case a person whose tenancy of the croft began after the commencement of this Act) held such tenancy as statutory successor to his immediate predecessor. [[6]and for the purposes of the said subsection the executor of a deceased crofter shall be deemed to be qualified if the deceased crofter would have been qualified as mentioned in the foregoing provisions of this subsection.]

(5) The Act of 1955 shall have effect subject to the amendments specified in Part I of the First Schedule to this Act, being amendments consequential on the foregoing provisions of this section.

(6) [*Repealed by Statute Law (Repeals) Act 1974 (c 22), Sch, Pt V.*]   [51]

Notes.—1 Words in sub-s (1) inserted by Law Reform (Miscellaneous Provisions) (Scotland) Act 1968 (c 70), Sch 2, Pt 1, para 19.
2 Words in sub-s (1), substituted by ibid, Sch 2, Pt I, para 19.
3 Section 6(3), modified by Highlands and Islands Development (Scotland) Act 1965 (c 46), s 8(3)(b).
4 Words in sub-s (3) repealed by Crofting Reform (Scotland) Act 1976 (c 21), Sch 3.
5 Words in sub-s (3) inserted by Law Reform (Miscellaneous Provisions) (Scotland) Act 1968 (c 70), Sch 2, Pt I, Para 20.
6 Words in sub-ss (3), (4) added by ibid, Sch 2, Pt I, para 21.

---

7. [*Repealed by Crofting Reform (Scotland) Act 1976 (c 21), s 22(3), Sch 3.*]   [52]

8. Reorganisation schemes

(1) Where in relation to any township the Commission—
(a) either of their own accord or on representations made to them by a crofter who is the tenant of a croft situated in the said township or by the landlord of such a croft or by a grazings committee appointed under section twenty-four of the

Act of 1955 in respect of common grazings shared in by any such crofter, and
  (b) after such consultation as is reasonably practicable with the tenants and the
landlords of crofts situated in the township and with any grazings committee
appointed as aforesaid, and
  (c) after making such inquiries as they think fit,
are satisfied that the township ought to be reorganised in order to secure the
preservation or the better development thereof, they may prepare a draft of a scheme
(in this Act referred to as a 'reorganisation scheme') for the reorganisation of the
township.

(2) A reorganisation scheme shall provide for the re-allocation of the land in the
township in such manner as is, in the opinion of the Commission, most conducive to
the proper and efficient use of that land and to the general benefit of the township, so,
however, that under the scheme every crofter who is the tenant of a croft situated in
the township and who so wishes shall be granted the tenancy of a croft and that such
croft shall—
  (a) if the crofter so wishes, include any dwelling-house which formed part of the
croft of which he was tenant immediately before the date on which the scheme
was put into effect, and
  (b) if he so wishes, be of a value not less than that of the croft of which he was tenant
as aforesaid.

(3) A reorganisation scheme may, if the Commission think fit, make provision with
respect to all or any of the following matters, that is to say—
  (a) the inclusion in the scheme of any land in the vicinity of the township, being
land to which the Act of 1955 and this Act do not apply, which in the opinion of
the Commission ought to be used for the enlargement of crofts in the township
or of common grazings used exclusively or shared in by the township;
  (b) the admission into the township of new crofters and the allocation to them of
shares in the common grazings;
  (c) the apportionment for the exclusive use of the township of a part of any
common grazings in which it shares;
  (d) the inclusion in any croft formed under the scheme of a part of the common
grazings or of any land held runrig;
  (e) [*Section 8(3)(e) repealed by Crofting Reform (Scotland) Act 1976 (c 21), Sch 3.*]
  (f) any other matter incidental to or consequential on the provisions of the scheme.

(4) For the purposes of a reorganisation scheme the Commission shall prepare such
maps and plans as may be necessary to indicate the general effect of the scheme and its
effects on each of the crofts in the township.

(5) The Commission shall serve on each crofter who is the tenant of a croft situated in
the township to which a draft reorganisation scheme relates a copy of such scheme
together with a notice—
  (a) naming a place within the locality in which the said township is situated where a
copy of the maps and plans prepared by the Commission under the last
foregoing subsection may be inspected at all reasonable hours, and
  (b) requesting that the crofter on whom the said notice is served shall, within four
months from the date of such service, intimate to the Commission in writing
whether he is in favour of the scheme or not.
Where any crofter on whom such a notice as aforesaid has been served fails to
comply with the request contained in such notice, he shall for the purposes of this
section be deemed to have intimated to the Commission in compliance with the said
request that he is in favour of the scheme.

(6) If within the said period of four months a majority of the crofters on whom a copy
of a draft reorganisation scheme and notice have been served in pursuance of the last
foregoing subsection have intimated to the Commission in compliance with the
request contained in such notice that they are in favour of the scheme, the
Commission shall submit to the Secretary of State the draft reorganisation scheme and

the maps and plans prepared by them under subsection (4) of this section together with such information as they may think necessary, or as the Secretary of State may require, for the purpose of informing him of the general purport and effect of the scheme, and shall submit also a statement of their views on the prospects of the development of agricultural and other industries in the township and in the locality in which the township is situated.

(7) The Secretary of State may confirm a draft reorganisation scheme submitted to him under the last foregoing subsection with or without modifications, and the provisions of the Second Schedule to this Act shall apply with respect to the confirmation and the validity of such a scheme.

[53]

9. Putting into effect of reorganisation schemes

(1) It shall be the duty of the Commission to put into effect any reorganisation scheme confirmed by the Secretary of State under the last foregoing section, and the Commission may, subject to any directions in that behalf given to them by the Secretary of State, do all such things as may be required for that purpose.

(2) A reorganisation scheme shall be put into effect on such date as may be appointed by the Commission, and the Commission may appoint different dates in respect of different provisions of the scheme, and any reference in this Act to the date on which a reorganisation scheme is put into effect shall, in relation to any land, be construed as a reference to the date on which the provisions of that scheme which apply to such land are put into effect.

(3) The Commission shall, on a reorganisation scheme being confirmed by the Secretary of State, remit the scheme to the Land Court to fix the sums which will become payable on the scheme being put into effect—
  (a) to each person who immediately before the said date was the tenant of a croft in the township, by way of compensation in respect of permanent improvements by reason of the termination of his tenancy by virtue of subsection (6) of this section;
  (b) by each person (whether or not he was immediately before the said date the tenant of a croft in the township) who under the scheme becomes the tenant of a croft, in respect of the permanent improvements on that croft; and
  (c) by way of rent in respect of each of the crofts formed under the scheme.

(4) In fixing rents under paragraph (c) of the last foregoing subsection the Land Court shall so proceed that the aggregate of the rents so fixed, so far as attributable to subjects which formed part of crofts comprised in the township at the date of the confirmation of the scheme—
  (a) does not exceed the aggregate of the rents payable in respect of those subjects at that date, and
  (b) is fairly apportioned amongst the said subjects.

(5) The rent fixed by the Land Court in pursuance of paragraph (c) of subsection (3) of this section in respect of any croft shall not be altered, except by agreement between the landlord and the crofter, for a period of seven years from the term at which it first became payable.

(6) For the purpose of putting into effect the provisions of a reorganisation scheme, the Commission shall serve on the tenant and on the landlord of every croft to which those provisions apply and on any person (other than such a tenant) who under the scheme is to become the tenant of a croft a notice specifying the date on which the scheme is to be put into effect, and where such notices have been served—
  (a) every such tenant shall be deemed to have given notice renouncing the tenancy of his croft immediately before the said date; and
  (b) each person (whether or not such a tenant) who under the scheme is to become the tenant of a croft shall on that date become the tenant of that croft.

(7) Where any buildings situated on land to which a reorganisation scheme applies will on the putting into effect of the scheme cease to be required in connection with the occupation of that land, the Commission shall, on the scheme being confirmed by the Secretary of State, give notice to that effect to the landlord of the land, and thereupon the provisions of subsections (6) and (8) of section sixteen of the Act of 1955 (under which the Secretary of State may be required to purchase buildings on certain crofts) shall apply in relation to the buildings first mentioned as if the said notice had been a notice given under the said subsection (6) to the landlord by the Commission immediately before the date of the putting into effect of the scheme.

A notice given under this subsection to a landlord by the Commission shall inform the landlord of the effect of this subsection in relation to the buildings in respect of which the notice is given.

(8) Where a reorganisation scheme provides, in pursuance of paragraph (a) of subsection (3) of the last foregoing section, for the inclusion in the scheme of land in the vicinity of the township, the Secretary of State shall, on confirming the scheme, serve—

(a) on the occupier of any such land who is not the owner thereof, a copy of the scheme together with a notice terminating his interest in the land on the expiry of three months from the date of the service of the notice; and

(b) on the owner of any such land a copy of the scheme together with a notice requiring him to enter into an undertaking that he will, on the date on which the scheme is put into effect, let the land in accordance with the provisions of the scheme.

(9) Where the interest in any land of the occupier of that land is terminated in pursuance of paragraph (a) of the last foregoing subsection, the Secretary of State shall be deemed to be authorised to purchase the said interest compulsorily and to have served notice to treat in respect thereof on the date on which the interest is terminated as aforesaid.

(10) Where—

(a) the owner of any land fails within two months from the date on which a notice is served on him under paragraph (b) of subsection (8) of this section to enter into such an undertaking as is mentioned in that paragraph or, having entered into such an undertaking, fails to let the land in accordance with the provisions of the scheme on the date on which the scheme is put into effect; or

(b) the owner of any land to which any provision contained in a reorganisation scheme applies gives to the Secretary of State, within two months from the date on which notice of the confirmation of the scheme is served on him under paragraph 7 of the Second Schedule to this Act, notice requiring the Secretary of State to purchase the land;

the Secretary of State shall be deemed to be authorised to purchase the said land compulsorily and to have served notice to treat in respect thereof immediately before the date on which the scheme is put into effect.

Any purchase of land under this subsection shall be deemed to be completed immediately before the date on which the scheme is put into effect, and the Secretary of State shall, as the landlord of such land, be liable to pay or, as the case may be, entitled to receive any such sum as is mentioned in paragraph (a) or (b) of subsection (3) of this section which becomes payable on the said date and any sum payable on that date under subsection (6) of section fourteen of the Act of 1955 by way of compensation for deterioration of, or damage to, fixed equipment on the land.

(11) The provisions of this and of the last foregoing section shall, unless the context otherwise requires, apply in relation to a group of neighbouring townships as they apply in relation to a township.

(12) [*Repealed by Statute Law (Repeals) Act 1974 (c 22), Sch, Pt V.*]

[54]

10. [*Repealed by Statute Law (Repeals) Act 1974 (c 22), Sch, Pt V.*]

[55]

11. Subletting of crofts

(1) [*Repealed by Statute Law (Repeals) Act 1974 (c 22), Sch, Pt V.*]

(2) Notwithstanding any enactment or rule of law a crofter shall be entitled after the commencement of this Act to sublet his croft without the consent of the landlord of the croft.

(3) A crofter shall not after the commencement of this Act sublet his croft otherwise than with the consent in writing of the Commission and in accordance with such conditions (which shall not include conditions relating to rent) as the Commission in giving their consent may impose; and any sublease of his croft granted by a crofter otherwise than as aforesaid shall be null and void:
    Providing that nothing in this subsection shall be construed as debarring a crofter from subletting any dwelling-house or other building forming part of his croft to holiday visitors.

(4) On applying to the Commission for their consent to a proposed sublease of his croft, a crofter shall furnish such information with respect to the proposed sublease, including the name of the subtenant, the duration of the sublease and the terms and conditions of the sublease (other than those relating to rent), as the Commission may require.

(5) The Commission shall, on an application being made to them by a crofter for their consent to a proposed sublease of a croft, serve on the landlord of the croft a notice stating that such application has been made and specifying the name and designation of the proposed subtenant, and in deciding whether to give or to refuse consent to such sublease the Commission shall have regard to any observatons made to them by the landlord within fourteen days from the date of the service of such notice.

(6) The Commission may, in giving their consent to a proposed sublease of a croft, impose such conditions (other than any relating to rent) as they may think fit.

[56]

12. Special provisions regarding subletting of crofts not adequately used

(1) Where the Commission are of the opinion that any crofter is failing to make adequate use of his croft, they may serve on him a preliminary notice setting out their opinion as aforesaid and stating that, unless he satisfies them within one year from the date of the service of such preliminary notice that he is making adequate use of his croft, the Commission may, in accordance with the provisions of the next following subsection, serve on him a notice of requirement to sublet.
    The Commission may at any time withdraw a preliminary notice served by them on a crofter under this subsection.

(2) Where a crofter on whom a preliminary notice has been served under the foregoing subsection fails to satisfy the Commission within the period mentioned in that subsection that he is making adequate use of his croft, the Commission may, within one month from the expiry of that period, serve on such crofter a notice stating that, subject to the provisions of the next following subsection, the croft will, on the expiry of one month from the date of the service of the notice or such longer period as may be specified in the notice, become subject to a requirement that it be sublet.

(3) A crofter on whom a notice is served under the last foregoing subsection by the Commission may, at any time before his croft becomes subject, in terms of such notice, to a requirement that it be sublet, refer to the Secretary of State the question whether he is making adequate use of his croft, and the Secretary of State, after affording to the crofter an opportunity of making representations to him and, if the crofter does not object to such consultation, after consulting with any grazings committee appointed under section twenty-four of the Act of 1955 in respect of

common grazings in the township in which the croft is situated, may annul the notice or may confirm it.

(4) Where a notice is served under subsection (2) of this section on a crofter by the Commission and either no reference is made under the last foregoing subsection to the Secretary of State by the crofter or on such a reference the Secretary of State confirms the notice, the Commission may, within one month from the last date on which a reference might have been made as aforesaid or from the date on which the notice was confirmed by the Secretary of State, as the case may be, serve on the crofter a further notice requiring that he shall, within three months from the date of the service of such further notice, submit to them for their approval proposals (other than any relating to rent) for subletting his croft.

(5) The Commission shall, on proposals for subletting a croft being submitted to them by a crofter as aforesaid, serve on the landlord of the croft a notice stating that such proposals have been submitted and specifying the name and designation of the proposed subtenant, and in deciding whether or not to approve such proposals the Commission shall have regard to any observations made to them by the landlord within fourteen days from the date of the service of such notice.

(6) The Commission may, in giving their approval to any proposals submitted to them by a crofter as aforesaid, impose such conditions (other than any relating to rent) as they may think fit, and any reference in this or the next following section to proposals submitted to the Commission under subsection (4) of this section and approved by them shall include a reference to conditions imposed by the Commission under this subsection in giving their approval to such proposals.

(7) If a crofter on whom a further notice is served under subsection (4) of this section by the Commission fails within the period mentioned in that subsection to submit proposals for subletting his croft, or if any proposals submitted by such a crofter are not approved by the Commission, or if such a crofter fails to sublet the croft in accordance with proposals approved by the Commission, the Commission themselves may, subject to the following provisions of this section, grant a sublease of the croft to such person as they may think fit.

(8) Before granting a sublease of any croft under the last foregoing subsection the Commission shall consult with any grazings committee appointed under section twenty-four of the Act of 1955 in respect of common grazings in the township in which the croft is situated, and thereafter the Commission shall, if they propose to grant such sublease, serve on the landlord of the croft and on the crofter a notice to that effect which shall also specify the name and designation of the proposed subtenant, and in deciding whether or not to grant the sublease the Commission shall have regard to any observations made to them by the landlord or by the crofter within fourteen days from the date of the service of such notice.

(9) Where the Commission grant a sublease of any croft under subsection (7) of this section, they shall forthwith give to the landlord of the croft, to the crofter and to the subtenant under the sublease a notice intimating that they have granted the sublease as aforesaid and setting out the name of the subtenant, the duration of the sublease, and the terms and conditions on which it has been granted, and the Commission shall also make a record of the condition as at the date of entry under the sublease of any fixed equipment let thereunder.

(10) A sublease of a croft granted by the crofter in accordance with proposals submitted to the Commission under subsection (4) of this section and approved by them, or by the Commission under subsection (7) of this section, shall not, unless the crofter so wishes, include—
  (a) any dwelling-house or garden ground forming part of the croft;
  (b) any buildings or other structures erected, or any works executed, on the croft which, by virtue of subsection (2) or (3) of section five of this Act, are permanent improvements on the croft;

(c) such part of the croft as the Commission shall determine, being a part which (taken together with the site of any dwelling-house, garden ground, buildings, structures or works which, by virtue of the foregoing provisions of this subsection, are not included in the sublease) extends to [¹one half hectare];

(d) any right pertaining to the tenancy of the croft to cut or take peat.

(11) A sublease of any croft granted under subsection (7) of this section by the Commission shall have effect in all respects as if it had been granted by the crofter in accordance with proposals submitted to the Commission under subsection (4) of this section and approved by them.

(12) The rent payable under a sublease granted under subsection (7) of this section by the Commission shall, in the case of a sublease of a whole croft, or of a whole croft other than any subjects which, by virtue of subsection (10) of this section, are not included in the sublease, be a sum equal to one and one quarter times the rent payable to the landlord by the crofter in respect of the croft, and, in any other case, be such proportion of the said sum as the Commission may determine:

Provided that the Land Court may, on an application in that behalf made by the crofter within six months from the date on which notice intimating the grant of the sublease was given to him under subsection (9) of this section by the Commission, vary the rent fixed by or under this subsection and substitute therefor such other rent, whether higher or lower than the rent so fixed, as may appear to the Land Court to be just in all the circumstances, and the rent determined by the Land Court in pursuance of this proviso shall be payable under the sublease, in place of the rent fixed as aforesaid, as from the date of entry under the sublease.

(13) The duration of any sublease granted under subsection (7) of this section by the Commission shall, subject to the provisions of the next following subsection and of subsection (3) of the next following section, be such number of years, not exceeding five, as the Commission may determine, and any such sublease shall be granted subject to the following terms and conditions, that is to say—

(a) the subtenant shall make adequate use of the land comprised in the sublease;

(b) the subtenant shall maintain any permanent improvements existing on such land at the date of the commencement of the sublease in as good a state of repair as they were in at the said date and, if he fails to do so, shall on the termination of the sublease pay to the crofter the cost, as at the date of such termination, of making good any deterioration of, or damage to, such improvements due to his failure, which cost shall, failing agreement between the subtenant and the crofter, be determined by the Land Court;

(c) the subtenant shall not make any permanent improvements on the land comprised in the sublease, other than an improvement falling under head 3, 4, 5 or 6 of the Fifth Schedule to the Act of 1955, and the crofter shall not be held responsible for the maintenance of any permanent improvements erected by the subtenant without the consent of the crofter;

and to such other terms and conditions as may be specified in the sublease.

(14) If the Commission are satisfied in relation to any sublease granted by them under subsection (7) of this section—

(a) that the subtenant has broken one or more of the terms or conditions of the sublease, or

(b) where representations in that behalf are made by the crofter or by the subtenant, that the circumstances of either of them have so materially altered that it is reasonable that the sublease should be terminated,

the Commission may serve on the crofter and on the subtenant a notice in writing terminating the sublease on such date as may be specified in the notice, being a date not later than one year from the date of the service of the notice.

(15) Where any person occupying a croft—

(a) has, by virtue of any of the provisions of this section, ceased to be entitled to occupy such croft; or

(b) is a subtenant to whom the croft has been sublet by the crofter after the date on which a further notice was served on the crofter by the Commission under subsection (4) of this section and otherwise than in accordance with proposals submitted to the Commission under that subsection and approved by them;

The Commission may serve on such person a notice in writing requiring him to give up his occupation of the croft on or before such date as may be specified in the notice, being a date not less than one month from the date of the service of the notice; and if he fails to give up his occupation of the croft on or before the date so specified, subsection (3) of section seventeen of the Act of 1955 (which provides for the ejection of a crofter from his croft in certain circumstances) shall, subject to any necessary modifications, apply as it applies where a crofter fails to give up the occupation of a croft as mentioned in that subsection.

(16) In this section 'adequate use' in relation to a croft means such use of the croft for agriculture as, having regard to its nature and location, a tenant reasonably skilled in husbandry might be expected to make of it.

[57]

Note.—1 Words in sub-s 10(c) substituted by Crofting Reform (Scotland) Act 1976 (c 21), Sch 2, para 20.

---

13. Miscellaneous provisions regarding subleases of crofts

(1) Subject to the provisions of the next following subsection, the subtenant under a sublease of a croft shall not be held to be a crofter or to be the tenant of an agricultural holding within the meaning of the Agricultural Holdings (Scotland) Act 1949.

(2)[1] Where under a sublease of any croft a right in any common grazing is let to the subtenant, and the sublease is one which—
  (a) has been intimated to the Commission under paragraph (a) or (b) of subsection (1) of section eleven of this Act, or
  (b) has been granted by the crofter with the consent of the Commission and in accordance with any conditions imposed by them, as mentioned in subsection (3) of section eleven of this Act, or
  (c) has been granted by the crofter in accordance with proposals submitted to the Commission under subsection (4) of the last foregoing section and approved by them, or
  (d) has been granted under subsection (7) of the last foregoing section by the Commission,
the subtenant shall come in place of the crofter in relation to any matter which concerns such right, and any grazings regulations applicable to such common grazing shall apply to the subtenant accordingly.

(3) Where the tenancy of a croft is terminated, any sublease of that croft subsisting immediately before the date of such termination shall come to an end on that date:

Provided that where a sublease comes to an end by virtue of the foregoing provisions of this subsection the Commission may, on an application in that behalf made to them by the subtenant within one month [2 or such longer period not exceeding three months as the Commission may in all the circumstances think reasonable] from the date on which the sublease came to an end as aforesaid, make an order permitting the subtenant to remain in occupation of the croft for such period, not exceeding one year from the said date, and subject to such conditions, as may be specified in the order; and no proceedings for the removal of the subtenant from the croft shall be taken by the owner of the croft before the expiry of the said period of one month [2or the said longer period] or, if an application is made under this subsection to the Commission by the subtenant within that period, before the date of the determination of the Commission on such application.

(4) In this and the last two foregoing sections any reference to a croft shall include a reference to a part of a croft.

[58]

Notes.—1 Section 13(2) modified by Crofters (Scotland) Act 1955 (c 21), s 25(1B) (as inserted by Crofting Reform (Scotland) Act 1976 (c 21), s 16(3)).
2 Words in proviso to sub-s (3) inserted by Crofting Reform (Scotland) Act 1976 (c 21), Sch 2, para 22(b).

14. Amendment of powers of Secretary of State with respect to giving of financial assistance in crofting counties

(1) The Secretary of State shall have the like power to provide financial assistance—

    (a) for occupiers of crofts who are also the owners thereof and who in the opinion of the Secretary of State are of substantially the same economic status as a crofter; and

    (b) for occupiers of holdings, other than crofts, situated in the crofting counties which are either holdings of which the area does not exceed [¹30 hectares] (exclusive of any common pasture or grazing held therewith) or holdings the annual rent of which, if they were crofts let to crofters under the Act of 1955 and this Act, would not, in the opinion of the Secretary of State, exceed [¹£100], being occupiers who in the opinion of the Secretary of State are of substantially the same economic status as a crofter; and

  [²(bb) for occupiers of holdings, other than crofts situated in the crofting counties which exceed 30 hectares (exclusive of any common pasture or grazing held therewith) and of which the annual rent if they were crofts so let would in the opinion of the Secretary of State exceed £100, but which in the opinion of the Secretary of State are not substantially larger than 30 hectares (exclusive of any common pasture or grazing held therewith) or are capable of being so let at an annual rent not substantially in excess of £100, being occupiers who in the opinion of the Secretary of State are of substantially the same economic status as a crofter; and]

    (c) for subtenants of crofts or parts of crofts occupying under subleases intimated or granted as mentioned in subsection (2) of the last foregoing section;

as he has by virtue of subsection (1) of section twenty-two of the Act of 1955 to provide financial assistance for crofters; and accordingly subsection (1) of the said section twenty-two shall have effect as if the reference therein to crofts included a reference to such holdings and to parts of crofts and as if the reference therein to crofters included a reference to occupiers of crofts who are also the owners thereof, to occupiers of such holdings and to subtenants of crofts or parts of crofts.

(2) The Secretary of State may make regulations providing that the conditions applied to any dwelling-house by regulations made under subsection (4) of section twenty-two of the Act of 1955 or subsection (3) of section seventy-seven of the Agriculture (Scotland) Act 1948 (which subsections provide for the making by the Secretary of State of regulations applying certain conditions to crofters' dwelling-houses in respect of which a grant has been made), shall not apply to such dwelling-house in such circumstances and to such extent as may be specified in the regulations made under this subsection.

[59]

Notes.—1 Words in sub-s (1)(b) substituted by Crofting Reform (Scotland) Act 1976 (c 21), Sch 2, para 22(a).
2 Section 14(1)(bb) inserted by ibid, Sch 2, para 22(b).

15. Amendment of law with respect to common grazings

(1) A person may be appointed in pursuance of section twenty-four of the Act of 1955 to be a member of a common grazings committee notwithstanding that he is not a crofter.

(2) The duty imposed on a grazings committee by subsection (2) of section twenty-six of the Act of 1955 to make provision in common grazings regulations for the recovery from certain crofters of the expenses incurred by the committee in the discharge of certain of their functions under that Act shall include a duty to provide in such regulations that the committee may from time to time levy on, and recover from, the crofters referred to in paragraph (a) or, as the case may be, [¹such of the crofters referred to in paragraph (b) of that subsection as are liable to pay any expenses in accordance with a proposed allocation of expenditure referred to in subsection (1A) of section 25 of that Act or, as the case may be, such a proposed allocation as approved or modified by the Commission under that subsection], in such proportions as may be specified in the regulations, such sums as will in the opinion of the committee be necessary to enable the committee to meet any expenses which they may incur in the [performance of the duties imposed on them by paragraphs (a) and (b) respectively of section 25(1) of that Act.]

(3) Common grazings regulations may—
   (a) restrict the use of any part of the common grazings on which works of improvement have been carried out to crofters who contribute towards the expenses incurred by the common grazings committee in carrying out those works;
   (b) where the use of any part of the common grazings is restricted as aforesaid, regulate the number and kinds of stock which each contributing crofter may put on that part and the number and kinds of stock which each crofter (whether or not he is a contributing crofter) may put on the remainder of the common grazings.

(4) Subsection (3) of section twenty-seven of the Act of 1955 (which empowers the Commission to apportion a common grazing shared by two or more townships into separate parts for the exclusive use of the several townships) shall have effect as if at the end thereof there were added the words 'or may apportion a part of such grazing for the exclusive use of one of the townships.'

(5) Where the Commission in pursuance of subsection (3) or (4) of section twenty-seven of the Act of 1955 apportion to a township or to an individual a part of a common grazing for its or his exclusive use, they may make the apportionment subject to such conditions, including conditions with respect to the fencing or the draining of the apportioned part, as they may think fit.

(6) For the purposes of the provisions of the Act of 1955 [²this Act and the Crofting Reform (Scotland) Act 1976] relating to common grazings references in [²any] of the said Acts to a crofter shall include references to any person who, not being a crofter, is entitled to share in a common grazing along with crofters.

[60]

Notes.—1 Words in sub-s (2) substituted by Crofting Reform (Scotland) Act 1976 (c 21), Sch 2, para 23(*a*).
2 Words in sub-s (6) substituted by ibid, (c 21), para 23(*b*).

---

16. Financial provisions

(1) Any increase in the expenses of the Commission attributable to the provisions of this Act shall be defrayed by the Secretary of State.

(2) All expenses incurred by the Secretary of State under the provisions of this Act shall be defrayed out of moneys provided by Parliament.

(3) All sums received by the Secretary of State under the provisions of this Act shall be paid into the Exchequer.

[61]

17. Interpretation

(1) In this Act the expression 'the Act of 1955' means the Crofters (Scotland) Act,

1955, and any expression used in this Act and in the Act of 1955 has the same meaning in this Act as in that Act.

(2) Any reference in this Act to any other enactment shall, unless the context otherwise requires, be construed as a reference to that enactment as amended by any other enactment including this Act

[62]

18. Amendments and repeals

(1) The Act of 1955 shall have effect subject to the amendments specified in Part II of the First Schedule to this Act, being minor amendments or amendments consequential on the provisions of this Act (other than section six thereof).

(2) [*Repealed by Statute Law (Repeals) Act 1974 (c 22), Sch, Pt V.*]

[63]

19. Citation and commencement

(1) This Act may be cited as the Crofters (Scotland) Act 1961, and the Crofters (Scotland) Act 1955, and this Act may be cited together as the Crofters (Scotland) Acts 1955 and 1961.

(2) This Act (other than section twelve thereof) shall come into operation on the expiry of the period of one month commencing with the date on which it is passed and section twelve of this Act shall come into operation on a day appointed by the Secretary of State by order made by statutory instrument, but no order shall be made under this subsection unless a draft of such order has been laid before Parliament and approved by resolution of each House thereof.

Any reference in this Act to the commencement of this Act shall be construed as a reference to the date on which this Act (other than section twelve thereof) comes into operation.

[64]

Note.—Power of appointment conferred by s 19(2) not exercised.

SCHEDULES

FIRST SCHEDULE

AMENDMENTS OF THE ACT OF 1955

PART I

AMENDMENTS CONSEQUENTIAL ON SECTION SIX OF THIS ACT

1. [Amends Crofters (Scotland) Act 1955 (c 21), s 7(2).]
2. [Inserts ibid, s 11(7)(A).]
3. [Amends ibid, s 13(3).]
4. [Amends ibid, s 14(7).]
5. [Amends ibid, s 16(8).]
6. [Repealed by Statute Law (Repeals) Act 1974 (c 22), Sch, Pt V.]
7. [Substitutes new s 28(2)–(2B) for s 28(2) in Crofters (Scotland) Act 1955 (c 21).]

PART II

MINOR AMENDMENTS AND GENERAL CONSEQUENTIAL AMENDMENTS

8.   Any reference in the Act of 1955 to that Act shall, unless the context otherwise requires, include a reference to this Act.
9.(a) [Amends Crofters (Scotland) Act 1955, s 3(1)(c).]
  (b) [Adds ibid, s 3(1)(d).]
10.(a) [Repealed by Statute Law (Repeals) Act 1974 (c 22), Sch, Pt V.]

   (b) [Amends Crofters (Scotland) Act 1955 (c 21), s 8(3).]
   (c), (d) [Repealed by Statute Law (Repeals) Act 1974 (c 22), Sch, Pt V.]
   (e) [Adds s 8(b) to Crofters (Scotland) Act 1955 (c 21).]
11.(a) [Amends ibid, s 12(2).]
   (b) [Adds ibid, s 12(4)]
12.(a) [Inserts ibid, s 16(3A).]
   (b) [Amends ibid, s 16(9).]
   (c) [Inserts ibid, s 16(11A).]
   (d) [Inserts ibid, s 16(13).]
13.   [Amends ibid, s 24(2).]
14.   [Amends ibid, s 25(1)(a).]
15.   [Amends ibid, s 26(2)(a).]
16.   [Amends ibid, s 32(2).]
17.   [Amends ibid, s 34(1).]
18.   [Amends ibid, s 37(1).]
19.   [Amends ibid, s 38(2).]
20.(a) [Amends ibid, Sch 2, para 3.]
   (b) [Inserts ibid, Sch 2, para 3A.]
   (c) [Substitutes ibid, new Sch 2, para 5.]
21.(a) [Amends ibid, Sch 5, para 10.]
   (b) [Inserts ibid, Sch 5, para 11.]

[65]

SECOND SCHEDULE

CONFIRMATION AND VALIDITY OF REORGANISATION SCHEMES

PART I

Procedure for confirming reorganisation schemes

1. Before confirming a reorganisation scheme the Secretary of State shall—
   (a) serve on every owner and every occupier of land to which the draft scheme applies a copy of the draft scheme together with a notice naming a place within the locality in which such land is situated where a copy of the maps and plans submitted with the draft scheme may be inspected at all reasonable hours and stating that such owner or occupier may, within twenty-eight days from the date of the service of the notice, object in such manner as may be specified in the notice to the draft scheme or to any provision contained therein; and
   (b) in two successive weeks publish in one or more newspapers circulating in the locality in which the land to which the scheme applies is situated a notice stating that the draft scheme has been submitted to him, specifying the land to which the scheme applies, naming a place within the locality where a copy of the draft scheme and of the maps and plans submitted therewith may be inspected at all reasonable hours, and stating that any person having an interest in any land to which the scheme applies may, within twenty-eight days from the date of the first publication of the notice, object in such manner as may be specified in the notice to the draft scheme or to any provision contained therein.

2. If no objection is made under the foregoing paragraph or if all objections so made are withdrawn, the Secretary of State may, subject to the provisions of paragraph 4 of this Schedule, confirm the draft scheme with or without modifications.

3. If any objection made as aforesaid is not withdrawn, the Secretary of State shall, before deciding whether to confirm the draft scheme, cause a public local inquiry to be held, and after considering the objection and the report of the person who held the inquiry the Secretary of State may, if he thinks fit and subject to the provisions of the next following paragraph, confirm the draft scheme with or without modifications.

4. Where the Secretary of State proposes to make any modification in the draft

scheme by virtue either of paragraph 2 of this Schedule or of the last foregoing paragraph, he shall, before deciding to confirm the draft scheme as so modified, serve on each of the persons referred to in sub-paragraph (a) of paragraph 1 of this Schedule and on any other person who in his opinion may be substantially affected by such modification a notice specifying the modification and stating that such person may, within fourteen days from the date of the service of the notice, make representations in writing concerning the modification to the Secretary of State, and the Secretary of State shall consider any representations so made before he decides whether to confirm the draft scheme as so modified.

5. Notwithstanding anything in paragraph 3 of this Schedule, the Secretary of State may require any person who has made an objection to state in writing the grounds thereof and may disregard the objection for the purposes of this Schedule if it is an objection which in the opinion of the Secretary of State is frivolous, or which relates exclusively to the assessment of any sum which will fall to be fixed under this Act or any other enactment by the Land Court, or which relates to the assessment of compensation on the compulsory acquisition of land or of an interest in land by virtue of section nine of this Act.

6. The provisions of [¹subsections (2) to (8) of section two hundred and ten of the Local Government (Scotland) Act 1973] (which relate to the holding of local inquiries) shall apply in relation to a public local inquiry held under paragraph 3 of this Schedule as they apply in relation to local inquiries held under the said section three hundred and fifty-five.

PART II

Validity of reorganisation schemes

7. On confirming a reorganisation scheme the Secretary of State shall forthwith—
    (a) serve on every person on whom a notice was required to be served under sub-paragraph (a) of paragraph 1 or paragraph 4 of this Schedule a notice stating that the scheme has been confirmed; and
    (b) publish in one or more newspapers circulating in the locality in which the land to which the scheme applies is situated a notice stating that the scheme has been confirmed and naming a place within the locality where a copy of the scheme and of the maps and plans relating thereto may be inspected at all reasonable hours.

8. If any person aggrieved by a reorganisation scheme desires to question its validity on the ground that it is not within the powers of this Act or that any requirement of this Act has not been complied with, he may, within six weeks from the date of the first publication of the notice referred to in sub-paragraph (b) of the last foregoing paragraph, make an application for the purpose to the Court of Session, and if any such application is made the Court, if satisfied that the scheme is not within the powers of this Act or that the interests of the applicant have been substantially prejudiced by a failure to comply with any requirement of this Act, may quash the scheme either generally or in so far as it affects any property or interest of the applicant; but except as aforesaid the scheme shall not at any time be questioned in any proceedings whatsoever.

[66]

Note.—1 Words in para 6 substituted by virtue of Local Government (Scotland) Act 1973 (c 65), s 237(2).

THIRD SCHEDULE

[*Repealed by Statute Law (Repeals) Act 1974 (c 22), Sch, Pt V.*]

[67]

Crofting Reform (Scotland) Act 1976 (c 21)

ARRANGEMENT OF SECTIONS

1. New rights of crofters and cottars to acquire their subjects

(1) A crofter may, failing agreement with the landlord as to the acquisition by the crofter of croft land tenanted by him, apply to the Land Court for an order authorising him to make such acquisition.

(2) A crofter shall be entitled to a conveyance of the site of the dwelling-house on or pertaining to the croft tenanted by him, and a cottar shall be entitled to a conveyance of the site of the dwelling-house on or pertaining to his subject, and the crofter or cottar may, failing agreement with the landlord, apply to the Land Court for an order requiring the landlord to grant such a conveyance.

(3) In this Act 'croft land' includes any land being part of a croft, other than—
    (a) the site of the dwelling-house on or pertaining to the croft;
    (b) any land, comprising any part of a common grazing, unless the land has been apportioned under section 27(4) of the Act of 1955 and is either—
        (i) adjacent or contiguous to any other part of the croft, or
        (ii) arable machair;
    (c) any right to mines, metals or minerals or salmon fishings (not being salmon fishings in Orkney or Shetland) pertaining to the croft.

(4) In this Act, 'the site of the dwelling-house' includes any building thereon and such extent of garden ground as, failing agreement with the landlord, may be determined by the Land Court by order under section 4(1) of this Act to be appropriate for the reasonable enjoyment of the dwelling-house as a residence but does not include—
    (a) any right to mines, metals or minerals pertaining thereto; or
    (b) where there is more than one dwelling-house on or pertaining to a croft or, as the case may be, the subject of a cottar, the site of more than one dwelling-house; or
    (c) where the site of the dwelling-house on or pertaining to a croft has been acquired by the crofter after the passing of this Act, the site of any dwelling-house erected after such acquisition on or pertaining to the remainder of the croft.

[68]

2. Authorisation by Land Court of acquisition of croft land

(1) The Land Court, on an application made to them under section 1(1) of this Act, may make an order—
    (a) authorising the crofter to acquire such croft land as may be specified in the order, subject to such terms and conditions as, failing agreement with the landlord, may be so specified, and requiring the landlord to convey the land to the crofter or his nominee in accordance with such terms and conditions; or
    (b) refusing the application.

(2) The Land Court shall not make an order in accordance with subsection (1)(a) above where they are satisfied by the landlord as to either or both of the following matters—
    (a) that, in all the circumstances pertaining to the landlord and having regard to the extent of land owned by him to which the Act of 1955 applies, the making of such an order would cause a substantial degree of hardship to the landlord;
    (b) that the making of such an order would be substantially detrimental to the interests of sound management of the estate of the landlord of which the croft land to which the application relates forms part.

(3) The Land Court, in making an order in accordance with subsection (1)(a) above, may provide that the authorisation to acquire is conditional on the crofter granting a lease to the landlord of the shooting rights over or the fishing rights pertaining to the croft land and shall so provide where they are satisfied that if such a lease were not granted the interests of the landlord in the shooting or fishing rights of which the rights being acquired by the crofter form part would be materially affected; and any such lease shall be at such nominal annual rent, for such period of not less than 20 years and subject to such other terms and conditions as the Land Court may specify.

(4) The Land Court, in making an order in accordance with subsection (1)(a) above, may include the condition that the crofter shall grant a standard security in favour of the landlord to secure any sum which may become payable to him or his personal representative under section 3(3) of this Act in the event of disposal of the croft land or any part thereof.

(5) Where the Land Court propose to make an order authorising the crofter to acquire—

(a) land comprising any part of a common grazing which has been apportioned under section 27(4) of the Act of 1955; or

(b) land held runrig which has been apportioned under section 27(7) of that Act, and they are satisfied that the apportionment has been made subject to conditions imposed by the Commission under section 15(5) of the Act of 1961, or, as the case may be, the said section 27(7), they shall have regard to the conditions so imposed.

[69]

3. Consideration payable in respect of acquisition of croft land

(1) Where the Land Court make an order in accordance with section 2(1)(a) of this Act and the crofter and the landlord have failed to reach agreement about the consideration payable in respect of the acquisition, the consideration shall, subject to subsection (3) below, be the crofting value of the croft land specified in the order as determined by the Land Court under subsection (2) below.

(2) The crofting value of the croft land, as determined by the Land Court for the purposes of subsection (1) above, shall be 15 years' purchase of such amount as the Land Court may determine to be the proportion attributable to the croft land of the current rent payable for the croft of which the croft land forms part:

Provided that the Land Court, on an application made to them by the landlord at any time before they make a final order under section 2(1) of this Act, may determine a fair rent for the croft which shall be deemed to be the current rent for the purposes of this subsection; and section 5(4) of the Act of 1955 shall apply for the purposes of this proviso as if for the word 'parties' there were substituted the words 'landlord and the crofter'.

(3) If the person who had acquired croft land by virtue of section 2(1) of this Act ('the former crofter') or a member of the former crofter's family who has obtained the title to that land either—

(i) as the nominee of the former crofter, or

(ii) from the former crofter or his nominee,

disposes of that land or any part of it ('the relevant land') to anyone who is not a member of the former crofter's family, by any means other than by a lease for crofting or agricultural purposes, forthwith or at any time within five years of the date of its acquisition by the former crofter then, subject to subsection (6) below, the person disposing of the relevant land shall pay to the landlord referred to in the said section 2(1) or to his personal representative a sum equal to one half of the difference between—

(a) the market value of the relevant land (on the date of such disposal) which, failing agreement between the parties concerned, shall be as determined by the Land Court under subsection (4) below on the application of such landlord or personal representative; and

(b) the consideration which was paid under subsection (1) above in respect of the relevant land.

(4) The market value of the relevant land as determined by the Land Court shall be the amount which the land, if sold in the open market by a willing seller (not being an authority as defined in section 1(1)(b) of the Community Land Act 1975), might be expected to realise assuming that on the date of the disposal—

(a) there were no improvements on the land which, if the land were let to a crofter, would be permanent improvements in respect of which the crofter would be entitled to compensation under section 14 of the Act of 1955 on renunciation of the tenancy of the croft of which the land formed part;

(b) no other development had been carried out on the land (not being development carried out on the land, when it was subject to the tenancy of the former crofter or any of his predecessors in the tenancy, by a person other than that crofter or any of such predecessors); and

(c) no development of the land which consisted of the making of such an improvement as is referred to in paragraph (a) above were or would be permitted in pursuance of the Town and Country Planning (Scotland) Act 1972.

(5) If the relevant land comprises only part of the land which was acquired under section 2(1) of this Act, the Land Court may, failing agreement between the parties concerned, on an application made to them by the person disposing of the relevant land or the landlord referred to in the said section 2(1) or his personal representative, determine for the purposes of subsection (3)(b) above the proportion of the amount of the consideration which was paid under subsection (1) above in respect of the relevant land.

(6) No payment shall be made under subsection (3) above in respect of the disposal of the relevant land in a case where payment is made in respect of such disposal in accordance with an agreement entered into between the landlord and the person disposing of that land.

[70]

4. Determination by Land Court of terms and conditions for conveyance of the site of the dwelling-house

(1) The Land Court, on an application made to them under section 1(2) of this Act, may make an order requiring the landlord to convey the site of the dwelling-house to the crofter or cottar or his nominee with such boundaries and subject to such terms and conditions as, failing agreement, may be specified in the order.

(2) Where the parties have failed to reach agreement about the consideration payable in respect of the conveyance the consideration shall be—
  (a) the amount as determined by the Land Court which the site, if sold in the open market by a willing seller, might be expected to realise assuming that—
    (i)   there were or would be no buildings on the site;
    (ii) the site were available with vacant possession;
    (iii) the site were not land to which the Crofters (Scotland) Acts 1955 and 1961 apply; and
    (iv) no development of the site were or would be permitted in pursuance of the Town and Country Planning (Scotland) Act 1972;
and in addition, in a case where the landlord has provided fixed equipment on the site—
  (b) an amount equal to one half of the proportion attributable to that fixed equipment, as determined by the Land Court, of the value of the site, such value being the amount as so determined which the site, if sold as aforesaid, might be expected to realise making the assumptions referred to in sub-paragraphs (ii), (iii) and (iv) of paragraph (a) above.

(3) The Land Court in making an order under subsection (1) above may determine that any of the expenses of the conveyance of the site and other expenses necessarily incurred by the landlord in relation thereto shall be borne by the crofter or cottar:
  Provided that where the order relates to the conveyance of the site of the dwelling-house on or pertaining to a croft, any such determination shall be subject to the condition that the conveyance is not included in a deed which also provides for the conveyance of croft land.

(4) Failing agreement between the parties as to the amount of such expenses, the auditor of the Land Court may, on the application of either party, determine such amount; and may determine that the expenses of taxing such expenses shall be borne by the parties in such proportion as he thinks fit.

[71]

5.   Provisions relating to conveyance

(1) A landlord shall have power to execute a valid conveyance in pursuance of the foregoing provisions of this Act, notwithstanding that he may be under any such disability as is mentioned in section 7 of the Lands Clauses Consolidation (Scotland) Act 1845.

(2) Where the Land Court are satisfied, on the application of the crofter or cottar or his nominee that the landlord has failed to execute a conveyance of land in favour of such person in compliance with an order under section 2(1) or 4(1) of this Act within such time as the Land Court consider reasonable, they shall make an order authorising their principal clerk to execute the conveyance and such other deeds as adjusted at his sight as may be necessary to give effect to the order; and a conveyance executed by the principal clerk under this subsection shall have the like force and effect in all respects as if it had been executed by the landlord.

(3) Where the principal clerk of the Land Court has executed a conveyance in pursuance of subsection (2) above, the Land Court may make such order as they think fit with regard to the payment of the consideration in respect of the conveyance and in particular providing for the distribution of the sum comprised in the consideration according to the respective estates or interests of persons making claim to such sum.

(4) Notwithstanding that the Land Court have made an order under section 2(1) or 4(1) of this Act determining the terms and conditions on which land is to be conveyed, the crofter or, as the case may be, the cottar and the landlord may arrange for the conveyance of the land on any other terms and conditions that they may agree.

(5) Where a person other than the landlord is infeft in the subjects to be conveyed, the second references in sections 1(2) and 2(1) of this Act and the reference in the said section 4(1) and in the foregoing provisions of this section to the landlord shall be construed as references to the landlord and such other person for their respective rights.

(6) The Land Court in specifying in an order under the said section 2(1) or 4(1) the terms and conditions on which land is to be conveyed shall have regard to any existing land obligations as defined in section 1(2) of the Conveyancing and Feudal Reform (Scotland) Act 1970 relating to such land.

(7) Where the landlords are the National Trust for Scotland, they shall not be required to convey land by an order of the Land Court under the said section 2(1) or 4(1) otherwise than by a grant in feu; but section 4(2) of the Order confirmed by the National Trust for Scotland Order Confirmation Act 1947 (which requires the consent of the Lord Advocate to grants in feu by the Trust exceeding 20 acres) shall not apply to such a grant.

(8) Where the Land Court are satisfied, on the application of the landlord, that the crofter or his nominee has failed to execute a standard security in favour of the landlord in compliance with a condition imposed by the Land Court under section 2(4) of this Act within such time as the Land Court consider reasonable, they shall make an order authorising their principal clerk to execute the standard security; and a standard security executed by the principal clerk under this subsection shall have the like force and effect in all respects as if it had been executed by the crofter or his nominee.

[72]

6.   Provisions supplementary to sections 2 and 4

(1) An order of the Land Court under section 2(1)(a) or 4(1) of this Act shall have effect for a period of two years from the date of intimation of the order or for such other period as may at any time be agreed to in writing by the crofter or, as the case may be, the cottar and the landlord or as may be determined by the Land Court on the application of either party.

(2) Where an order has been made by the Land Court under the said section 2(1)(a) or 4(1) in relation to croft land or the site of the dwelling-house on or pertaining to a croft or under the said section 4(1) in relation to the site of the dwelling-house on or pertaining to the subject of a cottar, then, so long as the order has effect—

(a) the crofter shall not be entitled under section 14(1) of the Act of 1955 to compensation for any permanent improvement made on the croft land or site; and

(b) the landlord of the croft shall not be entitled under section 14(6) of that Act to recover from the crofter compensation for any deterioration of, or damage to, any fixed equipment provided by the landlord in respect of the croft land or site; or

(c) the cottar shall not be entitled under section 28(1) of that Act to compensation for any permanent improvement made on the site,

being compensation to which the crofter and the landlord or, as the case may be, the cottar would be entitled but for this subsection.

(3) Any condition or provision to the effect that—

(a) the superior of any feu shall be entitled to a right of pre-emption in the event of a sale thereof or any part thereof by the proprietor of the feu, or

(b) any other person with an interest in land shall be entitled to a right of pre-emption in the event of a sale thereof or of any part thereof by the proprietor for the time being,

shall not be capable of being enforced where the sale is by a landlord to a crofter or his nominee of croft land or to a crofter or a cottar or his nominee of the site of the dwelling-house on or pertaining to the croft or the subject of the cottar in pursuance of an order under the said section 2(1) or, as the case may be, 4(1).

(4) Where the landlords are the National Trust for Scotland, the Land Court, in making an order under the said section 2(1) or 4(1), shall have regard to the purposes of the Trust.

(5) A compulsory purchase order which authorises the compulsory purchase of land, being land which was held inalienably by the National Trust for Scotland on the date of the passing of this Act and was acquired from the Trust by a crofter in pursuance of an order under section 2(1) or 4(1) of this Act, shall in so far as it so authorises be subject to special parliamentary procedure in any case where an objection has been duly made by the Trust under the Acquisition of Land (Authorisation Procedure) (Scotland) Act 1947 and has not been withdrawn; and in this subsection 'held inalienably' has the same meaning as in section 7(1) of the said Act of 1947.

(6) Where the site of the dwelling-house on or pertaining to a croft has been acquired after the passing of this Act by a person, who immediately before the acquisition was the tenant of the croft, that person and the wife or husband of that person may, so long as either of them continues to occupy the subjects conveyed, enjoy any right to cut and take peats for the use of those subjects which that person enjoyed immediately before the acquisition.

(7) Any person acquiring croft land shall, unless and until the land ceases to be a croft by a direction of the Commission under section 16(9) of the Act of 1955, be required to give notice to the Commission of the change of ownership of the land.

[73]

7. **Adjustment of rent for remainder of croft where part conveyed to crofter**

Where a crofter acquires the site of the dwelling-house on or pertaining to his croft or any croft land forming part of his croft, then, notwithstanding that it is less than seven years since the term at which the existing rent for the croft first became payable, the Land Court may, on the application of the crofter or his landlord, determine a fair rent for the part of the croft which remains subject to the tenancy of the crofter, and accordingly subsections (3) and (4) of section 5 of the Act of 1955 shall apply for the purposes of such a determination as if the provisos to subsection (3) were omitted; but thereafter the said provisos shall apply to a rent so determined.

[74]

8. Provisions relating to existing loans and heritable securities

(1) Where—
  (a) a crofter who acquires the site of the dwelling-house on or pertaining to his croft is on the date of the acquisition under any liability to the Secretary of State or the Highlands and Islands Development Board, or
  (b) a cottar who acquires the site of the dwelling-house on or pertaining to his subject is on the date of the acquisition under any liability to the Secretary of State,

in respect of any loan, the amount outstanding in respect of such liability shall be deemed, as from the last day on which the crofter or cottar was liable to pay rent in respect of that site or on which the cottar was entitled to occupy the site as a cottar, to be a loan by the Secretary of State to the crofter or cottar or, as the case may be, by the Board to the crofter, and the provisions of Schedule 3 to the Act of 1955 (provisions as to security, etc, of loans) shall apply in relation to any such loan by the Secretary of State and, subject to any necessary modifications, to any such loan by the Board.

(2) Any question arising under subsection (1) above as to the day from which the outstanding amount is deemed to be a loan shall be determined by the Land Court.

(3) Any rights of the Board created under subsection (1) above shall be postponed to any rights, whensoever constituted, of the Secretary of State under that subsection; and such rights of the Secretary of State and the Board shall have priority over any other loan in respect of which the crofter or the cottar or his nominee as owner of the site of the dwelling-house is under any liability and shall be postponed only to such items as are referred to in heads (i), (ii) and (iii) of paragraph 4(b) of Schedule 2 to the Housing (Scotland) Act 1969.

(4) Any heritable security which immediately before the execution of a conveyance in pursuance of the foregoing provisions of this Act burdened the subjects conveyed shall, as from the date of recording of the conveyance in the Register of Sasines—
  (a) in the case of a conveyance in feu, cease to burden the *dominium utile* of the subjects conveyed and burden only the superiority thereof;
  (b) in the case of a conveyance otherwise than in feu where the heritable security burdened only the subjects conveyed, cease to burden those subjects;
  (c) in the case of a conveyance otherwise than in feu where the heritable security also burdened other land, burden only that other land;
and, unless the creditors in right of any such security otherwise agree, the landlord shall pay to them according to their respective rights and preferences any sum paid to him by the crofter or cottar as consideration for the subjects conveyed.

[75]

9. Crofter's right to share in value of land resumed by landlord

(1) Where the Land Court authorise the resumption of a croft or a part thereof under section 12 of the Act of 1955, the crofter shall be entitled to receive from the landlord, in addition to any compensation payable to him under that section, a share in the value of the land so resumed the amount whereof shall be one half of the difference between, subject to subsection (5) below, the market value of the land (on the date on which resumption thereof is so authorised) as determined by the Land Court in accordance with subsections (2) and (3) below (less any compensation payable as aforesaid) and the crofting value thereof.

(2) Where the resumption of the land is so authorised for some reasonable purpose

which has been or is to be carried out by the landlord or by any person not being an authority possessing compulsory purchase powers, the market value for the purposes of subsection (1) above shall be a sum equal to the amount which the land, if sold in the open market by a willing seller (not being an authority as defined in section 1(1)(b) of the Community Land Act 1975) might be expected to realise.

(3) Where the resumption is so authorised for some reasonable purpose which has been or is to be carried out by an authority possessing compulsory purchase powers (not being the landlord) on the acquisition by them of the land so resumed, the market value for the purposes of subsection (1) above shall be a sum equal to the amount of compensation payable by the authority to the landlord in respect of the acquisition:

Provided that, where the land so resumed forms part only of the land acquired from the landlord by the authority, the market value shall be a sum equal to such amount as the Land Court may determine to be the proportion of the amount of compensation so payable by the authority which relates to the land so resumed.

(4) Where the land so resumed forms or forms part of a common grazing, the share of the value of that land payable to the crofters sharing in the common grazing shall be apportioned among such crofters according to the proportion that the right in the common grazing of each such crofter bears to the total of such rights; and any sum so apportioned to such a crofter shall be deemed to be the share in the value of such land resumed to which he is entitled under subsection (1) above.

(5) For the purposes of this section, where any development has been carried out by any person, other than the crofter or any of his predecessors in the tenancy, on the land which the Land Court have authorised the landlord to resume before such authorisation, there shall be deducted from the market value such amount thereof as, in the opinion of the Land Court, is attributable to that development.

[[1](5A) A sum awarded under this section shall, if the Land Court so determine, carry interest as from the date when such sum is payable at the same rate as would apply (in the absence of any such statement as is provided for in Rule 66 of the Act of Sederunt (Rules of Court, consolidation and amendment) 1965) in the case of a decree or extract in an action commenced on that date in the Court of Session if interest were included in or exigible under that decree or extract:

Provided that this subsection shall not affect any case in which the hearing has begun before the coming into force of section 30 of the Law Reform (Miscellaneous Provisions) (Scotland) Act 1985.]

(6) In this section—
'crofting value', in relation to land resumed, has the same meaning as it has in section 3 of this Act in relation to croft land;
'reasonable purpose' has the same meaning as in section 12(2) of the Act of 1955.

[76]

Note.—1 Section 9(5A) added by the Law Reform (Miscellaneous Provisions) (Scotland) Act 1985 (c 73), s 30(2).

---

10. Crofter's right to share in value of land taken possession of compulsorily

(1) Where in pursuance of any enactment providing for the acquisition and taking of possession of land compulsorily by any person (in this section referred to as an 'acquiring authority'), an acquiring authority acquire and take possession of a croft or a part thereof from a crofter, the crofter shall be entitled to receive from the acquiring authority, in addition to any compensation payable to him under section 114 of the Lands Clauses Consolidation (Scotland) Act 1845, a share in the value of the land of which possession has been taken, the amount whereof shall be one half of the difference between, subject to subsection (4) below, the market value of the land (on the date on which such possession is taken) as determined by the Land Court in

accordance with subsection (2) below (less any compensation payable as aforesaid) and the crofting value thereof.

(2) The market value for the purposes of subsection (1) above shall be a sum equal to the amount which the land, if sold in the open market by a willing seller (not being an authority as defined in section 1(1)(b) of the Community Land Act 1975) might be expected to realise assuming that the land were not land to which the Crofters (Scotland) Acts 1955 and 1961 apply.

(3) Section 9(4) of this Act shall apply to land which has been taken possession of compulsorily by an acquiring authority as it applies to land of which the Land Court have authorised resumption.

(4) For the purposes of this section, where any development has been carried out by any person, other than the crofter or any of his predecessors in the tenancy, on the land referred to in subsection (1) above before the land has been acquired by and taken possession of by the acquiring authority, there shall be deducted from the market value such amount thereof as, in the opinion of the Land Court, is attributable to that development.

(5) In this section 'crofting value', in relation to land which has been taken possession of compulsorily, has the same meaning as it has in section 3 of this Act in relation to croft land.

[77]

11. Protection of interests of crofters and cottars from planning blight

The interests qualifying for protection under sections 181 to 196 of the Town and Country Planning (Scotland) Act 1972 and sections 64 to 77 of the Land Compensation (Scotland) Act 1973 (planning blight) shall include the interest of a crofter in his croft or a cottar in his subject; and accordingly the aforesaid enactments shall have effect subject to the amendments set out in Schedule 1 to this Act.

[78]

12. Financial assistance to crofters, cottars and certain owner-occupiers

(1) The Secretary of State may provide assistance under section 22(2) of the Act of 1955 but not in respect of buildings other than dwelling-houses to—
   (a) a person, being a crofter who has acquired the site of the dwelling-house on or pertaining to his croft after the passing of this Act;
   (b) the nominee of such a person, being a member of his family, to whom the site was conveyed by the landlord of the croft;
   (c) a member of such a person's family who has acquired the title to the site from that person or such nominee;
   (d) a person, being a cottar who has acquired the site of the dwelling-house on or pertaining to his subject after the passing of this Act;
for a period of seven years from the date of the acquisition from the landlord.

(2) The Secretary of State may provide assistance under the said section 22(2) or under section 31(1) of the Act of 1955 (building grants and loans to owner-occupiers of like economic status as crofters) towards the provision or improvement of roads, or water or electricity or gas supplies.

(3) The provisions of Schedule 3 to the Act of 1955 (provisions as to security etc of loans) shall apply in relation to any loan made under the said section 22(2) by virtue of subsection (1) above.

(4) Where a person other than the landlord was infeft in the site of the dwelling-house immediately before the conveyance, the reference in subsection (1)(b) above to the landlord shall be construed as a reference to the landlord and such other person for their respective rights.

(5) If any person, for the purpose of obtaining for himself or any other person, a grant of loan under a scheme made under section 22(1) of the Act of 1955 or under the said section 22(2), knowingly or recklessly makes a false statement he shall be liable on summary conviction to a fine not exceeding £400.

(6) Any scheme made under the said section 22(1) may be varied or revoked by a subsequent scheme made in like manner.

[79]

13. Provision as respects removal of land from crofting tenure

(1) For subsection (7) of section 16 of the Act of 1955 (vacant crofts) there shall be substituted the following subsection—

'(7) Where a croft has, in consequence of the making of an order under section 17(1) of this Act, become vacant and has remained unlet for a period of six months beginning with the date on which the croft so became vacant, the Commission shall, if the landlord at any time within three months after the expiry of the period aforesaid gives notice to the Commission requiring them to do so, direct that the croft shall cease to be a croft; and if the landlord within one month after the issuing of such a direction gives notice to the Secretary of State requiring him to purchase the buildings on the croft, the Secretary of State shall purchase such buildings.'

(2) For subsection (9) of the said section 16 there shall be substituted the following subsections—

'(9) Where a croft is vacant, the Commission may, on the application of the landlord, direct that the croft shall cease to be a croft or refuse to grant the application; and if the Commission direct under this subsection or under subsection (7) above that a croft shall cease to be a croft, the provisions of this Act and, subject to subsection (9A) below, the Crofters (Scotland) Act 1961 shall cease to apply to the croft, without prejudice, however, to the subsequent exercise of any powers conferred by any enactment for the enlargement of existing crofts.

(9A) The coming into effect of a direction given by the Commission by virtue of section 16A(4) of this Act shall not affect the powers contained in the proviso to section 13(3) of the said Act of 1961 (subleases).'

(3) After the said section 16 there shall be inserted the following section—

'16A. Provisions supplementary to s 16(9)

(1) The Commission shall give a direction under section 16(9) of this Act that a croft shall cease to be a croft if—

(a) subject to subsection (2) below, they are satisfied that the applicant has applied for the direction in order that the croft may be used for or in connection with some reasonable purpose within the meaning of section 12(2) of this Act and that the extent of the land to which the application relates is not excessive in relation to that purpose; or

(b) the application is made in respect of a part of a croft, which consists only of the site of the dwelling-house on or pertaining to the croft and in respect of which a crofter is entitled at the time of the application, or has been entitled, to a conveyance by virtue of section 1(2) of the Crofting Reform (Scotland) Act 1976, and they are satisfied that the extent of garden ground included in that part is appropriate for the reasonable enjoyment of the dwelling-house as a residence.

(2) Without prejudice to subsection (1)(b) above, the Commission, in determining whether or not to give such a direction, shall have regard to the general interest of the crofting community in the district in which the croft is situated and in particular to the demand, if any, for a tenancy of the croft from persons who might reasonably be expected to obtain that tenancy if the croft were offered for letting on the open market on the date when they are considering the application.

(3) Where the Commission give such a direction on being satisfied as mentioned in subsection (1)(a) above, they may in the direction impose such conditions as appear to them requisite for securing that the land to which the direction relates is used for the proposed use; and if at any time they are satisfied that there has been a breach of any such condition, they may make a further direction that the land in respect of which there has been such a breach shall be a vacant croft.

(4) The Commission may, on the application of a crofter who is proposing to acquire croft land or the site of the dwelling-house on or pertaining to his croft, give a direction under the said section 16(9) as if the land were a vacant croft and the application was made by the landlord, that in the event of such acquisition of the land it shall cease to be a croft, or refuse the application; but such a direction shall not have effect until the land to which it relates has been acquired by the crofter or his nominee and unless the acquisition is made within five years of the date of the giving of the direction.

(5) A direction under the said section 16(9) may be given taking account of such modification of the application in relation to which the direction is given as the Commission consider appropriate.

(6) The Commission shall advertise all applications under the said section 16(9) or subsection (4) above (except in application made in respect of a part of a croft consisting only of the site of the dwelling-house on or pertaining to the croft) in one or more newspapers circulating in the district in which the croft to which the application relates is situated, and before disposing of such an application shall, if requested by the applicant, afford a hearing to the applicant and to such other person as they think fit.

(7) The Commission shall give notice in writing to the applicant of their proposed decision on an application made to them under the said section 16(9) or subsection (4) above, specifying the nature of and the reasons for such decision.

(8) The applicant may within 21 days of receipt of the notice under subsection (7) above, and the owner of land to which a further direction under subsection (3) above relates may within 21 days of the making of that further direction, appeal against the proposed decision or further direction to the Land Court who may hear or consider such evidence as they think fit in order to enable them to dispose of the appeal.

(9) The Commission shall give effect to the determination of the Land Court on an appeal under subsection (8) above.'.

[80]

14.   Extension of section 3 of Act of 1955

Section 3 of the Act of 1955 (definition of croft and crofter) shall have effect as if for subsection (5) there were substituted the following subsections—

'(5) For the purposes of this Act, the Crofters (Scotland) Act 1961 and the Crofting Reform (Scotland) Act 1976, any right in pasture or grazing land held or to be held by the tenant of a croft, whether alone or in common with others, and any land comprising any part of a common grazing which has been apportioned for the exclusive use of a crofter under section 27(4) of this Act and any land held runrig which has been apportioned under section 27(7) of this Act, shall be deemed to form part of the croft.

(6) For the purposes of the aforesaid Acts, where—
   (a) a crofter has acquired his entire croft other than any such right or land as is referred to in subsection (5) above, or
   (b) any person, not being a crofter, has obtained an apportionment of any land under the said section 27,

then the person referred to in paragraph (a) or (b) above shall be deemed to hold the right or land referred to therein in tenancy until held otherwise and that right or land shall be deemed to be a croft.'.

[81]

15. Assignation of croft

(1) Section 8 of the Act of 1955 (assignation of croft) shall apply to a part of a croft, being a part consisting of any right in pasture or grazing land deemed by virtue of section 3(5) of that Act to form part of a croft, as it applies to a croft.

(2) A crofter, who proposes to assign his croft or such a part as is referred to in subsection (1) above to a member of his family, shall not, if he obtains the consent of his landlord, be required to obtain the consent of the Commission under the said section 8; and a landlord who has given such consent shall notify the Commission of the assignation and the name of the assignee.

[81A]

16. Amendment of law with respect to common grazings

(1) At the end of section 24 of the Act of 1955 (appointment, etc, of grazings committee) there shall be added the following subsection—

'(9) A grazings committee shall pay such annual remuneration to the clerk appointed under subsection (6) or (8) of this section as they may determine; and they may recover from the crofters sharing in the common grazings all expenditure incurred by them in paying such remuneration.'.

(2) Nothing in paragraph (a) or (b) of section 25(1) of the Act of 1955 shall preclude a grazings committee from performing the duties therein specified on land other than the common grazings.

(3) After subsection (1) of the said section 25 there shall be inserted the following subsections—

'(1A) The grazings committee shall give notice to each crofter sharing in the common grazings of any proposals to carry out works in pursuance of the duty imposed by subsection (1)(b) above and the proposed allocation of the expenditure to be incurred in respect of those works among such crofters; and any such crofter may within one month of the date of such notice make representations in respect of the proposals or the proposed allocation to the Commission who may approve the proposals or proposed allocation with or without modifications or reject them.

(1B) Notwithstanding section 13(2) of the Act of 1961 (which provides that where a right in common grazings is sublet the subtenant comes in place of the crofter in relation to any matter which concerns such right), subsection (1A) above shall have effect in a case where such a right is sublet as if any reference to a crofter included a reference to a crofter in whose place a subtenant has come; but no liability to meet expenditure incurred by a grazings committee in the performance of the duties imposed on them by subsection (1)(b) above shall be imposed on such a crofter in respect of any period during which such a subtenancy subsists.'.

(4) For section 26(2)(b) of the Act of 1955 (common grazings regulations) there shall be substituted the following paragraph—

'(b) the recovery by the grazings committee from such crofters of all expenses incurred by the committee in the performance of the duties imposed on them by section 25(1)(b) of this Act according to the proposed allocation of expenditure referred to in subsection (1A) of the said section 25 or, as the case may be, that allocation as approved or modified by the Commission under that subsection;'.

(5) Section 27(7) of the said Act (apportionment by the Commission of lands held runrig) shall have effect as if after the word 'manner' there were inserted the words 'and subject to such conditions'.

[82]

17.   Extension of powers of Land Court

(1) An order or determination of the Land Court may be enforced as if it were a decree of the sheriff having jurisdiction in the area in which the order or determination is to be enforced; and accordingly section 25(6) of the Small Landholders (Scotland) Act 1911 (enforcement of Land Court orders) shall cease to have effect.

(2) The books called the 'Crofters Holdings Book' and the 'Landholders Holdings Book' kept in pursuance of section 27 of the Crofters Holdings (Scotland) Act 1886 shall be kept by the principal clerk of the Land Court; and accordingly the said section 27 shall cease to have effect.

[83]

18.   Pensions and compensation for members of Commission

Schedule 1 to the Act of 1955 (provisions as to the Crofters Commission) shall have effect as if after paragraph 4 there were inserted the following paragraphs—
> '4A. The Secretary of State shall, in the case of any member of the Commission to whom he may with the approval of the Minister for the Civil Service determine that this paragraph applies, pay such pension, allowance or gratuity to or in respect of the member on his retirement or death, or make such payments towards the provision of such a pension, allowance or gratuity, as he may, with the like approval, determine.

> 4B. If a person ceases to be a member of the Commission and it appears to the Secretary of State that there are special circumstances which makes it right that that person should receive compensation he may, with the approval of the said Minister, pay to that person a sum of such amount as he may, with the like approval, determine'.

[84]

19.   Application of Act to Crown

(1) This Act shall apply to land an interest in which belongs to Her Majesty in right of the Crown and land an interest in which belongs to a government department or is held in trust for Her Majesty for the purposes of a government department; but in its application to any land an interest in which belongs or is held as aforesaid this Act shall have effect subject to such modifications as may be prescribed by regulations made by the Secretary of State.

(2) Any regulations made by the Secretary of State under this section shall be embodied in a statutory instrument which shall be subject to annulment in pursuance of a resolution of either House of Parliament.

[84A]

20.   Financial provisions

(1) There shall be paid out of moneys provided by Parliament any increase attributable to this Act in the sums payable out of moneys so provided under section 3(10) of the Small Landholders (Scotland) Act 1911 and the Act of 1955.

(2) All sums received by the Secretary of State by virtue of this Act shall be paid into the Consolidated Fund.

[85]

21.   Interpretation

(1) Expressions used in this Act and the Act of 1955 have the same meanings in this Act as in that Act.

(2) In this Act—
  'the Act of 1955' means the Crofters (Scotland) Act 1955;
  'the Act of 1961' means the Crofters (Scotland) Act 1961;

'authority possessing compulsory purchase powers' has the same meaning as in the Town and Country Planning (Scotland) Act 1972;

'cottar' has the same meaning as in section 28 of that Act of 1955;

'croft land' has the meaning assigned to it by section 1(3) of this Act;

'development' has the same meaning as in section 19 of the Town and Country Planning (Scotland) Act 1972, except that it includes the operations and uses of land referred to in paragraphs (a) and (e) of subsection (2) of that section;

'landlord', in relation to the site of the dwelling-house on or pertaining to the subject of a cottar, means—

    (a) where the cottar is the tenant of the subject, the landlord thereof, and

    (b) where the cottar is the occupier of the subject who pays no rent, the owner thereof;

'National Trust for Scotland' means the National Trust for Scotland for Places of Historic Interest or Natural Beauty incorporated by the Order confirmed by the National Trust for Scotland Order Confirmation Act 1935;

'the site of the dwelling-house' has the meaning assigned to it by section 1(4) of this Act.

(3) Any reference in this Act to a member of a person's or crofter's or former crofter's family is a reference to the wife or husband of that person or crofter or former crofter or his son-in-law or daughter-in-law or anyone who would be, or would in any circumstances have been, entitled to succeed to his estate on intestacy by virtue of the Succession (Scotland) Act 1964.

(4) Any reference in this Act to any other enactment shall, unless the context otherwise requires, be construed as a reference to that enactment as amended, extended or applied by any other enactment including this Act.

[86]

22.   Minor and consequential amendments, repeals and savings

(1) The enactments mentioned in Schedule 2 to this Act shall have effect subject to the amendments respectively specified in that Schedule, being minor amendments or amendments consequential on the provisions of this Act.

(2) The enactments set out in Schedule 3 to this Act are hereby repealed to the extent specified in the third column of that Schedule.

(3) The repeal by this Act of part of section 17 of the Act of 1955 and of sections 18 of that Act and 7 of the Act of 1961 shall not affect anything done or any right established under any such provision before the passing of this Act.

[87]

23.   Short title and extent

(1) This Act may be cited as the Crofting Reform (Scotland) Act 1976.

(2) This Act extends to Scotland only.

[88]

SCHEDULES

SCHEDULE 1

AMENDMENT OF ENACTMENTS CONSEQUENTIAL ON SECTION 11

The Town and Country Planning (Scotland) Act 1972

1. At the end of section 182 (power to serve blight notice), there shall be added the following subsection—

'(5) Where the claimant is a crofter or cottar, this section shall have effect as if—
(a) in subsection 1(c) for the word "sell" there were substituted the word "assign";
(b) in subsection 1(d) for the words from "sell it" to "to sell" there were substituted the words "assign it except at a price substantially lower than that for which he might reasonably have expected to assign it";
(c) in subsections (1) and (4) for the word "purchase" there were substituted the words "take possession of".'.

2. In section 184 (reference of objections to Lands Tribunal), in subsection (6) after the word 'treat' there shall be inserted the words 'or, in a case where the claimant is a crofter or cottar, notice of entry'.

3. At the end of section 185 (effect of valid blight notice), there shall be added the following subsection—
'(5) Where the claimant is a crofter or cottar, this section shall have effect as if in subsections (1) and (3) for the words from "acquire" to "respect thereof" there were substituted the words "require the crofter or cottar to give up possession of the land occupied by him and to have served a notice of entry in respect thereof under paragraph 3 of Schedule 2 to the Acquisition of Land (Authorisation Procedure) (Scotland) Act 1947.'.

4. At the end of section 188 (effect on powers of compulsory acquisition of counter-notice disclaiming intention to acquire), there shall be added the following subsection—
'(5) Where a claimant is a crofter or cottar, this section shall have effect as if in subsections (2) and (4) for the words from "or by" to "claimant in" there were substituted the words "to require the crofter or cottar to give up possession of".'.

5. In section 192(4) (meaning of 'owner's interest'), after the words 'interest of' there shall be inserted the word '(a)' and after the word 'years' there shall be inserted the words 'and (b) a crofter or cottar therein'.

6. In section 196(1) (general interpretation), after the definition of 'the claimant' there shall be inserted the following definitions—
'"cottar" has the same meaning as in section 28(4) of the Crofters (Scotland) Act 1955;
"crofter" has the same meaning as in section 3(2) of the Crofters (Scotland) Act 1955'.

The Land Compensation (Scotland) Act 1973

7. At the end of section 68 (land affected by orders relating to new towns), there shall be added the following subsection—
'(6) This section shall have effect where the service of the blight notice by virtue of subsection (1) above is by a crofter or cottar as if—
(a) in subsection (4) for the words "acquire compulsorily any interest in land" and "acquires an interest" there were substituted respectively the words "take possession of any land occupied by the crofter or cottar" and "takes possession" and in paragraphs (a) and (b) for the word "interest" there were substituted the word "possession";
(b) in subsection (5) for the words from "acquisition of" to "acquisition were" there were substituted the words "taking of possession of land by the Secretary of State under subsection (4) above as if the taking of possession were".'

8. At the end of section 74 (blight notice requiring purchase of whole agricultural unit), there shall be added the following subsection—
'(3) This section shall have effect where the blight notice is served by a crofter or cottar as if for subsection (1)(b) there were substituted the following paragraph—

"(b) a requirement that the appropriate authority shall take possession of the
whole of the unit or, as the case may be, the whole of the part of it to which
the notice relates".'

9. At the end of section 76 (effect of blight notice requiring purchase of whole
agricultural unit), there shall be added the following subsection—
'(9) Where the claimant is a crofter or cottar this section shall have effect as if—
(a) in subsections (2) and (4) for the words from "acquire compulsorily" to
"interest" and for the words "to treat in respect thereof" there were
substituted respectively the words "take possession compulsorily of the
land" and the words "of entry in respect of that land under paragraph 3 of
Schedule 2 to the Acquisition of Land (Authorisation Procedure) (Scotland)
Act 1947";
(b) in subsection (4)(a) for the word "acquire" there were substituted the words
"take possession of".'

[89]

SCHEDULE 2

MINOR AND CONSEQUENTIAL AMENDMENTS

The Small Landholders (Scotland) Act 1911

1. In section 32(14) (provisions as to statutory small tenants), for the words 'twenty,
the section twenty-seven' there shall be substituted the words 'and section twenty'.

The Land Settlement (Scotland) Act 1919

2. At the end of section 6 (duty of Secretary of State with respect to sale or lease of
land), there shall be added the following subsection—
'(6) Subsections (3) and (4) above shall not apply to crofts as defined in section 3
of the Crofters (Scotland) Act 1955.'.

The Acquisition of Land (Authorisation Procedure) (Scotland) Act 1947

3. In Schedule 1 (procedure for authorising compulsory purchases), in paragraph 4(1)
after the word 'aforesaid' there shall be inserted the words 'or if no objection is duly
made by the National Trust for Scotland in a case where the land comprised in the
order was held inalienably by the Trust on the date of the passing of the Crofting
Reform (Scotland) Act 1976 and was acquired from the Trust by a crofter as defined in
section 3 of the Crofters (Scotland) Act 1955 in pursuance of an order under section
2(1) or 4(1) of the said Act of 1976'.

The Crofters (Scotland) Act 1955

4. At the end of section 1(1) (constitution and general functions of the Commission),
there shall be added the words 'and the Crofting Reform (Scotland) Act 1976.'.

5. In section 2 (particular powers and duties of the Commission)—
(a) in subsection (1)(d), after the word 'Act' there shall be inserted the words 'and
the Crofting Reform (Scotland) Act 1976';
(b) in subsection (3), for the words 'sheriff-clerk' there shall be substituted the
words 'principal clerk of the Land Court', and the words from 'and the
provisions' to the end shall cease to have effect;
(c) in subsection (4), after the word 'Act' there shall be inserted the words 'and the
Crofting Reform (Scotland) Act 1976.'

6. In section 8 (assignation of croft)—
(a) for subsections (1) and (2) there shall be substituted the following subsections—
'(1) A crofter shall not assign his croft—

(a) to a member of his family unless he obtains the consent in writing of his landlord or, failing such consent, the consent in writing of the Commission on an application made to them;

(b) to a person other than a member of his family unless he obtains the consent in writing of the Commission on an application made to them.

(2) A landlord who has given his consent in pursuance of subsection (1)(a) above shall notify the Commission of the assignation and the name of the assignee.';

(b) in subsection (5), after the word 'Commission' where it first occurs there shall be inserted the words 'in a case where he is required to obtain such consent in pursuance of subsection (1) above';

(c) at the end there shall be added the following subsections—

'(7) Any reference in this section to a croft shall include a reference to a part of a croft, being a part consisting of any right in pasture or grazing land deemed by virtue of section 3(5) of this Act to form part of a croft.

(8) In this section 'member of his family', in relation to a crofter, has the same meaning as 'member of the crofter's family' has in section 10(7) of this Act.'

7. In section 15(1) (Commission to obtain information and to compile register of crofts)—

(a) for the word 'acreage' there shall be substituted the word 'extent';

(b) at the end there shall be added the words 'and the Crofting Reform (Scotland) Act 1976.'

8. In section 16 (vacant crofts)—

(a) in the proviso to subsection (4), for the words from 'an application' to the end there shall be substituted the words 'the Secretary of State is considering an application made to him under subsection (3) above for consent to let, or the Commission are considering an application made to them under subsection (9) below for a direction that the croft shall cease to be a croft';

(b) in subsection (8), after the words 'section or' there shall be inserted the words 'by the landlord to the Secretary of State';

(c) in subsections (11A) and (13), after the word 'section' there shall be inserted the words 'and section 16A of this Act';

(d) at the end of the section there shall be added the following subsection—

'(14) For the avoidance of doubt it is hereby declared that this section has effect (and shall be deemed always to have had effect since 27th August 1961) as if—

(a) a person who has become the owner-occupier of a croft were required under subsection (1) above within one month of the date on which he became such owner-occupier to give notice thereof to the Commission; and

(b) any reference in the section other than in subsection (1) above to a landlord included a reference to an owner-occupier.'

9. In section 17(1)(a) (absentee crofters), for the words 'ten miles' there shall be substituted the words 'sixteen kilometres'.

10. In section 22(5) (power of Secretary of State to give financial assistance to crofters), after the word 'building' there shall be inserted the words 'or towards the provision or improvement of roads, or water or electricity or gas supplies' and for the words 'such erection, improvement or rebuilding' there shall be substituted the words 'the works in question'.

11. In section 27(1) (common grazings), for the words 'forty shillings' and 'five shillings' there shall be substituted respectively the words '£10' and '50 pence'.

12. In section 30(4) (provisions as to entry and inspection), for the words 'five pounds' there shall be substituted the word '£10'.

13. In section 31(2) (building grants and loans to owner-occupiers of like economic status as crofters), for paragraph (b) there shall be substituted the following paragraph—
'(b) is either—
(i) a holding of which the area does not exceed 30 hectares, or
(ii) a holding of which the annual rent, if it were a croft let to a crofter under this Act and the Crofters (Scotland) Act 1961, would not in the opinion of the Secretary of State exceed £100, or
(iii) a holding which exceeds 30 hectares and of which the annual rent if it were a croft so let would in the opinion of the Secretary of State exceed £100, but which in the opinion of the Secretary of State is not substantially larger than 30 hectares or is capable of being let as a croft at an annual rent not substantially in excess of £100;'.

14. In section 34(1) (determination of disputes, etc) after the word 'Act' there shall be inserted the words 'or the Crofting Reform (Scotland) Act 1976'.

15. In Schedule 3 (provisions as to security, etc, of loans)—
(a) in paragraph 1, for the words 'bond which shall be a charge on' there shall be substituted the words 'heritable security over';
(b) in paragraph 4, for the word 'bond' there shall be substituted the words 'heritable security'.

The Valuation and Rating (Scotland) Act 1956

16. In section 7 (provisions relating to agricultural lands and heritages and dwelling-houses occupied in connection therewith)—
(a) in subsection (6)(b) for the words 'fifty pounds' there shall be substituted the word '£100';
(b) at the end of subsection (8)(b) there shall be added the words
'and
(c) to a dwelling-house, comprised in a conveyance of the site of the dwelling-house on or pertaining to a croft or the subject of a cottar obtained after the passing of the Crofting Reform (Scotland) Act 1976 by a person who is the crofter of the croft or, as the case may be, the cottar of the subject of which the dwelling-house then forms part, and occupied by that person or the husband or wife of that person.'

The Crofters (Scotland) Act 1961

17. In section 2 (new crofts, enlarged crofts and common grazings)—
(a) subsection (1), and in subsection (5) the words from the beginning to 'section, and' shall cease to have effect;
(b) in subsections (2)(a) and (b) and (3) for the words 'and this Act' there shall be substituted the words 'this Act and the Crofting Reform (Scotland) Act 1976';
(c) in subsection 2(b)—
(i) for the words 'seventy-five acres' and 'fifty pounds' there shall be substituted respectively the words '30 hectares' and '£100',
(ii) for the words 'Secretary of State', 'him' and 'he makes' there shall be substituted respectively the words 'Commission', 'them' and 'they make';
(d) after subsection (2) there shall be inserted the following subsection—
'(2A) The Commission shall make a direction under subsection (2) above only if they are satisfied that such a direction—
(a) would be of benefit to the croft; and
(b) would not result in the croft as enlarged by the land referred to in that subsection being substantially larger than 30 hectares or capable of being let as a croft at an annual rent substantially in excess of £100.'

18. At the end of section 3(2) (Commission to maintain register of crofts), there shall be added the following proviso—

'Provided that the Commission shall not be required under this subsection to send a copy of any new entry or of any entry altered by them or to intimate the omission of any entry to any person who has to any extent assisted the Commission in the performance of their duties of inserting or, as the case may be, altering or omitting an entry by the furnishing of information to them.'.

19. In section 4 (determination of questions by Land Court), in subsections (1) and (2), after the words 'or this Act' and 'and this Act' wherever they occur there shall be inserted respectively the words 'or the Crofting Reform (Scotland) Act 1976' and 'and the Crofting Reform (Scotland) Act 1976'.

20. In section 12(10)(c) (subletting of crofts not adequately used), for the words 'one acre' there shall be substituted the words 'one half hectare'.

21. In section 13 (subleases of crofts), in the proviso to subsection (3) after the words 'one month' where they first occur there shall be inserted the words 'or such longer period not exceeding three months as the Commission may in all the circumstances think reasonable', and after the words 'one month' where they subsequently occur there shall be inserted the words 'or the said longer period'.

22. In section 14(1) (amendment of powers of Secretary of State with respect to giving of financial assistance in crofting counties)—
(a) in paragraph (b), for the words 'seventy-five acres' and 'fifty pounds' there shall be substituted respectively the words '30 hectares' and '£100';
(b) after paragraph (b) there shall be inserted the following paragraph—
'(bb) for occupiers of holdings, other than crofts situated in the crofting counties which exceed 30 hectares (exclusive of any common pasture or grazing held therewith) and of which the annual rent if they were crofts so let would in the opinion of the Secretary of State exceed £100, but which in the opinion of the Secretary of State are not substantially larger than 30 hectares (exclusive of any common pasture or grazing held therewith) or are capable of being so let at an annual rent not substantially in excess of £100, being occupiers who in the opinion of the Secretary of State are of substantially the same economic status as a crofter; and'.

23. In section 15 (amendment of law with respect to common grazings)—
(a) in subsection (2)—
(i) for the words 'paragraph (b) of the said subsection' there shall be substituted the words "such of the crofters referred to in paragraph (b) of that subsection as are liable to pay any expenses in accordance with a proposed allocation of expenditure referred to in subsection (1A) of section 25 of that Act or, as the case may be, such a proposed allocation as approved or modified by the Commission under that subsection';
(ii) for the words from 'discharge' to the end there shall be substituted the words 'performance of the duties imposed on them by paragraphs (a) and (b) respectively of section 25(1) of that Act.';
(b) in subsection (6) for the words 'and of this Act' and 'either' there shall be substituted respectively the words 'this Act and the Crofting Reform (Scotland) Act 1976' and 'any'.

The Countryside (Scotland) Act 1967

24. In section 13 (access agreements)—
(a) in subsection (9)(a), after the word 'either' there shall be inserted the word '(i)', and for the words from 'with the consent' to 'Commission' there shall be substituted the words '(ii) subject to subsection (9A) below';
(b) after subsection (9) there shall be inserted the following subsection—
'(9A) A grazings committee to whom such a payment as is referred to in paragraph (a) of subsection (9) above has been made and who are proposing to apply the payment in carrying out works in accordance with head (ii) of

that paragraph shall give notice in writing to each crofter sharing in the common grazings of their proposals; and any such crofter may within one month of the date of such notice make representations in respect of the proposals to the Crofters Commission who may approve them with or without modifications or reject them.'

The Agriculture (Miscellaneous Provisions) Act 1968

25. For section 11(8) (certain payments to tenant farmers), there shall be substituted the following subsection—

'(8) The provisions of the Small Landholders (Scotland) Acts 1886 to 1931 with regard to the Scottish Land Court shall, with any necessary modifications, apply for the purpose of the determination of any matter referred to them under subsection (7) of this section as they apply for the purpose of the determination by them of matters referred to them under those Acts.'.

[90]

SCHEDULE 3

REPEAL OF ENACTMENTS

Chapter	Short Title	Extent of Repeal
49 & 50 Vict (c 29)	The Crofters Holdings (Scotland) Act 1886	Section 27.
1 & 2 Geo 5 (c 49)	The Small Landholders (Scotland) Act 1911	Section 25(6).
3 & 4 Eliz 2 (c 21)	The Crofters (Scotland) Act 1955	In section 2(3), the words from 'and the provisions' to the end. In section 12(4), the words 'the constitution of new crofts or'. In section 16 subsection (2), in subsection (4) the words from the beginning of paragraph (a) to 'case' in paragraph (b). In section 17, subsections (4) to (8), in subsection (9) the words from the beginning to 'foregoing subsection' and subsection (10). Section 18. In section 22, subsections (4)(d) and (8). In section 25(1), the proviso. In Schedule 3, in paragraph 4, the word 'appropriate'.
9 & 10 Eliz 2 (c 58)	The Crofters (Scotland) Act 1961	In section 2, subsection (1), in subsection (5) the words from the beginning to 'section, and' and subsection (7). In section 6, in subsection (2) the words 'as a separate croft' and in subsection (3) the words 'or paragraph (a) of subsection (9) of section 19 of that Act'. Section 7. Section 8(3)(e).

Succession (Scotland) Act 1964 (c 41), section 16

[1]16. Provisions relating to leases

(1) This section applies to any interest, being the interest of a tenant under a lease, which is comprised in the estate of a deceased person and has accordingly vested in the deceased's executor by virtue of section 14 of this Act; and in the following provisions of this section 'interest' means an interest to which this section applies.

(2) Where an interest—
    (a) is not the subject of a valid bequest by the deceased, or
    (b) is the subject of such a bequest, but the bequest is not accepted by the legatee, or
    (c) being an interest under an agricultural lease, is the subject of such a bequest, but the bequest . . .[2] becomes null and void under section 10 of the Act of 1955,
. . .[2] the executor shall be entitled. . .[2] to transfer the interest to any one of the persons entitled to succeed to the deceased's intestate estate, or to claim legal rights or the prior rights of a surviving spouse out of the estate, in or towards satisfaction of that person's entitlement or claim; but shall not be entitled to transfer the interest to any other person without the consent—
    (i) in the case of an interest under an agricultural lease, being a lease of a croft within the meaning of section 3 (1) of the Act of 1955, of the Crofters Commission;
    (ii) . . .[2]

(3) If in the case of any interest—
    (a) at any time the executor is satisfied that the interest cannot be disposed of according to law and so informs the landlord, or
    (b) the interest is not so disposed of within a period of one year or such longer period as may be fixed by agreement between the landlord and the executor, or failing agreement, by the sheriff on summary application by the executor—
        (i) . . .[2]
        (ia) in the case of an interest under an agricultural lease which is the subject of an application by the legateee to the Crofters Commission under section 10 (1) of the Act of 1955, from the date of any refusal by the Commission to determine that the bequest shall not be null and void,
        (ib) in the case of an interest under an agricultural lease which is the subject of an intimation of objection by the landlord to the legatee and the Crofters Commission under section 10(3) of the Act of 1955, from the date of any decision of the Commission upholding the objection,
    (ii) in any other case, from the date of death of the deceased, either the landlord or the executor may, on giving notice in accordance with the next following subsection to the other, terminate the lease (in so far as it relates to the interest) notwithstanding any provision therein, or any enactment or rule of law, to the contrary effect.

(4) The period of notice given under the last foregoing subsection shall be—
    (a) in the case of an agricultural lease, such period as may be agreed, or, failing

agreement, a period of not less than one year and not more than two years ending with such term of Whitsunday or Martinmas as may be specified in the notice; and

(b) . . .[2]

(5) Subsection (3) of this section shall not prejudice any claim by any party to the lease for compensation or damages in respect of the termination of the lease (or any rights under it) in pursuance of that subsection; but any award of compensation or damages in respect of such termination at the instance of the executor shall be enforceable only against the estate of the deceased and not against the executor personally.

(6) Where an interest is an interest under an agricultural lease, and—

(a) an application is made under . . .[2] section 13 of the Act of 1955 to the Land Court for an order for removal . . .

(b) . . .

the Land Court shall not make the order . . .[2] unless the court . . .[2] is satisfied that it is reasonable having regard to the fact that the interest is vested in the executor in his capacity as executor, that it should be made.

(7) . . .[2]

(8) Where an interest is an interest under an agricultural lease and is the subject of a valid bequest by the deceased, the fact that the interest is vested in the executor under the said section 14 shall not prevent the operation, in relation to the legatee, of . . .[2] subsections (2) to (7) of section 10 of the Act of 1955.

(9) In this section—

'agricultural lease' means . . .[2] a lease of a croft within the meaning of section 3(1) of the Act of 1955;

. . .[2]

'the Act of 1955' means the Crofters (Scotland) Act 1955;

'lease' includes tenancy.

Notes.—1 As amended by Law Reform (Miscellaneous Provisions) (Scotland) Act 1968 (c 70), s 8, Sch 2.

2 Material omitted not relevant to this work.

[92]

APPENDIX B(1)

Rules of the Scottish Land Court

Coming into operation 1st May 1979

CONTENTS

DEFINITIONS

1. In the construction of these Rules (unless the context otherwise requires)—
    (a) The word 'Court' shall mean the Scottish Land Court and shall include the Full Court and any Divisional Court; the expression 'Full Court' shall mean the Court constituted for hearing appeals under section 25(5) of the Small Landholders (Scotland) Act 1911 and the expression 'Divisional Court' shall mean any member or any two members sitting or acting with any legal assessor in virtue of any powers delegated under the said subsection either by a quorum of the whole Court or by these Rules.
    (b) The word 'Chairman' shall mean the Chairman of the Court.
    (c) The expression 'Principal Clerk' shall mean the Principal Clerk and Legal Secretary to the Court and shall include every person who for the time being is authorised or deputed in the absence of the Principal Clerk to discharge the duties of Principal Clerk to the Court.

(d) The word 'Auditor' shall mean the Auditor of the Land Court.

(e) The word 'Order' shall include decree, award and determination in any proceeding before the Court.

(f) The word 'month' shall, in the computation of time for the purposes of these Rules and of any Order made by the Court, mean calendar month.

(g) The word 'revaluation' shall mean the fixing of a second and every subsequent Fair Rent or Equitable Rent for a holding.

(h) The word 'hearing' shall include trial, proof and debate in any Application or any proceeding accessory or incidental thereto.

(i) The word 'landlord' shall mean any person for the time being entitled to receive the rents and profits or to take possession of any holding and shall include the trustees, executors, administrators, assignees, legatee, disponee or next-of-kin, husband, guardian, curator bonis, trustee in bankruptcy or judicial factor of a landlord.

(j) The word 'person' shall include any body or association of persons, incorporated or unincorporated.

(k) The expression 'Final Order' shall mean an Order of the Court which, either by itself or taken along with a previous Order or Orders, disposes of the subject-matter of the Application, though all the questions of law or of fact arising in the Application shall not have been decided and though expenses, if found due, shall not have been modified, taxed or decerned for.

[93]

OFFICE AND SITTINGS OF THE COURT

2. The office of the Court in Edinburgh shall be open to the public on every day of the year from 9 o'clock am until 4 o'clock pm except Saturdays, Sundays, public holidays and any other days on which the office may be closed by Order of the Court.

[94]

3. The Court shall hold sittings for the purpose of hearing Applications, including Appeals and Motions for Rehearing, at such places as they shall from time to time intimate to parties.

[95]

4. Any sitting and any hearing in any Application or proceeding may be postponed or adjourned either to a fixed day or to a day to be afterwards fixed by the Court.

[96]

PROCEDURE

Applications

5. All Applications to the Court shall be framed as nearly as reasonably may be in accordance with the forms provided by the Court. These forms, with relative copy forms for service, may be procured by intending Applicants from the Court free of charge. They may be varied and the initial conclusions altered, supplemented or combined, so far as necessary to adapt the forms to any special case or to Applications for which no special form has been issued.

[97]

6. No Application shall be incompetent solely on the ground that a declaratory Order only is applied for.

[98]

7. Except as otherwise provided, Applications shall be signed by the Applicant or by a solicitor or counsel or, where an Applicant is furth of Scotland, by any person duly authorised in writing, on his behalf. Applications by a landlord may be signed by his factor.

[99]

8. Where an Applicant cannot sign his name and is not represented by a solicitor, he may instead adhibit his X or mark in the presence of at least one witness above eighteen years of age who shall certify in writing on the Application that it was read over and explained to the Applicant before his mark was adhibited.

[100]

9. All Applications shall be addressed to the Land Court at their office at 1 Grosvenor Crescent, Edinburgh, EH12 5ER and shall be posted to, or delivered at, the said office, together with (1) (except in the cases provided for under Rules 17 and 21 and in Applications where no service is necessary, eg joint Applications by landlord and tenant) a copy, or as many copies as are required, duly filled up, for service on the Respondent or Respondents and (2) the appropriate fee, as specified in the Table of Court Fees set forth in Appendix 1 to these Rules.

[101]

10. Tenants who hold pasture, grazing or other rights in common or whose holdings are situated in the same township and on the estate of the same landlord may join as Applicants, or be called by their landlord as Respondents, in one Application to fix fair rents for their holdings.

[102]

Service, intimation, etc.

11. If an Application, posted or delivered as aforesaid, appears to be in proper form and if the appropriate fee in accordance with the Table of Court Fees has been paid (unless the Application is one in which the Court fees fall to be assessed by the Court), the Principal Clerk shall, after satisfying himself of the accuracy of the service copy or copies lodged along with the Application, effect service of the Application by transmitting such copy or copies, duly certified, by first class recorded delivery service or registered post letter to the Respondent, or each Respondent, at the address, or addresses, stated in the Application.

[103]

12. Any notice, order, summons or proceeding in any Application shall similarly be served or intimated by first class recorded delivery service or registered post letter containing a certified copy of such notice, order, summons or proceeding, directed by the Principal Clerk (or by an Applicant or Respondent if so ordered) to the person, or persons, on or to whom such service or intimation is required.

[104]

13. Any period which begins to run from service or intimation shall be reckoned from the expiry of twenty-four hours after the time of posting such recorded delivery service or registered letter.

[105]

14. Service on, or intimation to, a landlord may be effected by first class recorded delivery service or registered post letter containing a certified copy of the Application, order, notice, summons or proceeding, of which service or intimation is required, directed to him at the address of his factor or the solicitor to whom the tenant, or other Applicant or Applicants, has usually paid rent.

[106]

15. Service on, or intimation to, any association, board, firm, company or corporation may be effected in like manner by first class recorded delivery service or registered post letter containing a certified copy as aforesaid, directed to such

association, board, firm, company or corporation under the name or description which they ordinarily use, at the principal office or place of business or (if the principal office or place of business be situated outwith Scotland) at any office or place within Scotland (including the office of a clerk, secretary or representative) where they carry on business.

[107]

16. In every case where a party to an Application is represented by a solicitor, any order, summons, notice or other proceeding may be served on, or intimated to, such party in like manner by first class recorded delivery service or registered post letter directed to such solicitor at his office or place of business, unless and until the other parties and the Principal Clerk are notified that such solicitor no longer acts for such party.

[108]

17. In any Application for resumption of, or otherwise relating to, common grazings, when the number of persons called as Respondents, or to whom intimation is ordered, exceeds twenty, the Court may allow the Applicant, or Applicants, or other parties, as the case may be, to give notice or intimation of the Application or any proceeding therein to all such persons by advertisement in each of two successive weeks in any newspaper circulating in the district or by service of such notice or intimation on the clerk to the grazings committee or in such other manner as the Court may think sufficient, in substitution for intimation or service made by recorded delivery service or registered post letter by the Principal Clerk to or on each Respondent so called or each person to whom intimation is so ordered.

[109]

18. If any person who is named as a Respondent or who has an interest to intervene in, or who is proposed to be made a party to, an Application has no known factor or solicitor and no known residence or place of business within Scotland, but has a known residence or place of business outwith Scotland, notice or intimation of such Application, or of any order or proceeding therein, shall be given to him by first class recorded delivery service or registered post letter containing a certified copy thereof directed to such residence or place of business.

[110]

19. The receipt of the Post Office for a first class recorded delivery service or registered post letter duly directed, which is certified by the Principal Clerk or is otherwise proved to have contained a true copy of the Application, order, notice, summons or proceeding intended to be served on, or intimated to, the person to whom such recorded delivery service or registered post letter was directed, shall be sufficient prima facie proof of due service on, or intimation to, such person of such Application, order, summons, notice or proceeding having been effected at the time at which said recorded delivery service or registered post letter would have been delivered in ordinary course of post. A first class recorded delivery service or registered post letter shall be deemed, until the contrary is proved, to have been duly directed to the person on or to whom service or intimation was intended to be so made, when it has been directed to him either (1) at the address stated by him in any Application or pleading or proceeding in the Application or (2) at the address of his factor or solicitor or (3) at his last known residence or place of business.

[111]

20. When intimation is made under Rule 17 copies of the newspaper containing the advertisement shall be deemed prima facie proof of such intimation.

[112]

21. Any person named as a Respondent in an Application or made a party thereto, may by a signed endorsement on the Application or by statement in open Court or by letter to the Appliant or other party moving, or entitled to move, for service or intimation or to the Principal Clerk, agree to dispense with service or intimation of such Application or order, summons, notice or proceeding therein.

[113]

22. No party who appears in Court or lodges objections or answers or other pleading shall be entitled to state any objection to the regularity of the service on, or of the intimation to, himself.

[114]

23. If there has been any insufficiency of, or irregularity in, any service on, or intimation to, a person who has not appeared in Court or lodged objections or answers or other pleading or if it seems expedient that service or intimation of any Application, order, notice, summons or proceeding on or to any person should be made of new or in any other or further manner than by first class recorded delivery service or registered post letter as aforesaid, the Court may authorise or direct new, or further, service or intimation accordingly, on such conditions as the Court may think proper, in any manner allowed by the law and practice of Scotland.

[115]

24. As soon as an Application has been received by the Principal Clerk, it shall be deemed to be in dependence before the Court and shall not be abandoned or withdrawn without leave of the Court on such conditions as to expenses or otherwise as the Court may think just.

[116]

Process

25. Any party to an Application or his solicitor or other authorised representative may (1) require the Principal Clerk to exhibit the Application, or any part of the process therein, in his custody at the office of the Court during office hours, free of charge; (2) make a copy of the Application or any order pronounced therein or any answers, minutes, writings, plans or other documents in process in such custody at the said office, during office hours, and under supervision of the Principal Clerk, free of charge.

[117]

26. No person shall be allowed, without leave of the Court, to borrow the principal Application or any original deed, writing, plan, document or other production forming part of the process therein: but the Principal Clerk may, when duly requested, issue a certified copy, or copies, thereof to any party to an Application or his solicitor or other authorised representative at the charge specified in the Table of Court Fees.

[118]

27. Any solicitor acting for a party to an Application may borrow (1) any part or parts of the process therein, other than those specified in the preceding Rule and (2) also the part or parts so specified, by leave of the Court, or by permission of the Principal Clerk, in each case upon granting a borrowing receipt and undertaking to return the productions borrowed to the office of the Court within 48 hours after demand by the Principal Clerk.

[119]

CONSIGNATION

28. In any application which raises questions regarding any claims for payment of money which the Court has power to decide, any party may consign a sum of money in Court to be dealt with according as rights of parties may be determined in course of the proceedings.

[120]

29. Any sum of money which a party desires, or has been ordered, to consign shall be consigned in the hands of the Principal Clerk in the same manner as in an ordinary action in the Sheriff Court and shall be held by the Principal Clerk subject to the

directions of the Court. No consigned money shall be paid or uplifted without leave of the Court or the consent in writing of all parties interested.

[121]

TIME LIMITS

30. Any period limited in these Rules, or in any Order, for any act or proceeding, which expires on a Saturday, Sunday, public holiday or any other day on which the office of the Court is closed by Order of the Court, shall be extended to the next lawful day.

[122]

31. Any period limited by an Order for any act or proceeding may be extended by the Court, on cause shown, either before or after the expiry of such period.

[123]

PLEADINGS

32. A Respondent is not required to lodge Answers unless, and until, Answers are ordered by the Court. Answers, Replies, Objections or other written pleadings shall be lodged with the Principal Clerk, unless otherwise directed by the Court, and the Principal Clerk shall note receipt of the same on the Application. If Answers ordered by the Court are not lodged within the time specified in the Order, the Principal Clerk shall certify to that effect on the Application.

[124]

33. The Court may, at any stage of an Application, order any party therein to lodge a statement or pleadings, where this has not been done, or to revise his statement or pleadings, and also to make specific any statement, answer or reply contained in his Application, Objections, Answers or other pleadings, relating to material facts disputed; and either to admit or deny definitely any statement, made by any opposing party in that party's Application or Answers or Objections or other pleadings, relating to disputed material facts, when the Court is of opinion that such statement or pleadings, specification, admission or denial is necessary to define, or determine, the real matter or matters is dispute; or to withdraw or expunge any irrelevant and improper matter contained in his Application, Answers, Replies, Objections or other pleadings.

[125]

34. All Objections, Answers, Replies, Statements, Minutes or other pleadings shall be subscribed as provided for under Rules 7 and 8.

[126]

35. Where a party is represented by a solicitor or factor, he shall lodge along with any Answers, Replies, Statements, Minutes or other pleadings a copy thereof for each of the other parties to the Application.

[127]

Amendment, Conjunction, etc.

36. The Court may, either of their own accord or on the motion of any person interested, at any time before a Final Order has been pronounced in an Application and upon such terms or conditions as to notice, intimation or service and expenses or otherwise, as the Court shall think proper,
   (a) amend any error, omission or defect in the Application or any pleadings or proceeding therein;
   (b) qualify, restrict, enlarge, or add new conclusions to, the conclusions of the Application, notwithstanding that, by such amendment or addition, additional or alternative remedies may be sought or a larger sum of money or an additional

area of land or other interests in land may thereby be subjected to the adjudication of the Court;

(c) strike out the names of any persons who have, improperly or unnecessarily, been made parties to the Application;

(d) substitute or add the names or proper characters of any persons as Applicants or Respondents who ought to have been, but were not, made parties, Applicant or Respondent as the case may be, or not made parties in their proper character, representative, individual or otherwise;

(e) substitute or add the names of any persons as parties, Applicant or Respondent as the case may be, who by reason of any assignation or renunciation by, or the marriage, bankruptcy or death of, any of the parties to the Application, or of any other event occurring during its dependence, have acquired any right or interest, or become subject to any liability, in respect of the matters to which the Application relates;

and, when necessary to enable the Court effectually to determine, or adjudicate on, the real matters in dispute, such amendments or additions shall be made or allowed.

[128]

37. Where the same, or similar, questions of law or fact arise in, or where there is a relation between, two or more depending Applications, the Court (1) may sist one or more of such Applications and appoint the other Application or Applications to proceed or (2) where it appears more convenient that they should be heard together, the Court may conjoin such Applications and dispose of them, either together or separately, as may be found expedient.

[129]

38. The Court may appoint a tutor or curator ad litem to any party in an Application who is in pupillarity or minority or is of defective capacity and has no known tutor, curator or other guardian.

[130]

ADMISSIONS, WITNESSES, PRODUCTION OF DOCUMENTS, ETC.

39. As soon as an Order appointing a time and place for hearing has been pronounced in any Application, any party thereto shall be entitled, unless the Order limits the hearing to matters of law or procedure,

(1) to call on any opposing party by written notice, delivered or transmitted by first class recorded delivery service or registered post letter, not less than seven days before the time so appointed, to admit, but only as between the parties giving and receiving such notice and solely for the purposes of the particular Application, any specific fact or facts stated in such notice and relating to the subject-matter of the Application. If the party so called on unnecessarily refuses or delays to admit such specific fact or facts, he may be found liable in the expenses incurred in proving any specific fact which he is so refused or delayed to admit; and

(2) to move the Court to grant a summons requiring the persons therein named and designed to attend at such appointed time and place, and any adjourned hearing, for the purpose of (a) giving evidence and/or (b) producing the writings, documents, business books, plans or articles therein specified or described.

40. Further, on special cause shown or of their own accord the Court may, at any stage of the proceedings in an Application—

(1) Order any party thereto (a) to lodge in process all writings, documents, business books, plans or articles in his possession or under his control, whether founded on by such party or not, relating to any matter in dispute therein, which are specified or described in such Order and (b) to state whether all or any writings, documents, business books, plans or articles specified or described in such Order are, or have at

any time been, in his possession or under his control and whether he has parted with the same and what has become of them or any of them; and

(2) Order any person to attend the Court at a fixed time and place, or a time and place to be afterwards notified to such person, and to produce all writings, documents, business books, plans or articles in his possession, or under his control, which are specified or described in such Order, the production of which may be deemed by the Court material and proper for the determination of matters in dispute.

[131]

41. All writings, plans, books, or excerpts from books, or other documents or productions which are founded on in any Application or in any Answers, Objections, Minutes or other pleadings, or certified copies thereof, shall be lodged in process along with such Application or Answers, Objections, Minutes or other pleadings.

[132]

42. All writings, plans, books, or excerpts from books, or other documents or productions which any party intends to refer to or to use or put in evidence at any hearing shall, if in his possession or under his control, be lodged in process by such party at least seven clear days before the time appointed for such hearing and the party lodging the same shall forthwith intimate to the other parties to the Application that he has done so.

[133]

43. The Court may allow any Answers, Objections, Minutes or other pleadings and any writing, plan, book, or excerpt from a book, or other document or productions, which ought to have been, but were not, timeously lodged, to be received or to be referred to or to be used or put in evidence at the hearing, if satisfied that such omission was in the circumstances excusable, upon such conditions as to expenses, adjournment, further allowance of proof or otherwise as the Court may think proper.

[134]

44. When an Application or pleading or other original document has been lost or destroyed, a copy thereof proved and authenticated to the satisfaction of the Court may be substituted for the original to all effects and purposes.

[135]

45. If any Applicant or Respondent fails to lodge any statement or pleading or to produce any writing, plan, book, or excerpt from a book, or other document or article, which the Court have ordered to be lodged or produced, or to obey any Order of Court (a) where the Applicant is the party in default, the Application may be in respect thereof dismissed, with expenses (b) where the Respondent is the party in default, any pleas, objections or claims stated by him may be in respect thereof repelled, with expenses or (c) the party in default, whether Applicant or Respondent, may be merely found liable in expenses occasioned by such default.

[136]

46. A copy of any Order summoning persons therein named to attend the Court for the purpose of giving evidence and/or producing documents, which has been certified by the Principal Clerk or by the solicitor of the party who obtained it as correct, in so far as concerns the person on or to whom the said Order is to be served, intimated or directed, shall be held as equivalent to the original Order to all effects and purposes.

[137]

47. Parties may, orally in open Court or by letters or Minutes, renounce proof or dispense with a hearing, either generally or as regards particular matters or questions.

[138]

HEARING

48. At the time and place appointed for the hearing of an Application the parties shall lead or tender such oral and documentary evidence as they desire to lead or tender on any matters of fact in dispute, unless the hearing has been, by Order, limited to matters of law or procedure.

[139]

49. When the Application is called in Court at the appointed time and place,
    (a) if no appearance is made by or on behalf of an Applicant, but appearance is made by or on behalf of a Respondent, (1) the Application may be continued, (2) the Applicant may be dismissed in respect of such failure to appear, with or without expenses or (3) the Respondent may proceed, on any matters of fact in dispute, to lead evidence, so far as consistent with the terms of the Order appointing a hearing, or as allowed by the Court, and may thereafter move for an Order disposing of the subject-matter of the Application;
    (b) if no appearance is made by or on behalf of a Respondent, but appearance is made by or on behalf of an Applicant, (1) the Application may be continued (2) any defence, objection or claim pleaded by such Respondent may be repelled in respect of such failure to appear, with or without expenses or (3) the Applicant may proceed to lead evidence, so far as consient with the terms of the Order appointing a hearing, or as allowed by the Court, either on any matters of fact in dispute or only on matters in regard to which the burden of proof rests upon him and may thereafter move for an Order disposing of the subject-matter of the Application;
    (c) if no appearance is made by any party, the Application may be continued indefinitely or dismissed, as the Court may think proper.

[140]

50. Any person who, after warning by the Court, (a) wilfully disobeys any Summons or Order of the Court to attend in open Court for the purpose of producing documents and/or of giving evidence or (b) having attended, wilfully refuses to be sworn or to affirm or to answer any proper question or to produce any book, or excerpt from a book, writing or plan or other document or article, which he has been lawfully required to produce, may be found liable in payment of expenses occasioned by any adjournment which such disobedience or refusal renders necessary and may also be dealt with by the Court for contempt of court.

[141]

51. The Court may call and examine, or grant commission to examine, as a witness in the cause any person whose evidence appears to them to be necessary for the purpose of determining the matters in dispute, though such person has not been called or adduced by any of the parties, and may direct his fees and expenses as a witness to be paid by the parties, or any of them, in such proportion as the Court may determine, as part of the expenses of the Application.

[142]

EVIDENCE

52. Evidence shall be taken, unless otherwise agreed by parties, upon oath or affirmation.

[143]

53. Any consent or undertaking in an Application may be given by or on behalf of any party or parties thereto in letters or Minutes or verbally, either in open Court or during an inspection, made by a member or members of the Court, of the lands or other subjects to which the Application relates, provided that, where such verbal consent or undertaking forms the basis of, or a material element in, any Order of Court, its tenor shall be set out in such Order or in a note appended thereto.

[144]

54. All relevant objections to any deed or writing which is founded on in any Application may be stated and maintained by way of exception and shall for the purposes of the Application be disposed of by the Court without the necessity of proceedings being sisted in order that a reduction may be brought in the appropriate Court, unless the Court think it necessary or more convenient in the circumstances that the party challenging such deed or writing should proceed by reduction.

[145]

55. Notes of evidence may be taken down by the Court or, where all parties so desire, by a shorthand writer appointed by the Court, whose fee shall be fixed by the Court and may be ordered to be paid by the parties equally or in such proportions as the Court may think fit. Such notes of evidence may be used by the Court in any Appeal in, or Rehearing of, the Application.

[146]

Evidence on commission

56. The Court may, at any stage of the proceedings in an Application, order that the evidence of any witness whose evidence is in danger of being lost or who is resident furth of Scotland or who by reason of age or infirmity or remoteness of place or residence or other reasonable cause is unable to attend at the time and place fixed for hearing the Application or at any adjourned hearing shall be taken on commission, with or without interrogatories, by any member of the Court and/or the Principal Clerk, or any Depute-Clerk of Court or other qualified person or persons delegated or appointed for this purpose, and shall be reported to the Court.

[147]

57. The Court, of consent of parties, or where satisfied that such course is expedient in the interests of all parties, may remit to one of their number or to the Principal Clerk or any Depute-Clerk of Court or other qualified person to take the whole evidence in the cause and report it to the Court.

[148]

APPOINTMENT OF REPORTERS, ASSESSORS, ETC

58. The Court, either of their own accord or on the motion of any party, at any time before a Final Order has been pronounced in an Application (1) if they consider that all, or any, of the material facts in dispute may be appropriately so ascertained, may remit to any person specially qualified by skill and experience to enquire into such matters of fact and to report and may, upon such report or a further report, after affording parties an opportunity of being heard or of lodging written pleadings, if they so desire, proceed, without further enquiry or evidence, to determine the said matters of fact and any questions arising thereon or to make such other Order as the Court think just (2) if they consider that the assistance of one or more persons specially qualified by skill and experience is desirable for the better disposal of the matters in dispute, may appoint one or more such persons to act as assessors and sit with the Court at any hearing or inspect the lands or buildings or other subjects to which the Application relates. Such reporters, valuers or assessors shall be appointed from lists prepared by the Court from time to time and shall receive remuneration for their services out of funds provided by Parliament at such rates as the Treasury may sanction.

[149]

INSPECTION

59. The Court, and any assessor, valuer, surveyor or other official authorised in writing by the Court, may at any time and from time to time, during reasonable hours on any lawful day, enter upon and inspect all or any lands or buildings after notice to the parties, either in writing or verbally in open Court, in order that parties may have an opportunity of attending, or being represented, at the inspection.   [150]

ABANDONMENT

60. Any Applicant, or Respondent may, at any time before final decision upon, or dismissal of, the Application, abandon or withdraw his Application or Answers or Objections or pleadings by leave of the Court on such conditions as to expenses or otherwise as the Court may consider just.

[151]

FALLING ASLEEP AND WAKENING

61. If no Order has been pronounced in an Application for a year and a day it shall be held to have fallen asleep.

[152]

62. The Court may either of consent of all the parties or on the motion of one of the parties duly intimated to the other parties pronounce an Order wakening the Application and thereafter proceed with it.

[153]

REPONING

63. Where, by reason of the failure of an Applicant or Respondent to lodge any statement or pleading or to produce any writing, plan, book, or excerpt from a book, or other document or article or to appear at a hearing or to obey any Order of Court or by reason of any other default, an Order has been pronounced (1) dismissing the Application or (2) repelling any pleas or objections or claims, the party in such default may within thirty days from the date of intimation of such Order move the Court to be reponed against such Order; and the Court, if satisfied that such default occurred through mistake or inadvertence or as in the circumstances excusable, may, upon such terms and conditions as to expenses or further hearing or otherwise as they shall think just, recall such Order and appoint the Application to proceed as if such default had not occurred.

[154]

64. When a party, who has obtained any Order in his favour upon terms or conditions therein expressed, has failed within the time limited by such Order or by any subsequent Order (or, if no time has been so limited, then within such time as the Court think reasonable) to perform or comply with such terms or conditions, it shall be competent for any party in whose interest such terms or conditions were imposed to move the Court in the Application before it has been disposed of by a Final Order, or afterwards in a Rehearing, to recall or vary such Order.

[155]

APPEAL AGAINST DIVISIONAL COURT ORDER

65. Any competent Appeal to the Full Court against an Order by a Divisional Court shall be taken by a note dated and signed by the appellant or his solicitor or counsel or factor or by any person duly authorised in writing on behalf of the appellant. An appellant who cannot sign his name may adhibit his mark as provided by Rule 8.

[156]

66. Such note shall be delivered, or transmitted by first class recorded delivery service or registered post letter, to the Principal Clerk and shall be in the following or similar terms:

'The Applicant,.., (or Respondent or other Party) appeals to the Full Court in the Application Record No......................... Region

of............................... District of............................... (or Islands Area of........................)
on the following grounds, namely, ...'

Dated   Signature

The appellant shall at the same time (1) lodge with the Principal Clerk a copy of the
said note for service, by the Principal Clerk, on each of the other parties and (2) pay to
the Principal Clerk the fee specified in the Table of Court Fees.

[157]

67. It shall not be competent to take any Appeal after the expiry of one month from
the date of intimation to parties of the Order complained of.

[158]

68. It shall not be competent to take any Appeal except to the Full Court or against
any Order other than
    (a) A Final Order, or
    (b) An Order against which the Court which pronounced it has granted leave to
        appeal.

[159]

69. The Full Court may give judgment in any Appeal—
    (a) Without ordering either written pleadings or a hearing, where all parties so
        agree
    (b) Upon written pleadings only, where all parties so agree.
Except as above provided, the Court shall appoint a time and place at which parties
shall be heard on the Appeal.

[160]

70. Every competent Appeal shall submit to review at the instance not only of the
appellant but of every other party appearing in the Appeal the whole Orders
pronounced in the Application, to the effect of enabling the Full Court to do justice
between the parties without hindrance from the terms of any previous Order.

[161]

71. In the event of an appellant obtaining leave to withdraw or abandon his Appeal,
any other party appearing in the Appeal may insist in such Appeal (if otherwise
competent) in the same manner and to the same effect as if it had originally been taken
by himself.

[162]

72. When the Order appealed against is a Final Order, the Application shall not be
remitted to the Court which pronounced it, unless special circumstances render a
remit expedient, but shall be completely decided by the Full Court.

[163]

73. When the Order appealed against is an Order appealed by leave of the Court, the
taking of the Appeal shall not stay procedure before the said Court in the Application.
The said Court may make such interim Order, or Orders, concerning the
preservation of evidence, consignation or payment of money, custody or production
of documents or other like matters as just regard to the manner in which the final
decision is likely to affect the parties' interests may require. Such interim Order or
Orders shall not be subject to review except by the Full Court when the Appeal is
heard or determined.

[164]

REHEARING

74. Any party to an Application whose interests are directly affected by a Final Order
pronounced in an Application may move the Court, on one or more of the grounds
enumerated in Rule 78, to order that the Application shall be reheard, in whole or in

part, upon such terms or conditions as to expenses, or otherwise, as the Court shall think right.

[165]

75. Such motion shall be made by a note dated and signed by the party moving or his solicitor or counsel or factor or by any person duly authorised in writing on behalf of such party. A party who cannot sign his name may adhibit his mark, as provided by Rule 8.

[166]

76. Such note shall be delivered, or transmitted by first class recorded delivery service or registered post letter, to the Principal Clerk and shall be in the following or similar terms:

'The Applicant,.., (or Respondent or other party) moves for a Rehearing of the Application Record No.........................Region of........................ District of .... (or Islands Area of ....), in which a Final Order was pronounced on .... (insert date) on the following grounds, namely...'

Dated   Signature

The party moving shall at the same time (1) lodge with the Principal Clerk a statement specifying (a) whether the whole, or a part (and, if so, what part), of the Final Order is craved to be varied, amended or recalled, (b) whether it is desired that proof should be led or allowed at the Rehearing and, if so, (c) to what points proof is to be directed and (d) whether it is desired that the land, or other subjects, to which the Application relates, should be inspected or reinspected, (2) lodge with the Principal Clerk a copy of the said note and statement for service, by the Principal Clerk, on each of the other parties and (3) pay to the Principal Clerk the fee specified in the Table of Court Fees.

[167]

77. It shall not be competent to move for Rehearing after the expiry of three months from the date of intimation to parties of the Final Order in the Application except (1) where all the parties whose interests may be directly affected concur in the motion or (2) where leave to move is granted on special cause shown.

[168]

78. A motion for Rehearing may be made upon one or more of the following grounds:
(1) that the Order or Orders sought to be varied, recalled or annulled
  (a) proceeded upon essential error, either shared by all the parties, or induced by one or more of the opposing parties, or
  (b) were obtained or procured by fraud or fabrication of documents or subornation of perjury or other like misconduct on the part of one or more of the opposing parties in course of the Application;
(2) that pertinent and important evidence as to disputed matters of fact was tendered and erroneously rejected or disallowed;
(3) that the party moving is prepared to adduce pertinent and important evidence, of the tenor set forth in his statement, which was unknown to, and could not reasonably have been discovered by, him before a Final Order was pronounced;
(4) that the opposing party or parties has or have, without reasonable excuse, failed substantially to fulfil or comply with conditions imposed in the interest of the party moving by the Order or Orders sought to be varied or recalled;
(5) that owing to a change of circumstances the Final Order sought to be recalled is no longer appropriate.

[169]

79. Every motion for Rehearing or for leave to move for Rehearing and every Rehearing ordered shall be determined, or adjudicated on, by the Full Court.

[170]

80. The Court may dispose of the motion for Rehearing or for leave to move for Rehearing, either after hearing parties or, if parties agree to dispense with a hearing, on their written pleadings only.

[171]

81. Where the Court are satisfied that if the Order or Orders complained of are allowed to stand, a substantial wrong, or miscarriage of justice, which cannot by any other process be so conveniently remedied or set right, is likely to be thereby occasioned, they may order a rehearing of the Application, in whole or in part, in such manner and on such terms and conditions as they shall think just.

[172]

82. Neither a motion for Rehearing nor an Order granting a Rehearing nor any subsequent procedure therein shall have the effect of staying proceedings under, or implement of, the Order or Orders complained of, unless it be so ordered.

[173]

83. In any Appeal or Rehearing the Court may vary, recall or annul any Orders appealed or complained against either (a) in whole or (b) in so far only as affecting any separate and distinct part of the matters in dispute or (c) as between some of the parties only, and may make any Order or Orders which should have been made and also such other or further Order or Orders as they may think necessary to deal with any change of circumstances occurring after the date of the Order or Orders appealed or complained against, or to set right any substantial error, omission, defect, wrong or miscarriage of justice, and that upon such terms and conditions as they shall think just.

[174]

SPECIAL CASE

84. Any party to an Application who intends to require that a special case shall be stated on any question, or questions, of law for the opinion of a Division of the Court of Session shall, within one month after the date of intimation to parties of the decision complained of, lodge with the Principal Clerk a requisition to that effect, and also a draft statement of the case specifying (a) the facts out of which such question, or questions, of law are alleged to have arisen, (b) the decision complained of, (c) in what respect and to what extent such decision is maintained to be erroneous in point of law and (d) the question, or questions, of law proposed to be submitted to the Court of Session.

[175]

85. The said party shall at the same time lodge with the Principal Clerk a copy of the said requisition and draft statement of the case for service, by the Principal Clerk, on each of the parties in the Application. Any of these parties may, within ten days after intimation of such copy or copies, lodge with the Principal Clerk a note of any proposed alterations, or observations, on the said draft statement and question or questions which they may deem necessary.

[176]

86. Thereafter the draft case shall be settled by the Court or the Chairman and returned by the Principal Clerk to the party making the requisition, in order that a fair copy of the same may be made for lodging. The fair copy special case and the settled draft shall, within seven days after the settled draft has been posted to such party, be lodged with the Principal Clerk in order that the special case may be authenticated by the Court.

[177]

87. On the special case being authenticated in terms of Rule 100, the Principal Clerk shall transmit the same, with relative productions, if any, which have been made part

of the case, to the Deputy Principal Clerk of the Court of Session and shall notify such transmission to the parties thereto.

Within fourteen days after the receipt of the special case by the said Deputy Principal Clerk of Session, or, where such fourteen days expire during a vacation or recess of the Court of Session, then on or before the first sederunt day of the Court of Session thereafter ensuing, the party on whose requisition the special case has been stated shall lodge the same, together with any productions made part of the case, in the General Department of the Court of Session, along with a process and copies of productions for the use of the Court in terms of Rules of the Court of Session Nos 20 and 26(b) and shall at the same time intimate the lodging of the special case to the opposite party or his solicitor and deliver to him at least ten copies of the said case; and shall also deliver three copies of the said case to the Principal Clerk of the Land Court.

In the event of such party failing to lodge the special case within the time above prescribed, any other party thereto may within the like period of time from such failure, lodge the special case and also lodge copies with the Principal Clerk of the Land Court all in like manner.

In the event of the special case not being lodged as above prescribed, the special case shall, unless the Court of Session otherwise orders, be deemed to have been withdrawn or abandoned by all the parties thereto and shall be re-transmitted by the Deputy Principal Clerk of Session to the Principal Clerk of the Land Court; and the Land Court may thereafter determine any questions of expenses relating to the preparation and settling of the special case and shall otherwise proceed where any further procedure is necessary or expedient, as if no special case had been required.

[178]

88. Neither the requisition for a special case nor any subsequent proceeding therein shall have the effect of staying procedure in the Application, or Applications, in course of which the said question, or questions, of law are alleged to have arisen, unless it be so ordered.

[179]

89. The party on whose requisition the special case has been stated, whom failing the other party or parties thereto, shall, as soon as reasonably may be after the Court of Session has pronounced opinion upon the question, or questions, of law therein set forth, take the proper steps to cause a certified copy of the said opinion together with the relative productions, if any, to be transmitted to the Principal Clerk of the Land Court.

[180]

90. When the opinion of the Court of Session has been received by the Principal Clerk, the Land Court shall, if and in so far as necessary, bring their decision on the matters in regard to which the said question or questions of law have arisen into conformity with the said opinion.

[181]

EXPENSES

91. In all proceedings before the Court the fees stated in the Table of Solicitors' Fees set forth in Appendix II to these Rules shall be the fees and emoluments ordinarily chargeable by, and payable to, solicitors for all professional services rendered in connection with an Application, but subject to the power of the Court, which is hereby reserved, to deal in such manner with expenses as shall in each case seem just. No higher fees or remuneration shall (unless specially sanctioned by the Court) be recoverable or be allowed between party and party or (except on such sanction or under special written agreement) between solicitor and client.

[182]

92. The Court may sanction the employment of counsel in Applications of difficulty and general importance and fix the fees payable or chargeable in such cases.

[183]

93. Accounts of expenses, charged by solicitors against clients, or awarded by the Court as between party and party, in relation to any proceeding before the Court may be remitted for taxation and report by the Auditor. Expenses may be modified at a fixed sum by the Court as between party and party.

[184]

94. When any person other than a solicitor or counsel appears by leave of the Court on behalf of any party or parties to an Application, the Court may allow, or direct the Auditor to allow, him reasonable outlays and also a remuneration for time and trouble proportionate to his services and the value of the cause.

[185]

95. When two or more Applications involving similar questions and arising with respect to holdings which are held under the same landlord are heard at the same sitting, whether formally conjoined or not, the Court may award to the solicitor, or the person appearing by leave of the Court, who conducts the same, an inclusive fee or remuneration in respect of all the Applications in which he so appears and may settle the proportions in which it shall be paid by the respective parties.

[186]

ORDERS OF THE COURT, ETC

96. Every Order shall be in writing and shall be signed by at least one member of the Court and initialled by the Principal Clerk or one of the Clerks of Court.

[187]

97. Any one member of the Court may sign, and power is hereby delegated to each member, to sign for the Court any Final Order in an unopposed Application and any Order which merely (a) appoints answers, replies, objections, minutes, statements or other pleadings or documents or articles founded on by a party to be lodged with the Principal Clerk or (b) directs any service, notice or intimation to be made or given on or to any party or parties or (c) grants a summons to attend a sitting of the Court for the purpose of giving evidence and/or producing documents or articles or (d) fixes or alters the date of any sitting of Court or hearing or (e) requires borrowed productions to be returned or (f) interpones authority or effect to a joint minute for parties or (g) allows any Application or Appeal or motion for Rehearing or other proceeding therein to be, by consent of all parties, amended or abandoned or withdrawn, as the case may be, or the like: and such signature shall in these cases be sufficient.

[188]

98. Any verbal, clerical or casual error or omission or informality in an Order may be corrected or supplied de recenti, or of consent of parties, by the member or members of Court who signed it.

[189]

99. Every Order which disposes of the subject-matter of an Application or of any separate controverted part thereof, otherwise than by consent of parties, shall be signed by the member, or members, of the Court by whom the case, or such separate part thereof, has been considered and determined; provided that in the event of a difference of opinion among such members it shall be competent for the minority to omit signing the Order and to record dissent from any of the findings in the Order by note appended thereto; and the signatures of the majority shall in that case be sufficient.

[190]

100. All extracts or copies of Orders by the Court, required for the purpose of being

used in any proceeding before any court of law, arbiter, public department or any public authority whatever, and all special cases stated shall be authenticated by the signature of the Chairman or of the Principal Clerk and sealed with the seal of the Court before being issued from the office.

[191]

101. Any party to an application may, after an Order has been pronounced, move the Court for decree in conformity with such Order on which execution and diligence shall proceed.

[192]

GENERAL

102. In matters of procedure or evidence which are not provided for by statute or by these Rules the Court shall have regard to the general practice of courts of law so far as applicable and appropriate to the conduct of its business.

[193]

Note for information: As Appendices I and II referred to in the Rules are subject to periodic amendment, these have not been included here. Copies of either Appendix may be obtained from The Principal Clerk, Scottish Land Court, 1 Grosvenor Crescent, Edinburgh EH12 5ER.

Forms available from the Land Court

1.	Form number 1	Application by crofter to fix a fair rent (Crofters (Scotland) Act 1955, s 5).
2.	Form number 2	Application by landlord to fix a fair rent (ibid, s 5).
3.	Form number 6	Application by landlord to resume from a croft (ibid, s 12).
4.	Form number 7	Application by landlord to resume from a common grazing (ibid, s 12).
5.	Form number 17	Application by crofter to fix compensation for permanent improvements (ibid, s 14).
6.	Form number 19	Application to determine whether a holding is a croft and/or who is the crofter (Crofters (Scotland) Act 1961, s 4(1)).
7.	Form removal	Application by landlord to remove a crofter (Crofters (Scotland) Act 1955, s 13).
8.	Form general	Open, ie, blank crave.

[194]

Rules of procedure of the Crofters Commission

Coming into operation on 4th September 1980

CONTENTS

GENERAL

1. The Crofters Commission are an administrative body whose functions are defined in the aftermentioned Acts of 1955, 1961 and 1976. The business of the Commission

shall be carried on in a simple and orderly manner and as free from formality as is consistent with efficient administration. In the exercise of certain of their functions the Commission are required to act in a *quasi*-judicial or tribunal capacity and there is need in the case of any Application or other proceeding so coming before them for a more formal procedure to ensure

(a) that the Commission are provided with all the information necessary to enable them to discharge such functions;

(b) that every party who has an interest in any such Application or other proceeding before the Commission receives full and timeous notice thereof and of any case he may have to meet, and reasonable opportunity to present his own case fully to the Commission;

(c) that every person who puts forward a case in any such Application or other proceeding before the Commission and who has not already been given an opportunity to ask for a Hearing is, if the Commission propose to arrive at a decision adverse to his case and no further right of appeal is available to him, given notice of the provisional decision and its grounds and an opportunity to make further representations in writing and also to ask for a Hearing;

(d) that the grounds on which the Commission arrive at their final decision in any such Application or proceeding are made known to every person who has an interest.

[195]

2. The Commission may refer, and any person having an interest may apply, to the Land Court to determine in terms of section 4 of the Act of 1961 any question of fact or law arising under the Acts of 1955, 1961 and 1976 in any Application or other proceeding before the Commission, but excepting (i) any question of a kind reserved to a court other than the Land Court, and (ii) any question (other than a question of law) decided by the Commission in the discharge of functions under the said Acts, subject always to the right of an Appellant to raise any such question in an appeal under section 16A(8) of the Act of 1955 (which is concerned with appeals against proposed decisions and further directions given or made by the Commission under section 16(9) or section 16A(3) of the Act of 1955).

[196]

INTERPRETATION

3.(1) In these Rules, unless the context otherwise requires, the following expressions have the meanings hereby respectively assigned to them—

'the Act of 1955' otherwise '1955 c 21' means the Crofters (Scotland) Act 1955;

'the Act of 1961' otherwise '1961 c 58' means the Crofters (Scotland) Act 1961;

'the Act of 1976' otherwise '1976 c 21' means the Crofting Reform (Scotland) Act 1976;

'Application' means an Application made to the Commission in accordance with the provisions of Rule 8 hereof;

'Hearing' means either (a) a hearing for which a party to an Application or other proceeding before the Commission has asked whether in pursuance of a right conferred on him by section 16A(6) of the Act of 1955 or by section 33 thereof or by these Rules, or (b) a Hearing which the Commission hold of their own accord, as provided in Rule 5 hereof.

(2) Other expressions used in the Rules and in the said Acts have the same meaning in the Rules as in the Acts.

(3) The Interpretation Act 1978 applies for the interpretation of these Rules as it applies for the interpretation of an Act of Parliament.

[197]

HEARINGS

4.(1) When any party to an Application or other proceeding before the Commission has asked for a Hearing the Commission shall appoint a person to take the Hearing and shall give not less than fourteen days' notice of the date and place of Hearing to the person requesting it and to any other person interested in the Application or proceeding. The person so appointed will normally be a Commissioner and the date and place of Hearing will be fixed with due regard to the convenience of parties.

(2) The Hearing shall be held in public, but the person taking the Hearing shall have a discretionary power to exclude the public in any case where he is satisfied that justice may be better done or the public interest better served by holding the Hearing in private.

(3) The person taking the Hearing shall have power to administer the oath in any case where the Commission, under paragraph 9 of the First Schedule to the Act of 1955, have ordered that the evidence shall be taken on oath.

(4) The person who requested the Hearing, and any other person interested in the Application or proceeding, shall have the right to call and examine witnesses and to cross-examine the witnesses called by any other party.

[198]

5. Where, by reason of the complexity of the questions at issue in any Application or other proceeding, or the importance thereof to the public interest or for any other reason, the Commission are satisfied that it would be expedient to hold a Hearing at which all parties having an interest would have an opportunity of making representations, the Commission may at any time, after giving not less than fourteen days' notice, of their own accord and without any request from an interested party, hold such a Hearing and if a Hearing is so held no party interested shall be entitled whether under these Rules or otherwise to ask for any further Hearing in that Application or proceeding.

[199]

INSPECTIONS

6. In any Application or proceeding before the Commission which relates to the assignation or re-let of a croft in which the Commission decide that there should be an inspection of the subjects, notice of the inspection shall be given to the landlord and to any other person who is a party to the Application and they shall be afforded an opportunity of attending, or being represented at, the inspection. Notice of the inspection shall be given in writing except when it is carried out in connection with a Hearing when notice may be given either in writing or orally at the Hearing.

[200]

AUTHORITY TO ENTER ON LAND

7. Commissioners and Commission officers whose duties involve entry on or inspection of land shall be provided with documents of authority under section 30 of the Act of 1955. The minimum period of notice of intended entry required to be given to the occupier of the land is seven days in the case of land used for residential purposes and twenty-four hours in the case of other land.

[201]

APPLICATIONS

8.(1) Applications to the Commission shall be framed as nearly as may be reasonably possible in accordance with the Forms provided by the Commission. These Forms shall be obtainable from the Head Office of the Commission at Inverness and from any of the Area Offices of the Department of Agriculture and Fisheries for Scotland throughout the former crofting counties. All applications shall be addressed to the Secretary of the Crofters Crommission, 4–6 Castle Wynd, Inverness.

(2) Except as otherwise provided, Applications shall be signed by the Applicants, or by a solicitor or counsel, or by any person duly authorised in writing, on their behalf. Applications by a landlord may be signed by his Factor.

(3) Where an Applicant is blind or is unable to read and/or write and is not represented by a solicitor, he may instead adhibit his 'X' or mark, in the presence of at least one witness above 18 years of age who shall certify in writing on the Application that it was read over and explained to the Applicant before his mark was adhibited.

[202]

SERVICE AND COPYING OF DOCUMENTS AND REPRESENTATIONS

9.(1) Any copy of an Application or other document and any notice or other document required to be served on or given to any person under these Rules shall be served or given in the manner prescribed in section 29 of the Act of 1955 for serving or giving notices or other documents under that Act.

(2) The Commission reserve the right at any time during the consideration of an Application or other matter to reject, withdraw or expunge any material which they consider scurrilous or obscene contained in representations, either oral or in writing, made by any person.

[203]

TIME LIMITS

10.(1) Any period limited by these Rules for any act or proceeding may be extended by the Commission, on cause shown, either before or after the expiry of such period.

(2) In the case of a party resident furth of Scotland, the Commission may substitute for any period prescribed by these Rules such longer period as they consider reasonable.

[204]

ASSIGNATION OF CROFT

(Crofters (Scotland) Act 1955 (c 21), s 8)
(Crofting Reform (Scotland) Act 1976 (c 21), s 15(1))

11.(1) Application by a crofter for the Commission's consent to assign a croft or part of a croft consisting of any right in pasture or grazing land shall be made in the appropriate form provided by the Commission.

(2) On receipt of an Application on the said Form, properly completed, the Commission shall serve on the landlord a copy of the Application, together with a notice affording him an opportunity, within fourteen days from the date of service, both to make representations in writing and to ask for a Hearing. If the landlord makes written representations against the Application, the Commission shall give the Applicant a copy of the representations.

(3) The Commission shall make such enquiry and carry out such inspection as they deem necessary to inform themselves about the family and other circumstances of the crofter and of the proposed assignee of the croft and the general interest of the township in which the croft is situated.

[205]

12.(1) The Commission shall consider all the information available, and
  (a) if they are satisfied that the Application should be granted, the Commission shall grant the Application and intimate their decision to the Applicant and the landlord;
  (b) if a Hearing has not already been held and they are not satisfied that the Application should be granted, the Commission shall serve on the Applicant notice that they propose to refuse the Application and shall afford him an opportunity, within fourteen days from the date of service, both to make representations in writing and to ask for a Hearing. The Commission shall consider any further representations made to them, whether in writing or at a Hearing, in response to the said notice and thereafter they shall intimate their final decision to the Applicant and the landlord;
  (c) if a Hearing has already been held and they are satisfied that the Application should be refused, the Commission shall refuse the Application and intimate their decision to the Applicant and the landlord.

(2) In each case, except where the decision is to grant the Application and the landlord has not maintained an objection, the Commission shall give the Applicant and the landlord a written statement specifying the nature of and the reasons for their decision or provisional decision.

[206]

RE-LET OF CROFT

(Crofters (Scotland) Act 1955 (c 21), s 16(3))

13.(1) Application by a landlord for the Commission's consent to the let of a croft, or part of a croft, shall be made on the appropriate form provided by the Commission.

(2) On receipt of an Application on the said Form, properly completed, the Commission shall make such enquiry and carry out such inspection as they deem necessary to inform themselves about local crofting conditions, the demand for crofts in the locality, and the quality of the landlord's nominee for the tenancy.

(3) The Commission shall consider all the information available, and
  (a) if they are satisfied that the Application should be granted, the Commission shall grant the Application and intimate their decision to the landlord;
  (b) if they are satisfied that the Application should be refused, the Commission shall refuse the Application and intimate their decision to the landlord together with a written statement specifying the nature of and the reasons for such decision, and reminding him that notwithstanding the Commission's decision to withhold their consent he may apply to the Secretary of State for his consent to the proposed re-let.

[207]

SUBLET OF CROFT

(Crofters (Scotland) Act 1961 (c 58), s 11(3))

14.(1) Application by a crofter for the Commission's consent to the sublet of a croft shall be made on the appropriate form provided by the Commission.

(2) On receipt of an Application on the said Form, properly completed, the Commission shall serve on the landlord of the croft a notice stating that such

Application has been made, specifying the name and designation of the proposed subtenant, and requesting the landlord to make in writing any observations he may wish to make within fourteen days from the date of service of the notice.

(3) If the landlord makes observations against the Application, the Commission shall give the Applicant a copy thereof.

(4) The Commission shall make such further enquiry and carry out such inspection as they consider necessary to inform themselves about the circumstances of the Applicant and of the proposed subtenant, local crofting conditions and any other matter on which they require information before reaching a decision.

[208]

15.(1) The Commission shall consider all the information available, and
 (a) if they are satisfied that the Application should be granted and the landlord is not maintaining an objection, the Commission shall grant the Application subject to such conditions (which shall not include conditions relating to rent) as they consider reasonable, and thereafter they shall intimate their decision to the Applicant and the landlord;
 (b) if they are satisfied that the Application should be granted but the landlord is maintaining an objection, the Commission shall serve on the Applicant and the landlord notice in writing that they propose to grant the Application together with a written statement specifying the nature of and the reasons for such provisional decision, and shall afford them an opportunity, within fourteen days from the date of service, both to make further representations in writing and to ask for a Hearing;
 (c) if they are not satisfied that the Application should be granted, the Commission shall serve on the Applicant and the landlord notice in writing that they propose to refuse the Application together with a written statement specifying the nature of and the reasons for such provisional decision and shall afford them an opportunity, within fourteen days from the date of service, both to make further representations in writing and to ask for a Hearing.

(2) The Commission shall consider any further representations made to them, whether in writing or at a Hearing, in response to the notice given under paragraph (1)(b) or (1)(c) of this Rule, and thereafter they shall intimate their final decision to the Applicant and the landlord, together with a written statement specifying the nature of and the reasons for such decision.

[209]

APPORTIONMENT OF COMMON GRAZINGS

(1) Apportionment to a crofter

(Crofters (Scotland) Act 1955 (c 21), s 27(4))
(Crofters (Scotland) Act 1961 (c 58), s 15(6))
(Crofting Reform (Scotland) Act 1976 (c 21), Sch 2, para 23(b))

16.(1) Application by a crofter for apportionment of part of a common grazing for his exclusive use shall be made on the appropriate form provided by the Commission.

(2) On receipt of an Application on the said Form, properly completed, the Commission shall serve on the landlord and on the Clerk of the Grazings Committee (or Grazings Constable) a copy of the Application together with a notice requesting them to make any representations they may wish to make in writing within fourteen days from the date of service.

(3) If the number of shareholders in the common grazings does not exceed twelve and there is reliable information as to their names and addresses, the Commission shall serve on each shareholder a notice informing him that a copy of the Application can be seen in the hands of the Clerk of the Grazings Committee (or Grazings Constable) and

that he can make representations in writing to the Commission within fourteen days from the date of service. If the number of shareholders exceeds twelve or there is lack of reliable information as to their names and addresses, the Commission shall give the shareholders notice to the same effect by advertisement in a newspaper circulating in the district, or by notice posted in such public place or places in the district as the Commission may specify or in such other manner as the Commission may think sufficient.

[210]

17.(1) The Commission shall make such enquiry and carry out such inspection as they consider necessary to inform themselves about local crofting conditions, the circumstances of the Applicant, the quality of the grazing, the effect the apportionment would have on the interests of other shareholders, and what conditions should be attached if apportionment were granted.

(2) If the Commission are satisfied that apportionment should be granted and that there is no objection from the landlord, the Grazings Committee (or Grazings Constable) or the other shareholders to the apportionment or the conditions to be attached thereto, they shall without further procedure grant the apportionment and intimate their decision to the interested parties. If the Commission are not so satisfied, the procedure specified in the following Rule shall apply.

[211]

18.(1) The Commission shall consider any representations received from the landlord, the Grazings Committee (or Grazings Constable) and the other shareholders and all the other information available and shall reach a provisional decision as to what apportionment, if any, should be granted and on what conditions.

(2) If the provisional decision is to grant an apportionment, the Commission shall give to the landlord, the Clerk of the Grazings Committee (or Grazings Constable) and the other shareholders, in the same manner as notice was given to them of the Application under Rule 16 hereof, notice of the proposed apportionment and conditions together with a written statement specifying the nature of and the reasons for such provisional decision and shall afford them an opportunity within fourteen days from the date of service both to make representations in writing and to ask for a Hearing. The Commission shall also give the Applicant notice in writing of their provisional decision and a like opportunity of making representations in writing and asking for a Hearing.

(3) If the provisional decision is to refuse an apportionment, the Commission shall serve on the Applicant, the landlord and the Clerk of the Grazings Committee (or Grazings Constable) notice in writing to that effect together with a written statement specifying the nature of and the reasons for such provisional decisions and shall afford them an opportunity, within fourteen days from the date of service, both to make further representations in writing and to ask for a Hearing.

(4) The Commission shall consider any further representations made to them, whether in writing or at a Hearing, in response to a notice given under paragraph (2) or (3) of this Rule, and thereafter they shall intimate their final decision to the Applicant, the landlord and the Clerk of the Grazings Committee (or Grazings Constable), together with a written statement specifying the nature of and the reasons for such decision.

[212]

(2) Apportionment to a township

(Crofters (Scotland) Act 1955 (c 21), s 27(3))
(Crofters (Scotland) Act 1961 (c 58), s 15(4))

19.(1) Application by any crofters interested for apportionment of a common grazing shared by two or more townships into separate parts for the exclusive use of the several townships, or for apportionment of a part of such grazing for the exclusive use of one of the townships, shall be made on the appropriate form provided by the Commission.

(2) On receipt of an Application on the said Form, properly completed, the Commission shall serve on the landlord, and on the Clerk of every Grazings Committee and every Grazings Constable interested in the common grazing, a copy of the Application together with a notice asking them to make any representations they may wish to make to the Commission in writing within fourteen days from the date of service.

(3) The Commission shall, either by advertisement in a newspaper circulating in the district or by notice posted in such public place or places in the district as the Commission may specify or in such other manner as the Commission may think sufficient, give the shareholders in the common grazing notice that a copy of the Application can be seen in the hands of the Clerks of the Grazings Committees (or Grazings Constables) and that representations in writing may be made to the Commission within fourteen days.

[213]

20.(1) The Commission shall make such enquiry and carry out such inspection as they consider necessary to inform themselves about local crofting conditions, the circumstances of the Applicants, the quality of the grazing, the effect the apportionment would have on the interests of other townships and shareholders, and what conditions should be attached if the apportionment were granted.

(2) If the Commission are satisfied that apportionment should be granted and that there is no objection from the landlord, the Grazings Committees or Grazings Constables, or the other shareholders to the apportionment or the conditions to be attached thereto, they shall without further procedure grant the apportionment and intimate their decision to the interested parties. If the Commission are not so satisfied, the procedure specified in the following Rule shall apply.

[214]

21.(1) The Commission shall consider any representations received from the landlord, the Grazings Committees or Grazings Constables and the other shareholders and all the other information available and shall reach a provisional decision as to what apportionment, if any, should be granted, and on what conditions.

(2) If the provisional decision is to grant an apportionment, the Commission shall give to the landlord, the Grazings Committees or Grazings Constables and the other shareholders, in the same manner as notice was given to them of the Application under Rule 19 hereof, notice of the proposed apportionment and conditions and shall afford them an opportunity, within fourteen days from the date of service, both to make representations in writing and to ask for a Hearing. The Commission shall also give the Applicants notice of their provisional decision and a like opportunity of making representations in writing and asking for a Hearing.

(3) If the provisional decision is to refuse an apportionment, the Commission shall serve on the Applicants, the landlord and the Clerks of the Grazing Committees or Grazing Contables notice in writing to that effect, together with a written statement specifying the nature of and the reasons for such provisional decision and shall afford them an opportunity, within fourteen days from the date of service, both to make further representations in writing, and to ask for a Hearing.

(4) The Commission shall consider any further representations made to them, whether in writing or at a Hearing, in response to the notice given under paragraph (2) or (3) of this Rule, and thereafter they shall intimate their final decision to the Applicants, the landlord and the Clerks of the Grazings Committees or Grazings Constables, together with a written statement specifying the nature of and the reasons for such decision.

[215]

APPORTIONMENT OF LANDS HELD RUNRIG

(Crofters (Scotland) Act 1955 (c 21), s 27(7))

22.(1) Application by a landlord or crofter interested for apportionment of lands held runrig shall be made on the appropriate form provided by the Commission.

(2) On receipt of an Application on the said Form, properly completed, the Commission shall serve on every person, other than the Applicant, who has a known interest in the runrig lands a copy of the Application together with a notice requesting him to make any representations he may wish to make in writing within fourteen days from the date of service.

[216]

23.(1) The Commission shall make such enquiry and carry out such inspection as they consider necessary to inform themselves about local crofting conditions, the quality of the runrig lands, the effect the apportionment would have on the interests of the crofters sharing therein and what conditions should be attached if the apportionment were granted.

(2) If the Commission are satisfied that apportionment should be granted, and that there is no objection from the landlord or the crofters who have an interest in the lands held runrig to the apportionment or the conditions to be attached thereto they shall without further procedure grant the apportionment and intimate their decision to the interested parties. If the Commission are not so satisfied, the procedure specified in the following Rule shall apply.

[217]

24.(1) The Commission shall consider any representations received from the interested parties and all the other information available and shall reach a provisional decision as to what apportionment, if any, should be granted and on what conditions.

(2) If the provisional decision is to grant apportionment, the Commission shall serve on each of the parties known to be interested notice in writing of the proposed apportionment and conditions and shall afford him an opportunity, within fourteen days from the date of service, both to make representations in writing and to ask for a Hearing.

(3) If the provisional decision is to refuse an apportionment, the Commission shall serve on each of the parties known to be interested notice in writing to that effect together with a written statement specifying the nature of and the reasons for such provisional decision and shall afford him an opportunity, within fourteen days from the date of service, both to make representations in writing and to ask for a Hearing.

(4) The Commission shall consider any further representations made to them, whether in writing or at a Hearing, in response to the notice given under paragraph (2) or (3) of this Rule, and thereafter they shall intimate their final decision to the Applicant and to all the other parties known to be interested, together with a written statement specifying the nature of and the reasons for such decision.

[218]

REORGANISATION SCHEME

(Crofters (Scotland) Act 1961 (c 58), ss 8, 9)
(Crofting Reform (Scotland) Act 1976 (c 21), Sch 3)

25.(1) Where the Commission have prepared a draft of a scheme for the reorganisation of a township and such maps and plans as may be necessary to indicate the general effect of the scheme and its effect on each of the crofts in the township, the Commission shall serve on each crofter who is the tenant of a croft situated in the township a copy of such draft scheme together with a notice

    (a) naming a place within the locality in which the said township is situated where a copy of the said maps and plans may be inspected at all reasonable hours, and

    (b) requesting that the crofter on whom the said notice is served shall, within four months from the date of such service, intimate to the Commission in writing whether he is in favour of the scheme or not.

(2) If within the said period of four months a majority of the crofters on whom a copy of the said draft scheme and notice have been served have intimated or are deemed in terms of section 8 of the Act of 1961 to have intimated, that they are in favour of the scheme, the Commission shall submit to the Secretary of State the draft reorganisation scheme and the maps and plans prepared by them together with such information as they may think necessary, or as the Secretary of State may require, for the purpose of informing him of the general purport and effect of the scheme, and shall submit also a statement of their views on the prospects of the development of agricultural and other industries in the township and in the locality in which the township is situated.

[219]

26.(1) Where the Secretary of State has confirmed the draft scheme submitted to him, with or without modifications, the Commission shall do all such things as may be required to put the scheme into effect, subject to any directions in that behalf given to them by the Secretary of State.

(2) Where any buildings situated on land to which the scheme applies will on the putting into effect of the scheme cease to be required in connection with the occupation of the land, the Commission shall, on the scheme being confirmed by the Secretary of State, give notice to that effect to the landlord of the land.

[220]

27. The Commission shall remit the scheme, as confirmed by the Secretary of State, to the Land Court to fix the sums which will become payable on the scheme being put into effect by way of compensation for permanent improvements and of rent.

[221]

28. The Commission shall appoint the date or dates on which the various provisions of the scheme, as confirmed, are to be put into effect, and they shall serve on the tenant and on the landlord of every croft to which the provisions of the scheme apply and on any person (other than such a tenant) who under the scheme is to become the tenant of a croft a notice specifying the date or dates on which the scheme is to be put into effect.

[222]

29. The provisions of Rules 25 to 28 hereof shall, unless the context otherwise requires, apply in relation to a group of neighbouring townships as they apply in relation to a township.

[223]

ABSENTEE CROFTERS

(Crofters (Scotland) Act 1955 (c 21), s 17(1), (2))
(Crofting Reform (Scotland) Act 1976 (c 21), Sch 2, para 9)

30.(1) When it comes to the notice of the Commission that a crofter is not ordinarily resident on, or within sixteen kilometres of his croft and there are no circumstances known to the Commission which indicate that action under section 17 of the Act of 1955 (as amended) should not be taken, the procedure specified in this Rule shall be followed.

(2) In order to ascertain whether it would be in the general interest of the crofting community in the district in which the croft is situate that the croft should be made available for re-letting the Commission shall ask the landlord for his observations and may make such other enquiry as they think fit.

(3) If as a result of these enquiries it appears that there is a *prima facie* case for action under the said section 17 (as amended), the Commission shall address a letter to the crofter explaining the Commission's interest and requesting him to declare his intentions for the future of the croft.

(4) On receipt of the crofter's reply all the available information shall be considered by the Commission. If they consider that the information justifies it, the Commission shall serve on both crofter and landlord a notice in writing informing them that they propose to make an order terminating the tenancy of the crofter at a term of Whitsunday or Martinmas not earlier than six months after the date of the said notice, and shall afford them an opportunity, within fourteen days from the date of service, both to make representations in writing and to ask for a Hearing.

(5) The Commission shall consider any representations made in response to the said notice and all the circumstances of the case, as required in terms of subsection (2) of the said section 17, and if they are satisfied that the requirements of paragraphs (a) and (b) of subsection (1) of the said section 17 are satisfied, the Commission shall make an order terminating the tenancy of the crofter at a term of Whitsunday or Martinmas not earlier than three months after the making of such order.

(6) The Commission shall give notice in writing to the crofter and the landlord of the making of the order, together with a certified copy thereof and a written statement specifying the nature of and the reasons for their decision.

[224]

DECROFTING

(1) Application for a direction that a croft shall cease to be a croft

(Crofters (Scotland) Act 1955 (c 21), s 16(9), (13), (14), s 16A)
(Crofting Reform (Scotland) Act 1976 (c 21), s 13, Sch 2, para 8)

31.(1) An Application by a Landlord or an owner-occupier of a croft or by a crofter proposing to acquire subjects tenanted by him for a direction that a croft or a part of a croft shall cease to be a croft or part of a croft shall be made on the appropriate form provided by the Commission.

(2) On receipt of an Application on the said Form properly completed the Commission shall (except in the case of an Application made in respect of a part of a croft consisting only of the site of the dwelling-house on or pertaining to the croft) advertise the Application in one or more newspapers circulating in the district in which the croft to which the Application relates is situated. If any written representations are made in respect of the Application the Commission shall give the Applicant a copy of the representations.

(3) The Commission shall make such further enquiry and carry out such inspection as they deem necessary—
  (a) in the case of an Application which relates to a part of a croft which consists only of the site of the dwelling-house on or pertaining to the croft, to ascertain whether the extent of garden ground included in that part is appropriate for the reasonable enjoyment of the dwelling-house as a residence;
  (b) In the case of any such Application as is mentioned in subsection (1)(a) of section 16A of the Act of 1955, to ascertain whether the purpose of the Application is a reasonable one within the meaning of section 12(2) thereof; whether or not the extent of the land to which the Application relates is excessive in relation to that purpose; and what conditions of a specific nature if any should be imposed for securing that the land is used for the proposed use (other than a general condition to that effect);
  (c) in the case of any other Application (not being an Application such as is mentioned in sub-paragraphs (a) and (b) of this paragraph) to inform

themselves about the purpose of the Application and any other matter on which they require information before reaching a proposed decision.

(4) In the case of every Application other than such an Application as is mentioned in sub-paragraph (a) of the preceding paragraph, the Commission shall have regard to the general interest of the crofting community in the district in which the croft is situated and in particular to the demand, if any, for a tenancy of the croft from persons who might reasonably be expected to obtain that tenancy if the croft were offered for letting on the open market on the date when they are considering the Application.

[225]

32. (1) The Commission shall consider all the information available to them and if they are satisfied that the Application should be granted they shall give notice in writing to the Applicant of their proposed decision specifying the nature of and the reasons for such decision.

(2) If after considering all the information available to them the Commission
  (a) are not satisfied that the Application should be granted; or
  (b) are satisfied that it should be granted but subject to modifications in terms of section 16A(5) of the Act of 1955; or
  (c) in the case of such an Application as is mentioned in paragraph (3)(b) of Rule 31 are satisfied that it should be granted but that the direction to be given should be subject to such conditions of a specific nature as are therein mentioned;
they shall give notice in writing to the Applicant to that effect specifying the reasons why they are not satisfied or as the case may be specifying such modifications or conditions and the reasons therefore and shall afford him an opportunity within fourteen days from the date of service both to make representations in writing and to ask for a Hearing.

(3) After considering such representations (if any) as may be made whether in writing or at a Hearing, the Commission shall give notice in writing to the Applicant of their proposed decision specifying the nature of and the reasons for such decision and, where the proposed decision is to refuse the Application or to grant it subject to modifications or where appropriate to grant it and give a direction subject to conditions of a specific nature they shall remind the Applicant that he may within twenty-one days of receipt of the notice appeal against the proposed decision to the Land Court.

[226]

33. (1) Where their proposed decision is to grant the Application, or as the case may be to grant it subject to modifications or to grant it and give a direction subject to conditions of a specific nature and no appeal is made to the Land Court in respect of such modifications or conditions of a specific nature the Commission shall as soon as may be reasonably practicable after giving notice of their proposed decision make a direction conform thereto and give notice in writing to the Applicant of the making of the direction together with a certified copy thereof.

(2) Where their proposed decision is to refuse the Application or to grant it subject to modifications or to grant it and give a direction subject to conditions of a specific nature and the Land Court on appeal have determined that a direction shall be given (whether taking account of such modifications or subject to such conditions of a specific nature or otherwise as the case may be) the Commission shall as soon as may be reasonably practicable thereafter make a direction conform to such determination and give notice in writing to the Applicant of the making of the direction together with a certified copy thereof.

[227]

34. (1) Where notice is given to the Applicant under any provision of Rule 32 or Rule 33 the Commission may give notice to the like effect by such means as may seem to them appropriate to such other persons as they think fit and if the Applicant in

response to a notice given under Rule 32(2) asks for a Hearing the Commission may likewise afford a Hearing on the same occasion to such other persons as they think fit.

(2) A direction in the case of an Application by a crofter proposing to acquire subjects tenanted by him shall not have effect until the land to which it relates has been acquired by the crofter or his nominee and unless the acquisition is made within 5 years of the date of the giving of the direction.

[228]

(2) Further direction that decrofted land shall be a vacant croft

(Crofters (Scotland) Act 1955 (c 21), s 16A(3)
(Crofting Reform (Scotland) Act 1976 (c 21), s 13)

35.(1) If in the case of any direction given subject to such conditions as are mentioned in Rule 31(3)(b) the Commission at any time subsequently are satisfied that there has been a breach of any such condition, they may make a further direction that the land in respect of which there has been such a breach shall be a vacant croft. In order to determine whether such a further direction should be made the procedure specified in this Rule shall be followed.

(2) The Commission shall make such enquiry (including enquiry of the owner of the land) and carry out such inspection as they deem necessary to ascertain whether there has *prima facie* been such a breach.

(3) After making such enquiry or carrying out such inspection the Commission shall consider all the information available to them and
  (a) if they are satisfied there has been no such breach, or that for any other reason no such further direction should be made, they shall give notice to the owner of the land to that effect;
  (b) if it appears to the Commission that there has been such a breach and that such a further direction should be made they shall give notice to the owner of the land to that effect together with a written statement specifying the nature of and reasons for such provisional decision, and shall afford him an opportunity within fourteen days from the date of service both to make representations in writing and to ask for a Hearing.

(4) The Commission shall consider any further representations made to them, whether in writing or at a Hearing, in response to the notice given under paragraph (3)(b) of this Rule and
  (a) if they are satisfied there has been no such breach, or that for any other reason no such further direction should be made, they shall give notice to the owner of the land to that effect;
  (b) if they are not so satisfied they shall make a further direction accordingly and give notice to the owner of the land of the making of the further direction together with a certified copy thereof and a written statement specifying the nature of and reasons for their decision and they shall remind him that he may within twenty-one days of the making of that further direction appeal against it to the Land Court.

[229]

36.(1) Where the Commission have made a further direction as aforesaid and the Land Court on appeal have determined that no such further direction should have been made the Commission shall as soon as may be reasonably practicable after such determination rescind by order their further direction and shall give notice in writing to the owner of the land of the making of the order together with a certified copy thereof.

(2) Where the Commission have given such a notice as is mentioned in paragraph (3)(a) of Rule 35 or make such an order as is mentioned in paragraph (1) of this Rule they may, if they consider it appropriate and after making such enquiry as they deem necessary, revoke or vary by order any condition or conditions contained in their original direction and shall give notice in writing to the owner of the land of the making of the order together with a certified copy thereof.

(3) Where notice is given to the owner of the land under any provision of Rule 35 or of this Rule the Commission may give notice to the like effect by such means as may seem to them appropriate to such other persons as they think fit and if the owner of the land in response to a notice given under Rule 35(3)(b) asks for a Hearing the Commission may likewise afford a Hearing on the same occasion to such other persons as they think fit.

[230]

BEQUEST OF CROFT

(1) Application by legatee outwith the family for approval of bequest

(Crofters (Scotland) Act 1955 (c 21), s 10(1), (7))
(Law Reform (Miscellaneous Provisions) (Scotland) Act 1968, Sch 2, Pt I, para 3)

37.(1) Application to the Commission for approval of the bequest of a croft to a person who is not a member of the crofter's family shall be made on the appropriate form provided by the Commission.

(2) On receipt of an Application on the said form, properly completed, the Commission shall serve a copy, together with a notice intimating that objections in writing to the Application may be lodged within fourteen days from the date of service, on (i) the landlord of the croft; (ii) any person who appears to be entitled to succeed to the intestate estate of the crofter (in this and the following Rule referred to as 'the successor') if the name and address of the successor are known to the Commission and (iii) the executor of the deceased crofter. If from the information provided by the Applicant the Commission are unable to identify the successor they themselves may make such enquiry as they think fit or as may appear to them to be reasonably practicable to establish his identity.

(3) If the landlord or the successor (if known) or the executor makes written objections to the Application, the Commission shall send the Applicant a copy thereof.

[231]

38.(1) The Commission shall make such enquiry as they consider necessary to inform themselves about the merits of the Application and any objections made by the landlord or the successor or by the executor. Thereafter the Commission shall consider all the information available, and
  (a) if they are satisfied that the Application should be granted and no objection to it is being maintained by the landlord or the successor (if known) or by the executor, the Commission shall grant the Application;
  (b) if they are not satisfied that the Application should be granted, the Commission shall serve on the Applicant, the landlord, the successor (if known) and the executor notice in writing that they propose to refuse the Application together with a written statement specifying the nature of and the reasons for such provisional decision and shall afford them an opportunity, within fourteen days from the date of service, both to make representations in writing and to ask for a Hearing;
  (c) if they are satisfied that the Application should be granted but an objection is being maintained by the landlord or the successor (if known) or by the executor, the Commission shall serve on the Applicant, the landlord, the successor (if known) and the executor notice in writing that they propose to grant the Application together with a written statement specifying the nature of and the reasons for such provisions decision and shall afford them an opportunity, within fourteen days from the date of service, both to make representations in writing and to ask for a Hearing.

(2) The Commission shall consider any further representations made to them, whether in writing or at a Hearing, in response to the notice given under paragraph

(1)(b) or (1)(c) of this Rule, and thereafter they shall intimate their final decision to the Applicant, the landlord, the successor (if known) and the executor together with a written statement specifying the nature of and the reasons for such decision.

[232]

(2) Objection to legatee

(Crofters (Scotland) Act 1955 (c 21), s 10(3))

39.(1) When a landlord has duly intimated to the Commission that he objects to receiving a legatee as tenant of a croft and has stated the grounds of his objections, the Commission shall serve on the legatee a notice affording him an opportunity, within fourteen days from the date of service, both to make representations in writing and to ask for a Hearing. The Commission shall give the landlord a copy of any representations in writing lodged by the legatee in response to this notice.

(2) The Commission shall make such enquiry and carry out such inspection as they deem necessary to inform themselves about the case.

(3) The Commission shall consider all the information available to them, and
  (a) if a Hearing has already been held and they are satisfied that the landlord's objections are reasonable, they shall declare the bequest to be null and void and notify the landlord and the legatee accordingly
  (b) if a Hearing has already been held and they are not so satisfied, they shall notify the landlord and the legatee to that effect;
  (c) if a Hearing has not been held, the Commission shall serve on the landlord and the legatee notice of the decision which they have reached provisionally on the information available to them and shall afford them an opportunity, within fourteen days from the date of service, both to make further representations in writing and to ask for a Hearing.

(4) The Commission shall consider any further representations made to them, whether in writing or at a Hearing, in response to the notice given under paragraph (3)(c) of this Rule, and thereafter they shall intimate their final decision to the landlord and the legatee.

(5) The Commission shall give the landlord and the legatee a written statement specifying the nature of and the reasons for the decision or provisional decision in each case.

[233]

TRANSFER OF CROFTER'S INTEREST BY EXECUTOR

(Succession (Scotland) Act 1964, s 16(2)(i))
(Law Reform (Miscellaneous Provisions) (Scotland) Act 1968, Sch 2, Pt I, para 22 and Pt II)

40.(1) Application by an executor for the Commission's consent to transfer the interest under a lease of a croft to a person not being a person entitled to succeed to the intestate estate of the crofter (hereinafter referred to as 'the transferee') shall be made on the appropriate form provided by the Commission.

(2) On receipt of an Application on the said form properly completed the Commission shall serve a copy together with a notice intimating that objections in writing to the Application may be lodged within fourteen days from the date of service on (i) the landlord of the croft; and (ii) any person who appears to be entitled to succeed to the intestate estate of the crofter (in this or the following Rule referred to as 'the successor') if the name and address of the successor are known to the Commission. If from the information provided by the Applicant the Commission are unable to identify the successor they themselves may make such enquiry as they think fit or as may appear to them to be reasonably practicable to establish his identity.

(3) If the landlord or the successor (if known) makes written objections to the Application the Commission shall send the Applicant a copy thereof.

[234]

41.(1) The Commission shall make such enquiry as they may consider necessary to inform themselves about the circumstances of the transferee and about the merits of the Application and any objections made by the landlord or the successor (if known). Thereafter the Commission shall consider all the information available and—

(a) if they are satisfied that the Application should be granted and no objection to it is being maintained by the landlord or the successor (if known) the Commission shall grant the Application;

(b) if they are not satisfied that the Application should be granted the Commission shall serve on the Applicant notice in writing that they propose to refuse the Application and shall afford him an opportunity within fourteen days from the date of service both to make representation in writing and to ask for a Hearing;

(c) if they are satisfied that the Application should be granted but an objection is being maintained by the landlord or the successor (if known) the Commission shall serve on the landlord or as the case may be the successor (if known) notice in writing that they propose to grant the Application and shall afford him an opportunity within fourteen days from the date of service both to make representations in writing and to ask for a Hearing.

(c) The Commission shall consider any further representations made to them whether in writing or at a Hearing in response to a notice given under paragraph (1)(b) or (1)(c) of this Rule and thereafter they shall intimate their final decision to the Applicant, the landlord and the successor (if known).

(3) In each case, except where the decision is to grant the Application and neither the landlord nor the successor has maintained an objection, the Commission shall give along with the notice of the decision or provisional decision a written statement specifying the nature of and the reasons for such decision or provisional decision.

[235]

SUBDIVISION OF CROFT

(Crofters (Scotland) Act 1955 (c 21), s 9)

42.(1) Application by a crofter for the Commission's consent to subdivide his croft shall be made on the appropriate form provided by the Commission.

(2) On receipt of an Application on the said form, properly completed and accompanied by the consent in writing of the landlord to the proposed subdivision, the Commission shall make such enquiry and carry out such inspection as they deem necessary to enable them to deal with the Application.

(3) The Commission shall consider the Application and all the available information and

(a) if they are satisfied that the Application should be granted, the Commission shall intimate their decision to that effect to the Applicant and to the landlord;

(b) if they are not so satisfied, the Commission shall serve on the Applicant and the landlord notice in writing of their provisional decision to refuse the Application specifying the nature of and the reasons for such provisional decision, and shall afford them an opportunity, within fourteen days from the date of service, both to make representations in writing and to ask for a Hearing.

(4) The Commission shall consider any further representations made to them, whether in writing or at a Hearing, in response to the notice given under paragraph (3)(b) of this Rule, and thereafter they shall intimate their final decision to the

Applicant and the landlord, together with a written statement, if the decision is to refuse the Application, specifying the nature of and the reasons for such decision.

[236]

APPEAL AGAINST NOTICE OF IMPROVEMENT PROPOSALS

(Crofters (Scotland) Act 1955 (c 21), s 25(1), (1A) and (1B))
(Crofting Reform (Scotland) Act 1976 (c 21), s 16(3), Sch 3)

43.(1) A crofter to whom a Grazings Committee has given notice of proposed works of improvement on the common grazing may within one month of the date of the notice make representations to the Commission in writing in respect of the proposal or the proposed allocation of expenditure to be incurred.

(2) The Commission shall serve a copy of any representations so made on the Clerk of the Grazings Committee together with a notice requesting him to make any representations he may wish to make in writing within fourteen days from the date of service. The Commission shall send a copy of any representations so made to the crofter (in this and the following Rule referred to as 'the Appellant').

(3) If the number of shareholders in the common grazing does not exceeds twelve and there is reliable information as to their names and addresses, the Commission shall serve on each shareholder a notice informing him that a copy of the Appellant's representations can be seen in the hands of the Clerk to the Grazings Committee and that he can make representations in writing to the Commission within fourteen days from the date of service. If the number of shareholders exceeds twelve or there is lack of reliable information as to their names and addresses the Commission shall either by advertisement in a newspaper circulating in the district or by notice posted in such public place or places in the district as the Commission may specify or in such other manner as the Commission may think sufficient give the shareholders notice to the same effect. The Commission shall send copies of any representations so made to the Appellant and to the Clerk of the Grazings Committee.

[237]

44.(1) The Commission shall make such enquiry and carry out such inspection as they consider necessary to inform themselves about the nature and quality of the common grazing, the proposals for improvement and the expenditure to be incurred thereon and the circumstances of the proposed allocation of expenditure.

(2) The Commission shall consider the representations they have received and all the information otherwise available and shall reach a provisional decision whether to approve the proposals and proposed allocation of expenditure with or without modifications or to reject them.

(3) The Commission shall give to the Appellant, the Clerk of the Grazings Committee and the other shareholders in the same manner as provided in paragraph (3) of the preceding Rule notice of their provisional decision specifying the nature of and reasons for such decision and shall afford them an opportunity within fourteen days from the date of service both to make representations in writing and to ask for a Hearing.

(4) After considering such representations (if any) as may be made whether in writing or at a Hearing the Commission shall intimate their final decision to the Appellant and the Clerk of the Grazings Committee together with a written statement specifying the nature of and the reasons for such decision. The Commission shall likewise intimate their final decision to the other shareholders in the same manner as provided in paragraph (3) of the preceding Rule.

[238]

Forms available from the Crofters Commission

1. Application by crofter for consent to assign croft (Crofters (Scotland) Act 1955, s 8).

2. Application by crofter for consent to subdivide croft (ibid, s 9).

3. Application by legatee outside crofter's family for approval of bequest (ibid, s 10(1)).

4. Application by executor for consent to transfer croft tenancy (Succession (Scotland) Act 1964, s 16(2)(i)).

5. Application by landlord for consent to let of croft (Crofters (Scotland) Act 1955, s 16).

6. Application for a decrofting direction (ibid, ss 16(9) and (13) and 16A(4)).

7. Application for apportionment (for a township) of a general common grazing (ibid, s 27(3)).

8. Application by a shareholder for apportionment of part of a township common grazing or general common grazing (ibid, s 27(4)).

9. Application for apportionment of lands held runrig (ibid, s 27(7)).

10. Application for consent to sublet croft (Crofters (Scotland) Act 1961, s 11).

[239]

APPENDIX D

Availability of legal aid

1. Legal advice and assistance will be available under the normal rules to a crofter or cottar wishing to negotiate with the landlord regarding the purchase of his subjects. It will not normally be available to carry through the conveyancing work consequent on successful negotiations for, in the absence of good and cogent reasons as to why public funds should be utilized, requests for increases in authorised expenditure are likely to be refused on the view that the applicant should be expected to take the cost of conveyancing into account before deciding to proceed with the transaction. If the negotiated agreement contains a provision to the effect that the purchaser will pay the seller's legal expenses, these would not be a competent charge under the legal advice and assistance scheme. Such expenses are viewed as a concealed addition to the price of the subjects and as such are not allowable.

[240]

2. If the negotiations fail then legal aid may be available to the crofter or cottar to apply to the Land Court for a purchase order. Where such an order is obtained and conveyancing work is necessary to implement that order, such work should be covered by the legal aid certificate. If the resultant conveyancing work for some reason cannot be effected under a certificate, it could be the subject of a separate application under the legal advice and assistance scheme. Similarly, if it is a condition of the purchase order that the crofter has to grant a standard security or a lease to the landlord of fishing and shooting rights over the croft land, this might be covered by the certificate or by legal advice and assistance separately. However, if the Land Court orders that the crofter or cottar should bear the landlord's expense of the conveyance of the site of the dwellinghouse, these expenses cannot be covered by the legal aid certificate nor by legal advice and assistance for the reasons already stated.

[241]

3. Legal aid will be available for all parties in other applications to the Land Court including the determination of a fair rent, resumption of land and removal of a tenant, subject to the question of financial eligibility. When a landlord who has obtained legal aid is to receive monies following the disposal of a croft, the price and expenses payable to him constitute property recovered or preserved and require to be paid into the legal aid fund. Under legal advice and assistance, the price and expenses received would require to be applied towards the solicitor's charges subject to dispensation on the grounds of hardship, etc. If the Land Court award expenses against an assisted party, then the award could be the subject of modification.

[242]

4. Legal advice and assistance is available for applications to the Crofters Commission. It would include preparing the application, obtaining any necessary supporting evidence and advising the client on how he should conduct the proceedings, but actual representation at a hearing is not included. A crofter may seek a decrofting direction in advance of purchase and this will be covered by legal advice and assistance for the application but not for representation. There is an appeal against a refusal to decroft for which a legal aid certificate might be available.

[243]

5. Legal aid can only be made available having regard to the statutory tests imposed in the Legal Aid (Scotland) Act 1986, sections 14 and 15, ie probable cause and reasonableness must be shown for the application to be admitted on the merits and financial eligibility assessed. Because crofting matters are infrequently considered, it is necessary to give detailed information of the steps proposed to be taken.

]244]

Further information can be obtained from the Scottish Legal Aid Board, 44 Drumsheugh Gardens, Edinburgh EH3 7SW

INDEX

References are to paragraph numbers; numbers in square brackets
refer to material in the appendices.